D0068451

'Fun, fast-paced, ironic, the reportage seems solid and the facts straight . . . Lawson's book is ridiculously readable, well written and hard to put down' *Library Journal*'s 'Books for Dudes'

'The reporting is rock solid and readable . . . Lawson's tale of how some youthful schmucks ended up in deep water is captivating' Lit/Rant

'Like the best stories about rogues, con artists and scammers, the magic is in the details. Guy Lawson's *War Dogs* misses nothing. He gets it all' Nick Pileggi, author of *Wiseguy*

'This is one of those books that, God help us, shouldn't be true – but is. US governmental bungling, war in Afghanistan going awry, foreign hustlers making millions out of bilking heroic soldiers, and in the middle of it all are two barely post-teenager dopers fumbling their way into and out of the highest level of the sleazy arms business. Guy Lawson tells the disturbing story brilliantly. You'll cringe, you'll want to look away (a lot), but you won't be able to stop turning the pages' Jeff Guinn, author of *Manson*

'Guy Lawson's *War Dogs* is a triumph of investigative reporting and storytelling. This book is a mind-blowing account of how two kids turned themselves into some of the world's biggest weapons dealers in the chaotic years of the Iraq war. I couldn't put it down. If it were on the fiction shelf, the rollicking, riveting tale told within these pages would seem wildly implausible. But it's not' Rajiv Chandrasekaran, author of *Imperial Life in the Emerald City* and *Little America*

ABOUT THE AUTHOR

Guy Lawson is a *New York Times* bestselling author and an award-winning investigative journalist whose articles on war, crime, culture and law have appeared in the *New York Times Magazine*, *Rolling Stone*, *GQ*, *Harper's Magazine* and many other publications.

THE TRUE STORY OF

HOW THREE STONERS

FROM MIAMI BEACH

BECAME THE MOST UNLIKELY

GUNRUNNERS IN HISTORY

WAR /////////// //////////// DOGS

GUY LAWSON

VIKING

an imprint of

PENGUIN BOOKS

VIKING

UK | USA | Canada | Ireland | Australia
India | New Zealand | South Africa

Viking is part of the Penguin Random House group of companies
whose addresses can be found at global.penguinrandomhouse.com.

Penguin
Random House
UK

First published in the United States of America as
Arms and the Dudes by Simon & Schuster 2015
First published as an electronic edition in Penguin Books 2015
First published in the United Kingdom as *War Dogs* by Viking 2016
001

Copyright © Guy Lawson, 2015

The moral right of the author has been asserted

Printed in Great Britain by Clays Ltd, St Ives plc

A CIP catalogue record for this book is available from the British Library

ISBN: 978–0–241–97565–7

www.greenpenguin.co.uk

MIX
Paper from
responsible sources
FSC® C018179

Penguin Random House is committed to a
sustainable future for our business, our readers
and our planet. This book is made from Forest
Stewardship Council® certified paper.

For my mother, Mary

Of arms and the man I sing.

—Virgil, *The Aeneid*

////// CONTENTS //////

////// AUTHOR'S NOTE //////

In January of 2007, two kids from Miami Beach won a Department of Defense contract to supply $300 million worth of ammunition to the Afghanistan military. David Packouz and Efraim Diveroli were still in their early twenties but they'd become good—very, very, very good—at bidding online for federal arms contracts. The dope-smoking buddies had become so skilled at winning Pentagon munitions deals they'd beaten a dozen corporate competitors to become the sole winners of the contract to provide the Afghan military with everything from 100 million rounds of AK-47 ammo to thousands of tons of grenades, mortar rounds, and aerial rockets. The massive contract called for enough ammunition to literally create an army—which was precisely what the United States was attempting to do at the time.

As Packouz and Diveroli set out to fulfill the $300 million contract, they were joined by another dude from their Miami Beach posse named Alex Podrizki. As it happened, the trio had picked an excellent moment to turn themselves into international gunrunners. In the early months of 2007, the wars in Afghanistan and Iraq were both going badly. Years earlier, the United States had invaded the two countries with little thought for the aftermath and the inevitable need to rebuild distant, fractious Muslim societies. As the nations simultaneously descended into the chaos of raging insurgencies, the Bush administration surged tens of thousands of American soldiers into Iraq. This left the Pentagon with few resources to deploy to Afghanistan, as an underdog presidential candidate named Barack Obama noted frequently on the campaign trail. In desperation, the United States decided it needed to provide greater strategic support to the Afghanistan military and police—and it needed to do so quickly. The ammunition contract was thus part of a major initiative to try to bolster Afghanistan's security forces and turn the tide against the Taliban.

The Afghanistan arms deal was a reflection of a change in defense contracting policy for the United States. In the early days of the conflicts in Afghanistan and Iraq, the Pentagon had awarded multibillion-dollar, no-bid contracts to companies like Halliburton and Blackwater, causing public outrage at the way well-connected insiders were profiting from the wars. In response, President Bush changed the rules to require that most defense contracts be posted on the government's website, be open to competition, and have terms that were favorable to small businesses, giving even tiny players such as Packouz and Diveroli and Podrizki a chance to go up against the largest conglomerates in the military-industrial complex.

The logistics of acquiring and transporting arms on this scale presented serious challenges. Adding another layer of difficulty, the Afghans and Iraqis both used Soviet Bloc weapon systems. This meant the ammunition for the Afghanistan contract would have to be sourced entirely from formerly Communist countries—many nations notorious for corruption and illegal arms dealing. For this strategically vital and politically sensitive endeavor, the Department of Defense relied on three twentysomethings—one a licensed masseur, another a ninth-grade dropout, the third a small-time pot dealer.

Incredibly, at least according to the official version of events, instead of supplying the Pentagon with high-quality ammunition, Packouz and Diveroli and Podrizki shipped a mountain of the cheapest possible surplus rounds from arms caches in the Balkans. A story that appeared on the front page of the *New York Times* in March of 2008 reported that they had the audacity to scam the federal government, supplying faulty, ancient, rusty munitions; cheating the Army; and endangering the lives of innocent Afghan soldiers. The *Times* article made the dudes celebrities, of a kind. But it also raised serious questions. How could three so obviously unqualified and inexperienced kids be trusted with such a massive defense contract? How had they fooled so many people for so long? Was the contract typical of the way the world's lone superpower was fighting the wars in Afghanistan and Iraq? What did the debacle say about America's ability to triumph in the war on terror?

As a writer for *Rolling Stone*, I knew the magazine was always looking for a certain kind of story—"tales about young people doing f—ked-up things," to use the precise words of my editors. The three friends from Miami Beach certainly seemed to qualify. It appeared they might also provide an interesting, even unique, prism into the secretive and mysterious world of international arms dealing. The improbable voyage Packouz, Diveroli, and Podrizki had taken included geopolitical intrigue, Albanian mobsters, a shady Swiss arms dealer, and an underhanded conspiracy to repackage millions of ancient surplus Chinese-made AK-47 cartridges—all leading to federal indictments for fraud, a congressional investigation, and a scandal that made the US government look not only ridiculous but incompetent.

I knew from experience—this is a trick of the trade—that the best time for a journalist to approach criminal defendants is after they've been sentenced and their legal jeopardy is at an end. So I waited until David Packouz and Alex Podrizki were about to be sentenced for the federal fraud counts they'd pleaded guilty to. When I contacted Packouz's attorney, he said his client was willing to meet, so I traveled to Florida; Podrizki wasn't interested in talking at the time. Standing before a judge in Miami's shiny, new federal courthouse, Packouz received a suspended sentence for his role in the Afghanistan contract fraud; Podrizki likewise avoided prison. Their buddy, Diveroli, wasn't so lucky, sentenced to four years behind bars because he was the mastermind of the operation.

In court, the government portrayed Packouz and Diveroli and Podrizki as low-life fraudsters, three sleazy kids who'd do anything to make money. In the *Times*, Packouz's qualifications as a massage therapist played prominently, along with detailed reporting on Diveroli's checkered personal history. The mug shots of Packouz and Diveroli that ran in the newspaper made them look like hardened criminals. But in person David Packouz was a surprise. He was smart and well-spoken, a sharp observer of events with a keen memory, an easy laugh, and an ironic appreciation for the absurdity of what he'd lived through. Unlike the Hollywood image of an arms dealer—a soulless thug merchandizing death—Packouz seemed like the kind of kid who could just as easily have started a dot-com business in Silicon Valley. Instead of inventing a killer app, Packouz and his friends had fashioned themselves into gunrunners—precocious, cunning, and astonishingly successful gunrunners. In winning the $300 million contract, three kids from Miami Beach had turned themselves into the least likely arms dealers in history—until their fraud was discovered and the Pentagon turned on them.

The *Rolling Stone* article I wrote attracted more attention than any other piece I'd ever published, the improbable tale somehow capturing a measure of the madness of a decade of war and lawlessness; it was a story so strange it could only be true. But I knew there was more to tell—much more. A federal judge had placed a number of documents in the case under seal. Unwilling to let the case go, I spent months paging through court transcripts, studying defense-contract regulations, and drafting Freedom of Information requests. When I pursued interviews with the officials involved, the silence was deafening—and highly suspicious. Finally, as I kept digging, I received documents from confidential sources determined to reveal the truth. Then the ringleader of the arms-dealing operation, the force of nature named Efraim Diveroli, began to talk to me from prison. Alex Podrizki agreed to tell me about his experiences in Albania. Likewise, an older Mormon businessman from Utah named Ralph Merrill, who'd financed the deal and was also convicted of fraud, wanted to have his say about how events had unfolded.

Another story began to take shape—one that had never been reported. The three stoners from Miami Beach had taken a wild, incredible trip into the innermost reaches of the world of international arms dealing. But the tale also had a serious side, with important political and legal implications. I discovered that during the wars in Iraq and Afghanistan the government of the United States had turned itself into the biggest gunrunning organization on the planet, with virtually no oversight from Congress, law enforcement, or the press. As the Pentagon desperately tried to stand up new armies in Kabul and Baghdad, paying private contractors billions to acquire a vast array of weapons from formerly Communist Bloc countries, it had made little attempt to vet its business partners and turned a blind eye to rampant fraud—sometimes with murderous consequences. The US government had used a string of brokers like Packouz and Diveroli and Podrizki to insulate it from the dirty work of arms dealing in the Balkans—the kickbacks and bribes and double-dealing. They also set up the brokers to act as scapegoats should the extralegal operation ever be exposed. The story of the three dudes from Miami Beach vividly illustrated the failures of the wars in Afghanistan and Iraq. It was a tale that the government tried to bury—until now.

This is a story you were never meant to read.

Guy Lawson
New York, New York
June 2015

Chapter One

HELL-BENT

The e-mail confirmed it: the delivery was back on track, after weeks of maddening, inexplicable delays. It was May 24, 2007, and the e-mail said that a cargo plane had just lifted off from a military airstrip in Hungary and was banking east over the Black Sea toward Kyrgyzstan, some three thousand miles away. After stopping to refuel at an air base in Bishkek, the plane would carry on to Kabul, the capital of Afghanistan. Aboard the plane were eighty pallets loaded with 5 million rounds of AK-47 ammunition, for the Soviet Bloc weapons preferred by the Afghan National Army.

Reading the e-mail in his tiny office in Miami Beach, David Packouz breathed a sigh of relief. The shipment was part of the $300 million ammunition contract Packouz and his friends Efraim Diveroli and Alex Podrizki were attempting to fulfill for the Department of Defense. Packouz and his buddies were still in their early twenties, but they'd been contracted by the US Army to deliver a huge amount of munitions to the Afghanistan military. Bidding online, on the website where the Pentagon posted defense contracts for public competition, the stoner dudes had beat major corporations to win the Afghan contract. For weeks in the spring of 2007, Packouz had toiled tirelessly trying to obtain flyover permissions for the ammo from the countries between Hungary and Afghanistan—all formerly part of the Soviet Bloc. Working with nothing more than a cell phone, an Internet connection, and a steady supply of high-quality weed, he'd finally succeeded in getting the ammo en route to Kabul. But along the way Packouz had repeatedly encountered mysterious, invisible forces seemingly conspiring to stop him from delivering the ammo—the kind of political complications inherent in gunrunning.

Five thousand miles away, in the Balkan city of Tirana, Albania, Packouz's friends Efraim Diveroli and Alex Podrizki were also dealing with menacing and mysterious forces as they tried to arrange for 100 million rounds of AK-47 ammo to be transported to Kabul. Alone in a notoriously lawless country, Diveroli and Podrizki were trying to negotiate with an Albanian mafioso taking kickbacks, as well as a Swiss gun dealer running the deal through a Cyprus company seemingly as a way to grease the palms of shadowy operators allegedly associated with the prime minister of Albania. Or so it appeared—knowing the underlying truth was often impossible in international arms dealing. As if those woes weren't enough, Diveroli and Podrizki were also overseeing an operation to deceive the Pentagon by covertly repacking the AK-47 rounds into cardboard boxes to disguise that they had been manufactured decades earlier in China—a possible violation of American law.

Gunrunning, the three dudes were learning the hard way, was a tough business.

In Miami, David Packouz replied to the e-mail about the Kyrgyz ammo with excitement: the ammo was finally on its way. His workday at an end, he got in his new Audi A4 and drove home through the warm South Florida spring evening, windows open, U2's "Beautiful Day" blasting on the stereo. What was happening was incredible to Packouz. He had no training as an international arms dealer, other than what he'd learned on the job from his friend, the twenty-one-year-old dynamo Efraim Diveroli. Packouz was only twenty-five years old, and his only postsecondary education was half a bachelor's degree's worth of chemistry credits, along with the diploma he'd earned from the Educating Hands School of Massage; until recently, he'd made his living as a masseur advertising his services on Craigslist. Now Packouz was a central player in the delivery of an entire arsenal to Afghanistan, responsible for chartering dozens of flights from all over Eastern Europe, obtaining flyover permissions from countries like Turkmenistan and Uzbekistan, and placating overwhelmed American soldiers on bombed-out tarmacs in Kabul trying to build the Afghan army in the midst of a hot war.

Winning the $300 million Afghan deal was changing Packouz's life in myriad ways. He'd moved out of his dive studio apartment, into a condo in a flashy seaside building called the Flamingo. According to his calculations, he was about to become a multimillionaire. And that was just the beginning. Soon he was going to have enough money to kickstart his dream of a career as a rock musician. No more fending off the advances of massage clients who assumed he was a prostitute. No more self-doubt. No more existential angst. Soon he was going to be rich—and he was going to be famous.

Arriving home at his condo, Packouz packed the cone of his new Volcano electronic bong, took a deep hit, and felt the pressures of the day drift away into a clean, crisp high. Dinner was at Sushi Samba, a hipster Asian-Latino fusion joint. Packouz was exhausted but exhilarated—the improbable turn his life was taking was thrilling, even if it required extremely hard work. As his miso-marinated Chilean sea bass arrived, his cell phone rang.

The freight-forwarding agent they'd hired was calling from New York and he sounded panicked: "We've got a problem. The plane has been seized on the runway in Kyrgyzstan. The Kyrgyz secret service won't let it take off for Kabul."

"What are you talking about?" Packouz said, straining to hear over the restaurant's pounding music.

"Local customs and security personnel—the local KGB—are fucking with us. They won't explain anything. I need diplomatic intervention from the United States."

"That's bullshit!" Packouz shouted. "We worked for weeks to get the permits."

"The Kyrgyz KGB is blackmailing us. They say you have to pay a three-hundred-thousand-dollar fine for every day the plane sits on the runway."

Packouz was baffled, stoned, unable to grasp the implications of what he was being told. He had no idea that the ammo he was attempting to ship to Afghanistan was now a bargaining chip in a game of geopolitical brinksmanship between George W. Bush and Vladimir Putin. The Russian president didn't like NATO expanding into Eastern Europe, nor did old-school Communist elements inside the Kyrgyz intelligence apparatus. The United States was also being extorted to pay a higher rent for its use of the Bishkek airport as a refueling and staging area—a vital strategic link for the war in Afghanistan. Then there was the recently imposed ban on Russian companies' selling arms to the US government, denying the Russians the chance to compete for the huge Afghan ammunition contract. The Russians were orchestrating a tit-for-tat reaction, it appeared; it was known in global arms circles that the Afghans were running out of ammunition, so slowing the supply line was a devilish way to hurt American interests.

"It was surreal," Packouz recalled. "Here I was dealing with matters of international security and I was half-baked. I didn't know anything about the situation in that part of the world. But I was a central player in the Afghan War—and if our ammo didn't make it to Kabul the entire strategy of building up the Afghanistan army was going to fail. It was totally killing my buzz. But I had to get my shit together. I had to put on my best arms-dealer face."

Stepping outside the restaurant, Packouz cupped a hand over his cell phone to shut out the noise. "Tell the Kyrgyz KGB that ammo needs to get to Afghanistan right now," he shouted into the phone. "This contract is part of a vital mission in the global war on terrorism. Tell them that if they fuck with us they're fucking with the government of the United States!"

Hanging up, panicking, Packouz decided he needed to talk to

Efraim Diveroli, the leader of their operation. Diveroli was asleep in his hotel in Tirana when Packouz reached him. Still groggy from a long night of carousing, Diveroli was sleeping next to a prostitute who'd been provided to him by an Albanian businessman hoping to ingratiate himself with the young American gunrunner.

"We have an emergency," Packouz said.

"Dude, I'm sleeping," Diveroli replied.

"Our plane got seized in Kyrgyzstan," Packouz said.

"Our plane was seized?" Diveroli said. "What the fuck you talking about?"

"The Hungarian ammo. Kyrgyz intelligence is saying we don't have the right paperwork to transit through their country. They say we'll be fined three hundred grand for every day we're stuck there."

Diveroli was now fully awake.

"Three hundred thousand dollars a day?" Diveroli asked, shouting into the phone. "That's insane. What the fuck is going on? Tell them this is a vital mission in the war on terror. Tell them that if they fuck with us they're fucking with the United States of America."

"Yeah, yeah, I said that. I'm going to call the American embassy when it's morning there."

"You got to fix this. We can't afford this kind of shit. This is unfuck-ingacceptable. Call the State Department, call the Pentagon—call any-one you can think of. Go over to Kyrgyzstan and give those mobsters a fucking blow job if you have to. Do whatever it takes to get this resolved—and I mean whatever it takes."

"I'm on it," Packouz said.

"You know I can't help from here—I got enough troubles dealing with the fucking Albanian mafia."

"I'll get to the Kyrgyz."

"Now if you'll excuse me, I'm going to get back to fucking this hooker," Diveroli concluded.

//////

To observe that these kids from Miami Beach—still in their early twenties—were in over their heads would be an understatement.

Despite their youth, all three of the dudes were highly capable, in their different ways. Efraim Diveroli was little short of a genius when it came to bidding on federal contracts and mastering the intricacies of dealing with the Pentagon's bureaucracy. David Packouz was inventive and steady under stress. Alex Podrizki, the only one with a college degree and a modicum of military experience, was taciturn, cautious, determined to ensure that none of the ammo they shipped to Afghanistan was substandard.

But they had no real experience, training, or preparation to fulfill a contract as complex and vital as the $300 million Afghanistan deal. Giant international conglomerates had entire departments staffed by military veterans designed to fulfill contracts like the one the dudes were working on. The Pentagon had established the Defense Acquisition University in the 1990s and trained thousands of specialists in the arcane world of military procurements, an industry rife with the perils of fraud and political intrigue. Scores of small companies were also competing for the Army's contracts in Afghanistan and Iraq, almost all run by men in their forties and fifties with arms-dealing experience and connections inside the military. To their rivals, the kids had been a joke at first, but then they'd become a major threat because of their uncanny ability to win contracts by underbidding the competition.

The story of how the three dudes exploded onto the international arms-dealing scene began three years earlier, in the summer of 2004. At the tender age of eighteen, Efraim Diveroli had resolved improbably—but with true fervor—to turn himself into a gunrunner. Diveroli and his pals David Packouz and Alex Podrizki had met as teenagers at a yeshiva in Miami Beach, where they routinely skipped prayers to smoke dope in a nearby abandoned house. They belonged to a posse of Orthodox Jewish kids who styled themselves as grunge punks. Chasing around the Art Deco hotels of Miami, their gang rejected the strictures of religious life for the pleasures and distractions of modern American youth. Until the youngest of their gang, Efraim Diveroli, stumbled onto the idea of making money from America's wars in Iraq and Afghanistan—and drew his friends into the nascent arms business he was going to construct.

"When I started working with Efraim, I knew nothing about war," David Packouz recalled. "I knew about the so-called global war on terror. But I'm talking about the business of war—because that's what it was, a business. It turned out that I had a great teacher in Efraim. He was only a kid, but arms dealing came naturally to him. He had an uncle who dealt arms, so the business was kind of in his family, but nothing like the level he took it to. Efraim was born to be a gunrunner."

At the time, the eighteen-year-old Diveroli was living near the beach in a back-room studio apartment he rented from a Hispanic family. Wake and bake was his daily ritual. The buzz from a couple of hits on the bong he kept on the kitchen table helped him focus as he spent the morning scanning the website Federal Business Opportunities, or FedBizOpps, as it was known in the arms-dealing trade. Here the US government publicly posted contracts for goods and services that were open to online bidding, including billions of dollars' worth of weapons. At lunchtime, Diveroli would take a walk to smoke a joint, then return to hunt for his first arms deal—one he might actually have a chance of winning. For months he worked deep into the night, searching, smoking, searching, smoking. Once a week or so, he'd meet up with Packouz and Podrizki and their other friends to hit the nightclubs along the beach to blow off steam, downing shots of Grey Goose, snorting lines of coke, hoping to get lucky.

To the outside world, the Miami Beach kids might have looked like any other rabble of layabouts. But Efraim Diveroli wasn't an ordinary rebellious teenager; he was an incredibly talented businessman. What Diveroli possessed—and what possessed him—was a single-minded ambition. He didn't regard FedBizOpps as a way to make money, though getting rich was supremely important to him. The website represented a deeper desire. The contracts posted on FedBizOpps were for rivets and forklifts and generators, but also for guns, grenades, and rocket launchers. Contracts were referred to as *opportunities*, but the term hardly captured their significance for Diveroli. Underneath the tedious-looking technical specifications and bureaucratic boilerplate, he saw the chance to live out his dream to become an international arms dealer.

Like most any teenage dude living on his own, Diveroli's home was a sty, with dishes piled in the sink, dirty laundry tossed everywhere, and nothing in the fridge apart from beer and leftover take-out food. He dressed like a slob, wearing the cheapest jeans and T-shirts he could find. His shock of brown hair was always messy, framing a face with dark brows, a large nose, peach fuzz on his cheeks and chin, and an expression that combined class-clown humor with punk defiance.

All day every day, Diveroli parsed the Pentagon's website looking for a way to obtain deals. The bidding on FedBizOpps was winner take all, so there was no consolation for coming close. Diveroli knew winning even one competition would require patience and persistence. But it cost nothing but time to bid on federal solicitations—and he had plenty of time on his hands. To Diveroli, competing on FedBizOpps was like rolling the dice in a vast game of craps.

One morning in the summer of 2004, Diveroli came across a posting for a contract for nine hundred thousand rounds of .223-caliber, fifty-five-gram ball ammunition to supply the Army's Special Operations Command in Fort Bragg, North Carolina. Reading the terms of the offer, Diveroli had only a tenuous grasp of the mechanics of defense contracting. *Single source,* the posting said, which meant there would be only one winner of the contract. The term *combined synopsis solicitation* indicated that the government had specifically allocated funds for the purchase.

Diveroli thought that the contract was so small, in the context of Pentagon procurements, it might just fall through the cracks and not come to the attention of the large corporations who dominated the business. Two-two-three ammo, as the .223 rounds were called, were extremely commonplace bullets. It would be a matter of competing on price, Diveroli reasoned.

To get more information, Diveroli called the Army contracting officer listed online—Jerry was his name. Diveroli adopted a deep baritone to try to sound older. But his boyish enthusiasm was infectious as he asked Jerry about the specifications of bidding for the ammo deal. Jerry seemed impressed by Diveroli's youth and obvious desire to learn. The Bush administration had recently created rules to favor small businesses in federal contracts—and what company could be smaller than a one-man operation apparently run by a kid?

Jerry explained that bidding on federal contracts wasn't like a normal business-to-business transaction. FedBizOpps had a vast array of rules, regulations, and laws. Dealing with the Pentagon presented logistical and practical considerations, like *performance*. The term referred to the record the government kept of how private contractors fulfilled the terms of the contracts—the quality, quantity, and timeliness of deliveries were all closely monitored. If a company failed to *perform*, Jerry explained, it would be noted in Diveroli's record, and it could even lead to disqualification from future government deals.

As Diveroli listened to Jerry, he had some slight experience to call upon. When he'd been kicked out of school in Miami in the ninth grade, his parents had sent him to work for his uncle BK in Los Angeles. Diveroli had been caught selling cigarettes and was running with David Packouz and Alex Podrizki and their crowd of delinquent Orthodox Jewish kids who smoked dope around the beachfront. In LA, Diveroli would be expected to live by BK's strict religious rules. For decades, BK had run a successful arms company called Botach, which sold guns and paramilitary paraphernalia to law-enforcement agencies across the country. Diveroli's father also had a company that bid on police-supply contracts, though not for lethal weapons, so in a way government contracting and arms dealing were the family business.

At first the fourteen-year-old Diveroli had been a laborer in Botach's warehouse, but within months he'd risen to become a salesman.

By the time he was sixteen, he'd begun trading handguns like Glocks and Sig Sauers seized from criminals by police. Diveroli obtained the weapons from law enforcement, then resold them on "gunboard" websites like subguns.com, where collectors traded their wares. Diveroli wasn't just good at his job—he was obsessed.

"From the beginning I was addicted to business," Diveroli recalled. "When I was working for my uncle, I had my own office and a couple of Mexican guys working for me, receiving and shipping the orders that I was bringing in. I was selling everything from guns and boots to flashlights to police all over the country. I was spending hours every day in my uncle's walk-in vault, where he kept a lot of machine guns, silencers, pistols."

Then Diveroli came across the FedBizOpps website and clicked through the government contracts posted there. The contracts were called *solicitations* or *requests for proposals*. They were for billions upon billions in goods and services the federal government was buying every day. The biggest customer by far was the Department of Defense, which posted hundreds of billions of dollars' worth of contracts. Toilet seats, screwdrivers, rocket-propelled grenades, tanks—the list seemed to never end. The website offered new opportunities every day; even obtaining a tiny fraction would amount to a fortune to a teenager.

"It was much bigger than I had ever imagined or hoped for," Diveroli recalled. "I wanted a piece of it. I was going to bid on federal defense contracts. I was hell-bent."

Diveroli began vying for contracts, using his uncle's money to finance the deals, along with his various gun licenses. The arrangement was that Diveroli would split the profits 60–40 with his uncle, with the youngster receiving the smaller share. In weeks, Diveroli had begun to win small contracts on FedBizOpps. Within eighteen months, he calculated that he'd earned $150,000 in commissions.

"But there was tension between me and my uncle," Diveroli recalled. "It was mainly to do with stuff outside the office—like me smoking weed with the guys in the warehouse, not keeping kosher, not following the Sabbath. I told him to leave me alone—to keep personal and business separate. But I could see real trouble was coming, so I demanded at least partial payment of what he owed me. He told me to fuck myself. Within forty-eight hours I was on a plane to Miami to start my own business. One thing I knew for sure was that I was never going to take shit from any tyrant ever again."*

Back in Miami Beach and in business on his own in the summer of 2004, Diveroli spent days searching the Internet for the best price for the .223 ammunition. He didn't tell the suppliers he approached about the contract on FedBizOpps, lest they bid on the deal themselves. Eventually he found a company in Kentucky that would sell him the ammo for $105 for each box of a thousand rounds, making the total price $94,500. Diveroli now had to calculate his profit margin. Try for too much and he'd lose the contract; bid too low and he'd miss out on potential earnings. He reasoned that an established contractor would command at least 10 percent profit. So Diveroli gave himself a 9 percent margin. He hoped the sliver of difference would tilt the deal his way.

Three days later, Jerry called: "You got it, kid."

"It was the most exciting and scary moment of my life all at once," Diveroli recalled. "On one hand, I'd just secured my first contract with the Department of Defense. On the other hand, I had no fucking idea how I was going to actually deliver the ammo. But that wasn't going to stop me from trying."

The first obstacle was money. Diveroli had a stake of $30,000. Not bad for an eighteen-year-old, but it wasn't enough to pay the full price for the ammo up front, as the seller demanded. When the company refused to change its requirement for payment before delivery, Diveroli panicked. He had to find another supplier, one that would let him purchase the rounds on credit.

"I began frantically calling every ammo company in the United

---

* Diveroli's uncle would later tell the *New York Times* that his nephew didn't leave empty-handed—but with his customers.

States, pulling off marathon eighteen-to-twenty-hour stretches of work," Diveroli recalled. "Not only did I not have enough money—I didn't have the product to supply."

Diveroli finally located a shady outfit near Miami run by a pair of Cuban expats. They agreed to sell him the ammo for $114 per thousand. His profit would be nearly cut in half, but he no longer cared. He just needed to get the ammo to Fort Bragg ASAP—he needed to perform. If he failed to fulfill the contract, it would affect his ability to get more deals, and Diveroli was determined to build a stellar performance record.

Then this vendor also demanded full payment before shipping the ammo. With nowhere else to turn and time running out, Diveroli begged his father to lend him the money. Diveroli's father had bid on government contracts as well, though for smaller law-enforcement deals, so he was familiar with the idea of having to pay for goods up front. Diveroli said he only needed the money for thirty days. The government wouldn't renege on the contract, he promised; no creditor was more reliable than the US Treasury. Reluctantly, his father relented.

Within weeks, the rounds arrived at Fort Bragg. Countless hours of hard work had resulted in a profit of $4,500. Measly money, Diveroli thought, especially considering all the stress. But he knew something momentous had occurred, something with staggering implications. It was as if he had been initiated into a secret society—he was now a federal contractor, an arms dealer, a gunrunner.

"I was at the point of no return," Diveroli recalled. "I was meant to do this shit, and that was what I was going to do."

Diveroli's company was named AEY, from the first initials of the three siblings in his family (Efraim, the eldest, was the *E*). His father had incorporated this shell company and allowed his son to use it. There was nothing illegal about what his son wanted to do, after all, even if he was extraordinarily young to go into the federal-contracting business. Indeed, Diveroli wasn't old enough to qualify for a federal firearms license—the minimum age was twenty-one—so he begged his father to apply for one on his behalf. Once he had the company, the license, an Internet connection, and an ample supply of pot to modulate his manic nature, Diveroli had everything he needed to succeed—except money.

Diveroli figured he needed to have a minimum of $100,000 in cash to be a player on FedBizOpps. Planning to vie for big international defense contracts in Iraq and Afghanistan, he initially found backers willing to finance domestic ammunition deals that had nothing to do with the government—with the goal of building a war chest.

"I'd buy a hundred thousand dollars' worth of ammo from a company in New York with fifty grand down and fifty grand on net-thirty-day terms," Diveroli recalled. "Then I'd chop the ammo into three different sales of forty grand each going to Arizona, Louisiana, and fucking Texas. That meant I had a profit of twenty thousand bucks. Not many eighteen-year-olds can make twenty grand in a week legitimately and consistently. But I was doing it."

The truly big money wasn't in arms dealing in America, Diveroli knew; it was in Iraq. As it happened, he'd picked the ideal moment to get into the arms business. To fight simultaneous wars in Afghanistan and Iraq, the Bush administration had decided to outsource virtually every facet of America's military operations, from building and staffing Army bases to hiring mercenaries to provide private security for diplomats abroad. The Bush administration's heavy reliance on private contractors was part of a broader ideological struggle to bring the efficiencies of private enterprise to government. At least that was the theory. With Bush in office, private military contracts soared from $145 billion in 2001 to $390 billion by 2008. Military-industrial giants like Raytheon and Lockheed Martin turned war profiteering from a crime into a business model. Why shouldn't a stoner in Miami Beach get in on the action?

Diveroli had only a ninth-grade education, but even he could see that a fortune was to be made in the war on terror. As he amassed the capital he needed, he turned his attention to federal arms contracts for Iraq. Creating an Iraqi military alone was going to cost billions because the Americans were starting from scratch. The reason was in good measure the result of a strategic error of biblical proportions. In the heady aftermath of the invasion of Iraq in 2003, a former diplomat named Paul Bremer had run the Coalition Provisional Authority, the title given to the governing organization the United States was attempting to establish. Staffed largely with young neoconservative operatives from Washington, DC, with little or no foreign or military experience, the new authority tried to impose a radical form of free-market economics in Iraq—in direct contradiction to the authoritarian rule of Saddam Hussein, as well as the traditional tribal social order. As part of this initiative, in an attempt to rid the country of any hint of Saddam's Ba'ath Party and the Republican Guard, Bremer had dismissed the entire Iraqi security apparatus, including every soldier in the land. The decision had enraged, humiliated, and deprived a livelihood to four hundred thousand Iraqi men; the blunder had directly led to the growing insurgency in the summer of 2004.

The US military had worked with foreign militaries in the past, aiding allies in Vietnam and elsewhere, though it had never attempted to create an entire national military in the middle of a war. But the Bush administration wasn't willing to rely on American soldiers. Private industry would do a superior job, it was believed, and also protect the government from the political complications of a large commitment of American forces. Initially, the Pentagon outsourced the effort to stand up the new Iraqi army and police force through a no-bid contract to an American corporation called Vinnell, a division of Northrop Grumman. Vinnell had done some security work with the military in Saudi Arabia, but the retired American soldiers sent to Baghdad were clueless about Iraq, its culture, and the difficulties of starting an entirely new military. Contracted to create nine battalions of 1,000 men each, at a cost of $48 million, more than half of the first battalion deserted, and authorities in Baghdad soon decided on a new approach without

Vinnell—but not before the company collected $24 million for not get-ting the job done.

The problems with using private contractors weren't limited to the Iraqi security forces. The US Army's use of Logistics Civil Augmenta-tion Programs (LOGCAP) meant that many no-bid contracts worth billions were still being given to companies like Halliburton—where Vice President Dick Cheney had been chairman and CEO. Worse, the open-ended, contingency-based contracts didn't state a fixed value but moved according to expenses incurred by the company, plus an agreed profit margin, an arrangement that encouraged contractors to pad their accounts, if not outright steal. Revelations that Kellogg Brown & Root couldn't justify more than $1 billion in charges in 2004 alone led to the resignation of the Pentagon's top civilian overseeing the contract—not because he was caught taking bribes but because he refused to release the funds until the company explained why it de-served the extra billion. Instead, the official was replaced and the money was given to the company—with no accountability or over-sight for the discrepancy. Likewise, in the early days of the war in Iraq $12 billion in $100 bills was transported in more than twenty flights from a vault in New Jersey to the Green Zone—only to vanish. The Pentagon's law-enforcement agency did nothing to investigate or stop this theft.

Inside the Green Zone, in the gardens of what had been the Repub-lican Palace under the rule of Saddam Hussein, a business center was established as the place for private contractors to gather to peruse the various contracts for goods and services posted on the bulletin board each day. Like the scores of other ambitious American entrepreneurs descending on Baghdad to get rich quick, the principals of a small start-up called Custer Battles won a multimillion-dollar contract to provide security at the airport, even though its staff had no relevant experience. Creating sham companies in the Cayman Islands and Leb-anon, Custer Battles used fake invoices to grossly inflate its prices. The scam was revealed when a spreadsheet was accidentally left on a conference table in Baghdad, showing that the company had charged nearly $10 million for work that had cost less than $4 million—a markup of 162 percent. But only a whistle-blower lawsuit brought by two employees against the company prompted a Pentagon investigation, and by then Custer Battles had won more than $100 million in contracts from the US government.*

Bremer departed in June of 2004, fleeing a few days earlier than scheduled to avoid a feared assault from insurgents. Authority was passed to an interim Iraqi government. By July, a new strategy was being implemented to stand up the Iraqi military. The Iraqis would be in charge of the task; at least, that was the hope. A small group of Iraqis were flown to America for a three-week crash course in weapons procurement. An Iraqi who'd previously worked as a used-car salesman while exiled in Poland for decades was put in charge, given a budget of $600 million to spend by the end of the year, and let loose to enrich his cronies through no-bid contracts for shoddy, overpriced arms that often weren't even delivered. Many Iraqi soldiers lacked guns and helmets and bulletproof vests, but the Iraqi procurement officials conspired to buy ancient Russian helicopters that couldn't fly and armored personnel carriers that couldn't climb a slight incline because they had only a 150-horsepower engine. The theft and waste had all happened directly under the supervision of the occupying Americans—though nothing was done to stop it.

"Before, I sold water, flowers, shoes, cars—but not weapons," the Iraqi who was eventually put in charge of spending $1.3 billion explained to the *Los Angeles Times*. "We didn't know nothing about weapons."** .

In desperation, the US Army decided to use the Pentagon's own procurement system to arm the Iraqis. A new organization was formed

---

* Rajiv Chandrasekaran, *Imperial Life in the Emerald City* (Vintage, 2007), 155–66.
** "Iraq: Before Rearming Iraq, He Sold Shoes and Flowers," *Los Angeles Times*, November 6, 2005.

called the Multi-National Security Transition Command, or Minsticky. General David Petraeus was put in charge. A vast array of matériel was needed for the Iraqis—guns, tanks, ammo, mortar rounds. Every day officers from Minsticky posted "wants and needs" in the business center in Baghdad and on the Internet. These deals were open to any qualified bidder—and as an approved contractor on FedBizOpps, that included Diveroli.

Sitting in his tiny apartment in Miami Beach, Diveroli watched longingly as scores of Iraq solicitations appeared on his computer screen. Some of the contracts were for nonlethal goods, like boots and helmets. Some were for lethal matériel, like AK-47s and RPGs. Encouraged by his initial success, Diveroli spent all his waking hours trying to find a way into the Iraq action. He didn't care what kind of deal he won; he just wanted to get in the game.

As he studied the website, Diveroli learned that the Pentagon had decided to use "nonstandard" weapons for the Iraqi army and police. The term was used to differentiate the two basic forms of arms in the world of war. The Pentagon called Soviet Bloc guns and bombs—based on the metric system and designed for cost-effectiveness and reliability—nonstandard. On the other side was American and NATO-style "standard" weaponry, created for accuracy and lethality and consequently expensive.

Weapons on both sides of the Cold War divide had merits, but there was no debate about price. An American M16 rifle cost at least $1,000. A used Communist AK-47 could be had for a few dollars, or a live chicken in some African countries. According to Donald Rumsfeld's memoir, *Known and Unknown*, it cost $107,000 to train and deploy an American soldier, while an Iraqi soldier cost $6,500, and an Afghan soldier was a mere $1,800. This calculation ran through the strategic planning for both wars, with profound implications.

When Diveroli saw a contract to supply ten thousand bulletproof helmets to the Iraqi army, he began to scour the Internet for potential suppliers. Eventually, he found a Korean company willing to sell him the requisite amount for $110 each. Diveroli put in a bid of $125 per helmet and crossed his fingers. Soon after, he received the giddy-making news. He'd won his second government contract on his own—and this one was in Iraq.

But there was a hitch once again: finance. The value of the contracts was $1.25 million, and he needed $300,000 up front to pay for the first shipment. Diveroli's father couldn't lend him that much, even if he wanted to. Diveroli frantically looked for someone willing to back him, but the only person who agreed to take the risk had such onerous terms that Diveroli would receive nothing—literally not one dollar—on the contract. Diveroli couldn't agree to such a deal, even if it meant defaulting on his first Iraq contract.

Unable to find a financial backer and at the end of his rope, Diveroli decided to try one last possibility. When he was living in LA working for his uncle, he'd done business with an older Mormon man in Utah. The transactions had been modest, mostly involving spare parts for Uzis. But the man—Ralph Merrill—had an entrepreneurial streak and the means to finance the deal. Diveroli's telephone pitch to Merrill lasted three minutes: in return for half of the profits, the Mormon had to risk his money for thirty days. Diveroli would take care of all the details—managing the supplier, overseeing delivery, and attending to the paperwork.

Merrill was conservative: trim and clean-cut, a military veteran in his sixties, he was a lifelong Republican and a devoted father of five who kept to the strict tenets of his faith. Merrill had made his fortune designing and installing ATMs in banks around the country, but a life-long interest in guns had led him to start his own arms company after he retired, dedicated mostly to rebuilding AK-47s and Uzis.

Merrill seemed an unlikely partner for a brash teenager like Diveroli. But Merrill was an adventurer at heart. Over the years, he'd been involved in deals to import Uzis from Zimbabwe and AK-47 ammo from China, and along the way he'd developed close relationships with a number of international arms dealers.

Considering Diveroli's proposal, Merrill reasoned that the Pentagon wasn't going to refuse to pay for the helmets. After sleeping on it, Merrill decided to back the kid; their prior dealings had gone well, and he liked working with young entrepreneurs. There was also the possibility of bidding on more contracts through Diveroli. Like anyone watching the nightly news, Merrill knew that large sums were being made in Iraq. Diveroli was only nineteen at the time, but he was bright, ambitious, and seemingly trustworthy.

To get Diveroli started on the helmet order, Merrill agreed to front AEY $200,000 for thirty days, with a 3 percent monthly rate of return. If the deal worked, Merrill would renew the loan every thirty days, on the same terms. The arrangement turned out to be mutually beneficial and highly promising.

"Smooth as a baby's ass was how the first helmet deal went," Diveroli recalled. "Ralph immediately said he was interested in doing more business together, particularly if the United States government was the customer. I was, too. So I started bidding on government contracts with him in mind. I had my sights on the big Iraq contracts for weapons and munitions. I knew the government required an enormous quantity of Soviet Bloc arms and munitions—nonstandard arms. I hadn't even heard of most of the stuff they were after, let alone dealt with the weapons. But I wasn't going to throw in the towel."

Diveroli asked Merrill if he knew anyone who could source the different kinds of nonstandard weapons that were appearing in the solicitations. Merrill said he knew a Swiss man by the name of Henri who'd sold him Uzi parts in the past. Merrill and Henri had a good working relationship and had met several times. Merrill started forwarding Diveroli's e-mails requesting quotes for AK-47s, heavy machine guns, and grenades to Henri. Diveroli had no direct contact with Henri, but he was able to quote aggressively, using Henri's low prices on surplus munitions.

With Henri's connections, Diveroli was soon winning multimillion-dollar Iraqi arms contracts. His business model was brilliant. Most companies try to develop more customers as they grow. Not the young gunrunner. Diveroli concentrated exclusively on a single customer: the US government. No organization on the planet spent more money than the Pentagon, he knew.

Like an aspiring samurai, Diveroli set about mastering the art of arms dealing. He had little formal education but was blessed with an intuitive grasp of the art of deal-making as well as the gift of gab. Studying FedBizOpps wasn't tedious for him—it was the pursuit of a dream.

And it was profitable. Diveroli had virtually no overhead, no staff, and few of the expenses normally associated with running a company. Within months he'd started making serious money, amassing hundreds of thousands of dollars in profit. But Diveroli still maintained a tightfisted lifestyle. He drove an old, junk-box Daewoo Leganza sedan and dressed like a slob. His main expenses were drugs and the tabs he ran up at Miami Beach nightclubs.

The launch of the American offensive called Phantom Fury in the city of Fallujah, Iraq, in the fall of 2004 did nothing to slow the insurgency. Car bombs exploded in markets, suicide bombers attacked American outposts, and soldiers began to refuse to transport goods within Iraq, citing the lack of safety and protection.

As the insurgency intensified, so did the volume of solicitations appearing on FedBizOpps. Like the contract for ten thousand AK-47 rifles Diveroli bid on. Trying to get a price for the guns without relying on Henri, Diveroli found an Italian lawyer who brokered arms deals. Arnaldo La Scala claimed to have "bound" a cache of guns in a warehouse in Croatia—he didn't own them, but he said he was the exclusive broker. Diveroli bid on the contract using La Scala's price and his now trademark 9 percent profit margin. And Diveroli won. But when he tried to arrange for delivery of the weapons to Iraq, La Scala said he wasn't able to get them out of Croatia because the government refused to approve the sale. Diveroli couldn't accept excuses. He knew the Army didn't accept excuses. He had to deliver to protect his performance record, as best he could, in the chaos that was enveloping Iraq and grinding flights to a halt because of insurgent RPG fire.

Panicking, as any nineteen-year-old might, Diveroli called Ralph Merrill to ask if he had any other contacts who could supply the AK-47s quickly. Merrill explained that La Scala was really just a broker for Henri, the Swiss arms dealer Merrill was friendly with. Merrill said Diveroli should cut out the middleman and go directly to Henri. He gave Diveroli Henri's e-mail address and phone number. Merrill said his last name was Thomet, pronounced in the German way— *toe-met*.

When Diveroli called Thomet, the Swiss broker said the Croatian AK-47s couldn't be shipped to Iraq. But Thomet said he had access to another stockpile of AK-47s in Bosnia. Relieved, Diveroli was able to get the guns to Baghdad and reap a nice profit. It was another break-through. Diveroli was now dealing directly with a serious arms dealer who had high-level contacts throughout the Balkans. In a business that revolved around relationships, Diveroli had just acquired a major-league connection.

But the AK-47 shipment had a problem. Nothing major—the kind of thing that happened often in the gun trade, especially in the unfolding disaster of the war in Iraq. The Bosnians had slipped a thousand substandard AK-47 rifles alongside nine thousand good-quality guns that were delivered to Baghdad. Getting guns to pass muster with the procurement officers in Iraq usually wasn't hard: as long as the guns worked, they were okayed. *Serviceable without qualification* was the term of art on FedBizOpps. It essentially meant the guns had to fire, no matter how old they were or where they came from.

The poor quality of weapons being issued to the Iraqis was one of countless double standards on display in Baghdad. Often American soldiers were armed with the latest high-tech weapons, and ammunition was plentiful; when IEDs began to rip apart Humvees, soldiers campaigned to have their vehicles "up-armored." The benighted Iraqis got ancient Serbian AK-47s, Polish tanks that didn't start, and the cheapest, nastiest surplus ammo private contractors like AEY could find in dank bunkers in Eastern Europe.

A thousand of the Bosnian guns Diveroli shipped failed to meet even the abysmal standards the Army applied to Iraqi matériel. When the guns were rejected, Diveroli insisted that Thomet get the Bosnians to send replacements, which duly arrived in Baghdad. The faulty weapons were then "abandoned" in the field. There was no way for Diveroli to know what happened to them, if he'd cared to find out, just as there was no reliable method for the Army to ensure they didn't wind up in the hands of the enemy.

Elections in Iraq early in 2005 only quickened the daily thrum of roadside bombings, kidnappings, and sectarian fighting between Sunni and Shiite Muslims. The violence caused a thrilling upswing in business for AEY, and the Swiss broker became Diveroli's ideal collaborator. Thomet provided a "delivered" price. This meant that he took care of the logistics—the packing and shipping, obtaining the necessary permissions to transport hazardous goods, as well as the chartering of the planes to carry the goods to Iraq. Despite millions being spent on security, simply landing at Baghdad International Airport was extremely perilous, due to insurgent RPG and sniper fire; then followed the six-mile ride to the Green Zone along Route Irish—or ambush alley, as it was known. Thomet was able to navigate these obstacles with a skill and discretion Diveroli didn't possess. In the Balkans, men like Thomet used bribes, kickbacks, and numbered Swiss bank accounts as standard operating procedure, or so everyone in the business assumed—including, inevitably, the Pentagon.

At the time, Diveroli's buddy David Packouz was plying his trade as a massage therapist and taking a couple of chemistry classes at a local college. Alex Podrizki was still finishing an undergraduate degree in international relations. After he graduated, Podrizki had planned to join the US military, to follow in his veteran father's footsteps. But the invasion of Iraq had appalled Podrizki as a naked theft of Iraq's oil fields based on lies about Saddam Hussein's alleged connection to the attack on 9/11. Podrizki had become radicalized politically, attending protests and questioning America's role in the world. Over time, as the lack of weapons of mass destruction in Iraq became apparent, David Packouz had come to share his friend's dim view of the war. Efraim Diveroli had a different response.

"Do I agree with the Iraq War?" Diveroli asked Packouz and Podrizki one night as they passed a bong around. "Do I think George Bush did the right thing for the country by invading Iraq? No. But am I happy about it? Absofuckinglutely. I hope Bush invades more countries, because it's good for business."

The dudes rolled their eyes. Among his friends, Diveroli's act was a running joke—but it was getting old for Alex Podrizki.

"Efraim used to be a very funny guy," Podrizki recalled. "Cynical but hilarious. We used to sell pot and jewelry to tourists together along Miami Beach. He had an old .22 that we'd take to the range to shoot, and we used to joke about sawing off the barrel and attaching laser sights and a fifty-round clip—making this shitty gun super-tactical. But then Efraim changed when he started to be an arms dealer. He became all about making money. He wasn't funny anymore—he became controlling, overbearing, arrogant. He was a smart guy, in a lot of ways, but he became one-dimensional."

///////

In the spring of 2005, Diveroli came across an opportunity on FedBizOpps that promised to give him a chance to win a contract far larger than anything he'd attempted. The $51 million contract was called an ID/IQ, meaning an Indefinite Delivery, Indefinite Quantity solicitation. Diveroli learned that in an ID/IQ contract the Army couldn't say with certainty the amount of arms it wanted, or how long the deal would run. But it wanted to select a single company to fulfill the many orders that would follow as the United States tried to prepare Iraqis for combat.

The previous ID/IQ deal in Iraq, which was about to expire, had been won by a company called Taos. In the normal course of business, Taos would be the strong favorite to retain the deal. But Diveroli had other ideas. As usual, he contacted Thomet for quotes. Rocket-propelled grenades, mortar rounds, Russian-style machine guns—Thomet had access to matériel all over the Balkans. Diveroli entered his bid, heaving a large sigh.

"Then I got an e-mail saying that I'd won the contract," Diveroli recalled. "I'd won a fifty-one-million-dollar deal! I went out and celebrated like crazy. But the next day I found out that there was one major caveat. The same damn contract had been awarded to four other companies at the same time."

Instead of giving the whole ID/IQ contract to one winner, the Pentagon was going to conduct "mini-competes." AEY received an initial order for $500,000 in ammunition, but the rest of the order was cut into small contracts for Diveroli and his adversaries to bid on—companies like Taos, DLS, Blane International.

"Later on I would learn the significance of these companies," Diveroli recalled. "But at the time I figured they were big companies and I was the little guy. Right away I started winning the mini-competes. I was beating the big boys at their own game."

A normal commercial enterprise would assign perhaps a dozen people to the job. Not AEY: Diveroli worked alone. He was now on the phone with Thomet two, three, four times a day. The individual contracts were relatively small—a thousand pistols, half a million dollars' worth of a specific kind of ammo, a million dollars' worth of grenades. Whatever he was after, Diveroli knew that if anyone could find the arms, it was Thomet. He'd bound large quantities of weapons and ammos in storehouses in Bosnia, Croatia, and Albania. It made Thomet one of the few reliable sources in the market.

Diveroli didn't know or care what Thomet did to get the arms to Baghdad—nor did the US government. The Army wanted guns and ammunition in Iraq as quickly and cheaply as possible, and Diveroli was delighted to do the job.

As he continued to triumph on FedBizOpps, Diveroli was acquiring a reputation inside the Green Zone in Iraq. A Texan named Howard Lowry, who operated his own one-man company in Baghdad, also competed for the ID/IQ deals. Working in a war zone, Lowry had first-hand knowledge of the dangers of being an arms dealer. The Army's procurement officers were sometimes on the take, Lowry learned, but in such a lawless environment nobody was investigating or prosecuting the crimes. Rival contractors roamed Baghdad in armored vehicles, notoriously shooting at Iraqi civilians with impunity, and competitors sometimes uttered violent threats to each other. Lowry recalled talking to Diveroli during the ID/IQs competition and being struck by both his youth and his lack of awareness of the nature of the world he'd entered.

"The Army's contracting officers told me Diveroli was an arrogant little snot," Lowry recalled. "There were rumors floating around that he was a cocaine dealer. No one could understand how this kid could come up with the money to bid on contracts."

On the phone one day, Diveroli boasted to Lowry that he was going to "kick his ass" in the mini-competes. Lowry laughed, but he wasn't impressed by Diveroli's manner, which came across as insolent and immature.

"I told him that he didn't understand that he was in a very danger-ous business," Lowry recalled. "I wasn't threatening him. I was letting him know that arms dealing was a very, very high-testosterone busi-ness. There were a lot of big egos. Diveroli told me not to worry. He said he knew everything about the business—literally everything. I told him he had no idea what he was getting himself into."

As he neared his twentieth birthday, Diveroli imagined he was forg-ing an identity as a gunrunner. He was beginning to believe he was the equal of or even better than hardened arms dealers like Henri Thomet. As Diveroli sat in his apartment in Miami Beach lighting a bong, the perils of war were little more than an abstraction.

Chapter Two

SAVE THE KING

In 2004 Efraim Diveroli did $1,043,869 in business with the US government. In 2005 that number leaped to $7,238,329, as he liked to boast to his buddies David Packouz and Alex Podrizki. Diveroli was getting rich, and he reveled in his triumphs. He finally moved out of his tiny studio into a one-bedroom apartment overlooking the ocean in a building called Executive Condos. He hired a cleaning lady to come to his place once a week to get rid of the worst of the squalor. He treated himself to a black Mercedes. It was used, but still: the luxury sedan spoke to the status he'd achieved in such an improbable way at such a young age.

Smoking dope with David Packouz, Alex Podrizki, and their gang of Orthodox kids, Diveroli constantly bragged about the deals he was doing. Diveroli was younger than the other dudes in their posse, who were now in their early twenties and mostly going to college. Diveroli had always been the designated clown, the one who mooned patrons in the Eden Roc's exclusive dining room and was willing to take up any dare. But his personality was changing as he grew more obsessed with business. So were his appetites.

"I started to see my first girlfriend," Diveroli recalled. "She was a Jewish girl, artsy, pretty. My second love was drugs and alcohol. I loved to get high. I couldn't enjoy life sober. I would wake up to a joint. I'd smoke another for lunch. In the evening, I'd drink and snort cocaine.

My buddies would all get high, too, but I was always the extremist, doing the most drugs and making an asshole out of myself when I was wasted. My girlfriend hated all the drugs—the weed, the Ecstasy, the mescaline, the ketamine, the hallucinogenic mushrooms, and probably some other shit I can't remember."

Nothing mattered to Diveroli as much as business and money and getting high. He started to fight with his girlfriend more and more often. The couple broke up, got together, and broke up again, every few weeks—an emotional roller coaster.

Then a friend told Diveroli that his girlfriend had cheated on him. Diveroli got drunk that night and drove over to her parents' house, where she lived, parking his car on the front lawn.

"I started to bang on her bedroom window, demanding to talk to her," Diveroli recalled. "Her mother came out and threatened to call the police—which she then did. In a matter of minutes the relationship was gone forever."

Diveroli's ex-girlfriend obtained a restraining order. The brush with the law could have chastened Diveroli, but he was heedless. He was too caught up in his new life as an arms dealer to care—or to worry that he might be spinning out of control.

On the contrary, Diveroli was convinced he needed to expand his business. He was going to turn AEY into a conglomerate. But his bandwidth was already stretched to the breaking point. He needed help. Whom in his posse could he trust? Who was smart, ambitious, and looking to make a lot of money?

David Packouz was a few years older than Diveroli and studying science at college—an attribute that impressed the younger man greatly. They'd been friends since Diveroli was twelve and Packouz was sixteen, and both attended the same synagogue—or, to be more accurate, both skipped the services to smoke reefer and wreak havoc.

"Efraim would steal the yarmulkes of older kids," Packouz recalled. "He'd pick on the boys with short tempers, the ones he knew he could get a reaction from. He'd run off with their yarmulke and they'd chase him and finally catch him and beat him a little. Then when they'd walk away, he'd steal the yarmulke again. He was an annoying kid who enjoyed being an annoying kid. My friends liked him because it was fun watching him annoy uptight people. I wasn't so crazy about him."

Now twenty-four, Packouz was good at school, but he couldn't imagine spending his life as a scientist in a lab coat doing research. Privately, he longed to be a rock star. He spent hours practicing the guitar and dreaming of performing in front of arena-size audiences. His music was soulful, layered with complex movements, a blend of Pink Floyd, Alice in Chains, and Simon and Garfunkel—though he knew that sounded like a strange combination.

To get the chance to sing, sometimes Packouz went to open-microphone nights at clubs in Miami, but his main outlet was karaoke in a basement bar called the Studio. While others treated karaoke as an excuse to get drunk and bellow power ballads, Packouz took his performances seriously, concentrating on pitch and timbre as he imagined himself to be a real rock and roller. To develop a distinctive look, and to hide premature balding, he'd shaved his head, making his sharp blue eyes more striking.

"I planned on recording an album one day when I had enough money," Packouz recalled. "But the truth is that I didn't know what I was going to do with myself."

To support himself, Packouz advertised his services as a masseur on Craigslist. He figured that massage beat flipping burgers for minimum wage, even if fending off the sexual advances of clients was often a problem.

But Packouz had found another way to make money. He told Diveroli that he'd started to trade goods on the Internet to supplement his income. Packouz bought textiles online on websites like Alibaba.com, purchasing bibs and towels and sheets from manufacturers in Pakistan and India, then selling them to a contact in Miami who supplied old folks' homes. The business was tiny, with deals worth only a couple of thousand dollars for each transaction, but he'd fulfilled a few contracts and was starting to concentrate more on the Web—in essence, the same twenty-first-century business model Diveroli was following on a much larger scale.

Apart from their burgeoning online businesses, the thing that Diveroli and Packouz had most in common was money. Both were very, very interested in money. Diveroli was already well off, at least for someone so young, but the early wealth only made him want more. Packouz was effectively broke, but he didn't want to stay that way. Massage was never going to allow him the means to pursue a professional music career, he figured, nor would a job as a scientist. He was looking for a way to make a lot of money—the faster the better.

Diveroli and Packouz had other characteristics in common. Like a fondness for pot and the propensity to get in trouble. Both were raised in Orthodox Jewish families, but they'd rebelled against the rules and rites of their faith. Both had been kicked out of Hebrew school. When Packouz was booted for failing a drug test, his parents sent him to Israel, to a school that specialized in helping Jewish kids with substance-abuse issues. It turned out to be a great place to get high.

"I took acid by the Dead Sea," Packouz said. "I came across this guy, an American hippie, who said his name was Moses. I had a transcendental experience. I experienced infinity."

The son of a rabbi, Packouz grappled with his faith. At college, he'd taken an anthropology class and learned about the many cultures of the world. The experience changed his view of religion. Packouz wanted to know why there were so many events in the Bible that couldn't literally be true, as he'd been taught in Hebrew school—like Noah's flood, or so-called facts in the Torah that were obviously contradicted by scientific evidence.

"I started to ask real questions," Packouz said. "I talked to the rabbis, and they didn't have good answers. They just wound up using insults and put-downs, like I was a kid who knew nothing. I finally realized that there weren't answers to these questions because human beings wrote the Bible, not God. I realized I had to develop my own philosophy—my own morality and ethics. So I became an atheist. Science became my religion. I came to hope that science could deliver what religion had always promised. I figured that was a much more likely scenario than an invisible man in the sky who was full of contradictions."

When Packouz got together with Diveroli and Alex Podrizki and the others in their group to smoke dope, he shared his thoughts. The gathering of a dozen or so Orthodox kids might have looked like any other collection of stoners telling each other not to bogart the spliff. But despite the slacker appearances they were intelligent and engaged. They had long, involved conversations about science, geopolitics, Miles Davis, religion. All except Diveroli. He talked about business: Guns and money, money and guns—that was all he was interested in. And war.

Diveroli told his friends he was going to turn AEY into a multibillion-dollar company. He wanted to trade weapons on a global scale. He wanted a Gulfstream V private jet and a staff of hundreds. That was the kind of success Diveroli imagined for himself: the life of a billionaire. But with the added degree of difficulty—and frisson of excitement—that came with making his fortune practicing the black art of arms dealing.

Packouz didn't share Diveroli's outlandish hopes, at least not yet, but he was impressed by his friend's determination and success. In December of 2005 Diveroli decided to approach Packouz about working together. By then, Diveroli had decided from his experience that hard work and the ability to make a deal were what mattered, not the amount of money or the thing being traded. Bidding on bibs in Karachi to catch the drool of a septuagenarian in Miami Beach was no different from buying a cache of AK-47s from a Bosnian thug via a Swiss arms dealer for delivery to Baghdad. In theory.

One evening Diveroli made plans to go out with Packouz. The pair rarely hung out together alone; they were both much closer to others in their circle. Diveroli was in an expansive mood when he picked up Packouz in his Mercedes to go to a party a local rabbi was throwing.

The party was designed to entice kids like Diveroli and Packouz back to the straight and narrow, to meet someone nice, to settle down, to stay in the fold—free liquor, good food, and a gathering of pretty Jewish girls. Packouz recalled that for them it was just a cheap night out—and a chance to get lucky.

"You and me, let's talk some business," Diveroli said as they drove through the warm winter evening. *You and me:* the sentence structure was part of the persona Diveroli was perfecting—the swaggering, tough-guy cadence that matched his idea of how a gunrunner should talk.

"You and me, we can make money together," Diveroli said.

"You know I'm interested in making money," Packouz said.

"I know you're a real smart guy. You've done some business. I could really use a guy like you."

Passing Biscayne Bay, luxury cruise ships in one direction, the silver skyscrapers of Miami in the other, Packouz turned to Diveroli. "What do you actually do?" Like the other friends in their group, Packouz knew that Diveroli was an arms dealer, but he didn't know any of the details.

"I sell all sorts of stuff to the United States government. Let me tell you, in Iraq there's a gold rush going on. George Bush has opened the money floodgates."

"So I read in the papers."

"I'm in a prime position to capture quite a bit of that money. I have been getting a lot of it already. I'm doing all kinds of deals, selling the weapons and ammo to the government that they're giving to the Iraqi national army."

"What kind of weapons?"

"You name it. AK-47s, RPKs, light machine guns, grenades, 7.62-by-39 ammo, 7.62-by-54 ammo. I'm wrapping up a big contract right now."

Packouz said it sounded like a risky business.

"It is," Diveroli said. "That's what keeps all the schmucks and pussies out."

Diveroli grinned in his peculiar way—half smirk, half wink. He had a talent for making deals, and one of the components of being successful in business was knowing how to seduce the other party.

"You and me, we've known each other forever," Diveroli said. "I know you're smart and you've got balls. That's why I've picked you to be my partner."

Packouz hadn't agreed to be Diveroli's partner, of course—but the presumption was typical. Diveroli assumed that, because he'd selected Packouz, he'd obviously want to sign on. Diveroli explained that he had more work than he could handle himself. With Packouz on board, Diveroli said they could blow AEY into something big.

"I'm flattered," Packouz said. "Fortune favors the brave."

"Absofuckinglutely."

They rode in silence for a time as Packouz contemplated the proposal. Where did selling guns fit in his worldview? Was it morally permissible to be an arms dealer? The guns were being used to fight Islamist extremists, after all. The business was perfectly legal, and the customer was the US government. But wasn't there an inherent evil to selling death—wasn't profiting from the blood and suffering of others wrong?

Something about Diveroli was irresistible. Not charismatic, quite, but funny in a half-crazy and fearless way. He was somehow larger-than-life. Not physically: Diveroli wasn't large in stature, but his personality was forceful. He was obviously going to make it to the big time, come what may.

They arrived at the rabbi's house.

"How much money are you making?" Packouz asked.

"Serious money," said Diveroli.

"How much?"

"That's confidential information." The car came to a stop.

"If you had to leave the country tomorrow, how much money would you be able to take with you?"

"In cash?"

"Cold, hard cash."

"I'm going to tell you, buddy. But not to impress you. Not because I'm bragging." Diveroli paused, as if he were about to reveal his deepest secret. "I have one point eight million dollars in cash in the bank."

Packouz stared in disbelief. He'd expected a significant amount, given Diveroli's incessant talk about money. But nearly $2 million? Diveroli was only twenty years old. He was a ninth-grade dropout.

Diveroli grinned at Packouz with a glint in his eye, as if to say, *Can you fucking believe it?*

"Dude" was all Packouz said.

/////

AEY now had a staff of two. The global headquarters was Efraim Diveroli's oceanfront one-bedroom apartment. In its small alcove, the pair sat on opposite sides of a table. Diveroli and Packouz each had a laptop computer, one a beaten-up Dell, the other a junker Toshiba. A desktop computer sat on the table but it was useless because it constantly froze. Each also had a cell phone and a subscription to a discount Internet phone service. The bong lived on the coffee table in the living room—an essential home appliance.

"I figured I was going to make millions," Packouz said. "I didn't plan on being an arms dealer forever, like Efraim. I'd never even owned a gun."

Their agreement stipulated that Packouz would work entirely on commission, with no salary. Account Executive was his title. Diveroli would stake his money to finance the contracts Packouz found on FedBizOpps. Packouz had a little money saved, so he figured he could live on that while he tried to make his first transaction—supplemented by the occasional massage gig.

But the first opportunity Packouz brought to the new relationship had nothing to do with arms. Before joining up with Diveroli, Packouz had come across an offer on Alibaba.com for a large number of Xbox 360s. At the time, the video-game console was a worldwide craze, with stores unable to keep up with demand. Packouz had found a supply quoted online at $320 per unit. Retail was $400. But he knew that Xboxes were being sold on eBay for double and triple the retail price. He figured he could buy the Xboxes online and sell them to local big-box stores like Costco and Sears and make a fortune.

But there was a catch: the minimum order was one hundred thousand units and payment had to be made at the time of delivery. The total cost would be $32 million. Diveroli didn't have anything like that amount of money. But if they could find someone to finance the deal they stood to make millions. For two weeks the pair worked the phones trying to find a hedge fund or high-net-worth individual willing to take the risk. They agreed that they'd split the profits fifty-fifty.

"I quickly saw how talented at business Efraim was," Packouz recalled.

The broker running the deal on Alibaba.com didn't want to tell Packouz and Diveroli where he was getting the Xboxes, lest he get cut out of the transaction. But Diveroli persuaded him to reveal his source by saying he had a guaranteed buyer and he'd split the profit with the broker. As soon as Diveroli had the name, he dumped the broker and moved on through a daisy chain of three other brokers until they reached the large electronics company behind the deal.

"Efraim was only a kid, but he was too smart for grown men," Packouz recalled. "I was sure I was going to be rich. It was very exciting. But first we needed to finance the deal."

"Gentlemen," Diveroli said to a New York hedge fund they approached to lend them the money. "I need thirty-two million dollars, and I happen to be thirty million dollars short."

Packouz smiled at Diveroli's audacity. But no one was willing to back such a dicey deal relying on the word of two kids. Packouz was crestfallen. In days he'd gone from being a broke massage therapist to a multimillionaire and then back to penury. Being around Diveroli was dizzying—but in a thrilling way.

"Look, buddy, we tried to make a lot of money fast but it didn't work out," Diveroli said, consoling Packouz over a bong that evening. "You and me, let's get started on some real business—the business I know."

Diveroli logged on to FedBizOpps and showed Packouz what a Pentagon solicitation looked like. He explained the various meanings behind technical terms like *single source*, which indicated that the government was going to award the contract to only one bidder. *Best value* required the government to weigh a number of factors in awarding contracts, including that AEY was a small business and should thus be viewed more favorably than the large corporations who'd long dominated federal procurement.

Packouz was impressed by Diveroli's command of the language of defense contracting. The solicitations ran to thirty or forty pages. Each word and phrase in the long, dense paragraphs of technical terms was pregnant with legal meaning. For a high school dropout, Diveroli was incredibly sophisticated when it came to business, Packouz could see.

Scanning FedBizOpps, it occurred to Packouz that he and Diveroli had the perfect education for the devilishly difficult task of navigating the website. As religious students in Hebrew school, they'd been forced to study documents that bore an uncanny resemblance to government contracts.

"Reading the Talmud as Orthodox Jewish kids had prepared us for this kind of work," Packouz recalled. "The Talmud is a complex legal document written in a foreign language. You've got to study it line by line. There are references to other sections and other books, just like there was in the contracts. As a kid in the super-religious school I went to, I was forced to study the Talmud for four hours every day. Efraim and I had been taught how to really concentrate on concepts that other people would find mind-numbingly boring.

"There were a lot of suppliers who didn't know how to work FedBiz-Opps as well as we did. I'm talking about big companies with experienced adult staff. Diveroli really had mastered the system, and he was teaching me the secrets. You had to read the solicitations religiously."

Working alongside Diveroli, Packouz saw that searching FedBiz-Opps and working on winning contracts was all that he did. Diveroli never read a book or a magazine. He didn't watch television or follow the news. His sole focus in life was poring over the website, looking for deals.

"Money was all he cared about," Packouz recalled. "Literally. He didn't talk about sports or politics or culture. He would do anything to make money."

Packouz was mesmerized by Diveroli's work ethic—if not his ethics. Even as Diveroli was occupied fulfilling the Iraq contracts he'd already won, he constantly bid on new contracts. Eighteen-hour shifts blurred one into the next. Days were spent contacting manufacturers in the United States to find the cheapest prices for weapons for AEY to bid on. Nights, the pair worked the phones with arms dealers in Eastern Europe, who had the Communist Bloc weapons the Army was desperate to get to Iraq. At two or three in the morning, Packouz would crash on Diveroli's couch to save the time it took to drive to his studio apartment. As dawn broke, Packouz would wake to find his new partner hitting the bong and scanning FedBizOpps.

"Working with Efraim was a twenty-four-hour ordeal," Packouz recalled. "I had never seen anyone work so hard. It didn't matter if Efraim was tripling his money on a deal, he always tried to squeeze every last penny. One of his favorite lines was 'If the other guy's happy, then there's still money left on the table.'"

A solicitation for night-vision goggles was a typical example of Diveroli in action. The manufacturer Diveroli contacted for a quote was a giant defense company. If the company's executives knew about the contract on FedBizOpps, they would likely bid on it themselves, so Diveroli went for a diversion. He said he was buying thousands of goggles for an unnamed foreign government. He said he was competing with a Chinese goggles manufacturer so he needed a low price. Then Diveroli held out the promise of more orders in the future.

Ordinarily, a corporation would protect its pricing structure, particularly for its network of dealers. But Diveroli knew how to play on the venality of the executives: promise excellent volume, no hassles, no harm, easy money. Lured by Diveroli's sleight of hand, the manufacturer agreed to give AEY a price even lower than it gave to its own dealers. Adding his usual 9 percent profit margin, Diveroli won the contract by underbidding the competition—including the company's regular dealers.

Trouble appeared when Diveroli actually placed the purchase order and the manufacturer learned that the customer was really the US Army. Furious, it refused to sell to him. Fine, Diveroli said, I'll tell the government you reneged on the deal and substitute Chinese goggles. Diveroli was talking on the speakerphone, smiling at Packouz. They could hear the men on the other end of the line cursing. Who is this little motherfucker? Who does he think he's dealing with? He's going to snitch on us to the federal government? Diveroli stifled a laugh when they buckled and agreed to the sale.

"That's how you squeeze yourself into the middle of a deal," Diveroli said afterward.

Under Diveroli's guidance, Packouz prepared a bid on a multimillion-dollar contract to supply hundreds of SUVs to the US Embassy in Pakistan. The size of the deal promised to make Packouz a huge profit. The scale of the stakes was one of the most astonishing aspects of FedBizOpps: just winning one medium-size contract could make Packouz a millionaire.

Packouz spent weeks tirelessly trying to source the vehicles, eventually finding a dealer in Karachi with a supply of cheap SUVs. But the solicitation required ongoing service for the vehicles, which AEY wasn't able to provide. Packouz didn't win the contract, but simply going through the bidding had been uplifting. FedBizOpps was like a casino, Packouz realized. Even if there was only a 10 percent chance of success—even if there was only a 1 percent chance—the sums of money were so large it seemed just a matter of time before he won a contract and made a fortune. After all, the living proof of that possibility was sitting on the far side of the table, talking to his drug dealer about scoring cocaine for that night.

In the early months of their new business relationship, Packouz won a couple of small contracts—seventeen thousand gallons of propane to an Air Force base in Wyoming, $70,000 worth of Second World War–era rifles to train Special Forces at Fort Bragg. The profits were tiny. Packouz was learning, watching, whetting his appetite, biding his time.

But dealing with Diveroli had a flip side. Packouz watched his friend with a sense of wonder—but also sometimes dread. Packouz clearly saw that Diveroli was a genius. He was also a liar. He misled directly, indirectly, compulsively—almost as if telling a lie were better than telling the truth as a matter of principle.

When the pair traveled to Las Vegas for an arms trade show, Packouz watched in disbelief as Diveroli received a call from a procurement officer in Iraq threatening to cancel a contract because of repeated delays in the delivery of a large shipment of helmets for the Iraq army. The first load of helmets had arrived late, and then they'd been sent to the Abu Ghraib prison, not Baghdad. The mistakes were typical of Iraq: transportation was incredibly dangerous, with roadside bombings occurring daily, and tracking goods was essentially impossible.

But the procurement officer in Baghdad didn't seem to care about the realities on the ground, at least not in this instance. He told Diveroli he was going to kick AEY off the contract. This was worrisome. The government could cancel a contract *for convenience*, which meant it had changed its mind and was no longer going to purchase the goods. The other form of cancellation was *for cause*. Losing a contract for cause was a serious matter. It could be disastrous for AEY's performance rating with the Pentagon; one of the main considerations the government used in awarding contracts was prior performance; a canceled contract would be a permanent blot on the company's record. Diveroli needed to persuade the procurement officer to change his mind. The line was poor. Standing in the middle of the SHOT Show—a huge gun show held in a cavernous convention center in Vegas—Diveroli had to yell into his cell phone to be heard.

"Efraim launched into one of the most intricate and heartfelt sob stories I'd ever heard," Packouz recalled. "He gave a barrage of excuses for the delayed delivery. It was everyone else's fault."

Diveroli begged the procurement officer not to cancel the contract. His voice was shaking and his eyes were welling with tears. He said that if the deal fell through he'd be ruined. His tiny business would go into bankruptcy. He was going to lose his house. His children would go hungry. His wife would leave him. He was begging for his life—and all of it was completely made up. But he was totally convincing. The procurement officer backed down.

"I'd never seen more skillful lying," Packouz said. "I didn't know if Efraim was psychotic, or if he was acting. But he believed what he was saying—at least while he was talking.

"There was no doubt that Efraim knew how to make money, and how to get people to do what he wanted. I figured that after I made a couple of million I'd go out on my own. I told myself that I would never deal dishonestly with anyone myself."

It seemed to Packouz that Diveroli was so consumed he'd come to inhabit an alternate reality. His conversations often sounded as if he were acting in a scripted movie, like Diveroli's collection of sayings. Some were taken from *Lord of War*, one of the rare movies he took the time to see—not once or twice but over and over. "Where there's a will, there's a weapon," Diveroli would say. Or: "There are three basic types of arms deals—white being legal, black being illegal, and my personal favorite, gray."

Other sayings were his own. Packouz began to write them down, partly for entertainment, partly to keep track of the morality—or amorality—of the world he now inhabited. "You can fuck almost everybody once and get away with it," Diveroli would say. Or: "I don't care if I have the smallest dick in the room, as long as I have the biggest wallet." Or: "If you see a crack in the door, kick the fucker open." And: "Once a gunrunner, always a gunrunner."

"Efraim was still a kid, but he didn't see himself that way," Packouz recalled. "He would go toe-to-toe with high-ranking military officials, Eastern European mobsters, executives for Fortune 500 companies. He didn't give a fuck. He'd take them on and win, and then give them the finger. And I was following in his footsteps."

Once a week, or so, the pair hit the clubs of South Beach. Diveroli kept his cocaine in a small plastic bullet, retiring to the bathroom every half hour for another snort. After pounding Grey Goose, Diveroli would be high and drunk and ready to pick up a girl. His opening lines were beyond terrible: "Hey, baby, everybody's got a price, so what's yours?" Or: "Your pants are like a mirror, baby—I can see myself in them."

The Rodney Dangerfield–like approach often ended in disaster. Once, reaching out to grab the backside of a passing woman, Diveroli said, "You and me, baby, the backseat of my car in ten minutes." The woman's boyfriend wasn't amused. A mountain of a man, he grabbed Diveroli by the scruff of his neck and threw him against the wall. Packouz jumped in the middle.

"He's drunk," Packouz said. "He's really, really drunk. He didn't mean anything by it."

Kicked out by the bouncers, Diveroli was giddy as they walked to his car.

"The world is full of shitheads," Diveroli said, throwing his arm around Packouz. "You're the only guy I can trust. I consider you my best friend. You watch, we're going to become billionaires one day. You and me, we're going to be flying around in our own private jets soon. You and me, we'll come back and crush those motherfuckers."

Packouz was unnerved by Diveroli's calling him his best friend. Packouz certainly didn't feel the same way. But he wasn't going to express his ambivalence. Not when the promise of riches was so temptingly close.

One evening, Packouz convinced Diveroli to go to his favorite karaoke joint. Packouz wanted to sing, not just get wasted. Diveroli loved the idea, if not the idea of staying sober. The Studio was an underground bar with no cover charge and big crowds on the weekend. When Packouz went onstage, he sang U2's "With or Without You," followed by Pearl Jam's "Black." As always, he took the performance seriously, singing gently, careful to stay in key, and drawing a nice round of applause when he was done.

Diveroli jumped onstage with mock bravado. His voice was loud and completely off-key—for comic effect. He sang "It's My Life" by Bon Jovi, followed by "Rape Me" by Nirvana. For an encore, he sang Tim McGraw's country power ballad "Live Like You Were Dying." As he bellowed out the tunes, Diveroli tore off his shirt and gyrated his hips in mock-rock-star fashion, garnering whoops and hollers.

Afterward, Diveroli went to the bathroom to do a line of coke. Walking out of the men's room, he saw an attractive young Asian woman sitting on a couch by herself. Diveroli sat down next to her.

"So, do you do coke?" he asked.

The woman appeared shocked, but she answered. "Well, not in a really long time."

"Do you want to?"

"Why not?"

The pair vanished into the men's room. The woman, Suzie,* was a college student. She gave Diveroli her number, but when he called her the next day she didn't pick up. Diveroli dialed and redialed and redialed until she relented and answered. He persuaded her to have dinner that night. So began a tumultuous two-year relationship.

In contrast to Diveroli, Packouz was shy around girls. He was twenty-four years old at the time and he'd had only one serious girlfriend. But his luck was about to change. Entering the lobby of an upscale condo called the Flamingo in Miami Beach one afternoon, he

---

* Not her real name.

caught the eye of a pretty young woman. Packouz was carrying his massage table on his shoulder. He'd continued to advertise his services on Craigslist to support himself until he made his fortune with Diveroli. The woman was wheeling a massage table on a cart. She was lithe and lean and looked to be around his age. Packouz had been rushing to his appointment, but now he slowed down.

"I've got to get one of those carts for my table," Packouz said to the woman.

"You should," she replied. "Carrying your table over your shoulder like that will give you neck and shoulder problems."

"I'm very strong. I can handle it."

She laughed.

Packouz wondered if she might be flirting and asked, "Where did you study massage?"

"Educating Hands."

"Me, too," Packouz said excitedly. "Here's my card. If you want to trade massages sometime, let me know. I could really use one."

"Sounds good. Here's my card."

Packouz had her number. Sara was her name. She was Spanish— and she was a knockout. He'd taken the risk and it had paid off; fortune favored the brave, as he'd decided when he signed on with Diveroli. He disciplined himself and waited two days before calling, time calculated to make him look interested but not desperate. She offered to host, and after a few sessions of exchanged massages they went out for sushi and started to date.

The dudes both had girlfriends. FedBizOpps was humming with opportunities as the unfolding fiasco in Iraq fueled the tiny company. Packouz was receiving a rare education. He wasn't learning how to make a living—he was learning how to make a killing.

In Baghdad, the pickings were easy for Diveroli. Because procurement officers were rotated in and out of Iraq, Diveroli could rely on their inexperience. He won the soldiers over with fake wild-eyed patriotism and a keen sense of how to play to the military; he could "Yes, sir" and "No, sir," with the best of them. To get the inside dirt on a so-licitation, he'd call the soldier in charge in Baghdad and pretend to be a colonel or even a general seeking an update on the progress of the contract.

"He'd be toasted and you wouldn't know it," Packouz recalled. "He was incredibly effective. And relentless. He seemed to know every trick in the book. Business just came naturally to him. He was always look-ing for an edge. He was always looking to *squeeze* himself into deals—that's the word he used. I started calling him Squeeze-a-Roli. Or Sleaze-a-Roli. It was truly unbelievable to watch."

Scanning FedBizOpps, Diveroli didn't limit himself to Iraq. Pack-ouz watched as Diveroli won a State Department contract to supply high-grade FN Herstal machine guns to the Colombian army. The guns were to be used in the fight against FARC rebels in the mountains of Colombia, a hot war that had caused mass casualties. The deal was lucrative for Diveroli, but he wasn't satisfied—as usual, he wanted more and more. Using his wiles, he convinced the procurement officer from the State Department to allow him to substitute Korean-made knockoff guns, instead of the top-quality, Belgian-made Herstal—a swap that doubled his earnings.

As they toiled away, a story appeared in the newspapers about a rebellion in Nepal. The country was ruled by a repressive regime led by King Gyanendra. The reports said that the Nepali civilian popula-tion was fighting for its freedom. Loktantrik Andolan was the name given to the revolution, translated as "democracy movement." Accord-ing to the coverage, in this dirty civil war civilians regularly "disap-peared."

Diveroli didn't read the stories about Nepal for their news content. He didn't care about politics or human rights. To the young gunrunner, Nepal looked like a business opportunity.

Diveroli named his initiative to supply King Gyanendra with what he needed—ammo, RPGs, mortars—the Save the King Package. Pack-ouz watched in silence as Diveroli hunted for quotes for enough weapons to start a small army—or suppress a democratic movement. Attack helicopters were the first priority—the aircraft that would enable the king to strafe his Maoist enemies. The mysterious Swiss arms dealer Henri Thomet was Diveroli's collaborator, just as he was on the Iraq contracts. Diveroli and Thomet talked on the phone constantly and exchanged countless e-mails as they tried to source Balkan matériel for Nepal.

"People are rebelling against their king and you're going to help crush them?" Packouz finally asked, incredulous.

"Don't be an idiot," Diveroli said. "If it isn't me, it'll be someone else."

"That's probably true, but it doesn't make what you're doing right."

"It's a good thing you're not involved in this deal."

Packouz could feel that things were changing—and getting more dangerous. Selling arms to the US government to fight insurgents in Iraq was one thing. He could believe in that cause, at least enough not to wonder if he was participating in a criminal conspiracy. As long as the weapons he was trying to trade weren't being used for a specifically evil purpose, Packouz had no qualms. But Diveroli never had qualms, Packouz was beginning to realize. If he kept going with Diveroli, Packouz could easily wind up involved in something illegal, morally repugnant, or both.

"Efraim was devoid of moral purpose," Packouz recalled. "He understood that the Nepal deal was wrong, but he chose not to care. It bothered me. His skills as an arms dealer came at a price. I was getting nervous, on edge. I thought I could learn a lot from him. I was learning a lot, actually. Not all of it very nice. I was caught up in the money. But I could also see the danger."

Packouz's life was changing in other ways. One evening his girlfriend told him she was pregnant. It was an accident. Packouz was stunned into silence. She said she was going to keep the baby, no matter what. If Packouz was willing to help her, she'd stay in Miami, but if he wasn't going to step up and take responsibility she was going to move back to Spain to be close to her parents.

"I was very torn," Packouz recalled. "We didn't have a strong foundation for our relationship. She was a very strong-willed person and I'm a lifelong rebel, so we'd had some conflict. But in the end I decided that I wasn't going to let my child grow up without a father. Diveroli and I were about to travel to Paris, to a big arms show. I told my girlfriend that I was going to stand by her and the baby. Now I knew I had no choice about arms dealing. I had to sell a ton of guns."

Packouz pushed his ambivalence and fear aside. He was now in—all the way in.

Chapter Three

CRASH AND BURN

Eurosatory was one of the world's largest trade shows dedicated to the arms industry. Packouz and Diveroli flew to France in June of 2006 to walk the miles of booths inside the gigantic Paris Nord Villepinte exhibition center. The vast rooms were filled with arms dealers hawking the latest instruments of death—tanks, robots, drones. American generals and military officers from tin-pot dictatorships mingled at cocktail receptions, bedecked in medals, chatting with kaffiyeh-wearing sheikhs and South American colonels. Mixed into this group were the well-dressed, smooth-talking, amoral businessmen Diveroli most admired—international arms dealers who worked the space between legal and illegal arms deals, the "gray market."

Billed as a trade show specializing in land and air defense, Eurosatory was in reality a biannual celebration of man's endless desire to kill man. War was not only glorified in the halls of the conference center; it was institutionalized, commercialized, and monetized. Moët champagne and canapés and caviar were served in booths offering the latest inventions for death.

Entering the giant trade show, Packouz looked around with a mixture of excitement and horror, like a kid entering the Disneyland of death. Diveroli was enthralled. They were by far the youngest people there. They had dressed the part of international arms dealers—or how they imagined they should look. Each wore a suit, a dark shirt, and a striped tie. Inside their briefcases, the pair had photocopies of AEY's licenses to deal in arms, along with copies of the contracts the company had completed in Iraq, to prove that they were serious players, not just a couple of kids.

"We were so young we had a very hard time convincing people that we were really doing deals," Packouz recalled.

The pair were wowed watching live demonstrations of tanks jumping over sand dunes as if they were fighting a real war. They went to an exhibit where they could sit in a swivel seat and pretend to shoot heavy machine guns. But the AK-47 made the biggest impression on Packouz: the weapon was so perfectly designed, so simple, and yet so lethal.

Diveroli was swept up into the entire atmosphere. "Wait until I'm really in the big time," Diveroli boasted as he strode the aisles. "I will *own* this fucking show."

In Paris, Diveroli and Packouz found the booth of Henri Thomet, the Swiss arms dealer from whom Diveroli had been buying large amounts of weapons and ammunition for his Iraq contracts. Through Thomet, Diveroli had high-level contacts in Russia, Israel, Bulgaria, Ukraine, and throughout the Balkans. As a broker, Thomet had set up an array of shell companies and bank accounts in countries with financial-secrecy laws, like Cyprus and Switzerland. Packouz knew that Thomet had been behind much of Diveroli's success as an arms dealer—but he didn't know what really transpired between them.

Thomet's main business with AEY was brokering deals for Soviet Bloc nonstandard weapons for Iraq. But at the show he was exhibiting a new robotic reconnaissance device, a small-dog-size machine that could scale walls and enable unmanned surveillance behind enemy lines. In person, Thomet was tall, handsome, suave. In his late thirties, he had dark brown hair, light blue eyes, and an eerily calm demeanor. He was impeccably dressed. He spoke perfect English with a slight German accent. He had the odd tic of saying *okay* at the beginning and end of every sentence ("Okay, so the price of the AKs is firm, okay").

"Efraim told me that Henri could get body armor, machine guns, antiaircraft rockets—anything," Packouz recalled. "He was one of the best middlemen in the business, a real-life Lord of War. Henri definitely looked like the kind of guy who'd sell arms to anyone."

Packouz's intuition was more accurate than he knew. Indeed, Thomet's name was reportedly on the State Department's "watch list" of individuals and companies suspected of participating in black-market arms transactions. State's Directorate of Defense Trade Controls—the DDTC—was primarily charged with controlling arms exports to ensure America's "adversaries" didn't gain access to sensitive defense technology. Overseeing the $100 billion American international-arms business, the DDTC developed protocols for identifying people who were ineligible to receive export licenses or to contract with the federal government. Some eighty thousand names were on the watch list, which was continually reviewed based on intelligence reports, law-enforcement information, and open-source material.

If Thomet's name was on the DDTC watch list it didn't necessarily disqualify him from dealing with the government. The list was primarily informational, providing officials involved in arms deals with warnings about investigations and suspicious activity. If Thomet's name was on the list, though, it would indicate the government should use increased scrutiny in any dealings with him. But Thomet was openly doing business with the Pentagon through AEY; there was no attempt to hide his name, or the documents with his company's name on them. The munitions Thomet sourced from the Balkans routinely arrived in Baghdad with bills of lading saying they'd come from his company, which was also reportedly on the list. For the past year Thomet had sourced millions of dollars' worth of matériel for Diveroli and other American companies. All of the arms had gratefully been accepted by the US Army.

Thomet wasn't the only questionable arms dealer doing business with the United States in Iraq. The most notorious gun smuggler alive was a Russian named Viktor Bout, who was at that time using his fleet of cargo planes to deliver weapons to Baghdad. The planes were the same ones used to fly guns to men like Charles Taylor of Liberia, a war criminal responsible for the murder of thousands of innocent civilians. But in Baghdad no attempt was made to ensure that the American military wasn't transacting with men like Bout. The Army didn't care who its contractors hired as subcontractors—even if they were known to be responsible for supplying arms that resulted in mass murder.

The apparent lack of controls wasn't an oversight. The DDTC system was designed to make coordination between government departments easy and reliable. But the Army didn't want to coordinate its efforts; the Army was fighting a war and needed to act with dispatch. Procurement officers in Iraq weren't consulting State's watch list, because they weren't required to.

The legal exemption was accomplished by the use of a term deceptive for its seeming simplicity. When Congress authorized the Pentagon to set up new systems for training and equipping foreign forces in Iraq and Afghanistan, the law began with a preamble stating, "Notwithstanding any other provision of law." Page upon page of detailed regulations followed, all appearing like any other complex and legally binding act of Congress. But the words "notwithstanding any other provision of law" worked the magic of exempting the Department of Defense from responsibility to follow *any other laws*— including human rights laws, international treaties, and the State Department's foreign-military sales regime. The provision made the regulations a self-contained reality, subject to no outside legal authority or scrutiny. The sweep of the exclusion was as broad as imaginable—and it went completely unremarked upon in the press, and in Congress.

There was a further legal loophole created for the Pentagon, and this was equally audacious—and achieved by omission. Under the

State Department's regulations, companies doing business with the US government had to name all subcontractors. So if AEY's contracts were ruled by State's laws, the company would be required to disclose that it was doing business with Henri Thomet and his name would be checked against the DDTC watch list. But the Pentagon's system had no such requirement. The trick was accomplished by a simple omission of the word "subcontractor," an elision invisible to the untrained eye that enabled the Pentagon to deal indirectly with even the most corrupt warlords and gunrunners.*

Although it would never be fully reported in the press, the Pentagon, in effect, had enabled itself to legally deal with anyone it pleased, including arms dealers like Thomet, by using proxies like Diveroli and Packouz. In truth, AEY was in effect a front for the real transaction between Thomet and the Pentagon. Officially, AEY's contracts were governed by the Defense Federal Acquisition Regulation Supplement, or DFARS, as it was known in the trade. To the layman, the DFARS, looked like a complex mesh of laws intended to closely regulate the Pentagon's weapons purchasing. But beneath the surface of the extremely legalistic regulations lurked a darker reality. The Pentagon had set up a parallel system for buying arms that bypassed State's protocols and watch lists designed to avoid the US government's doing business with—and enriching—illegal arms dealers.

The two young partners didn't know it—couldn't imagine it—but they were in the middle of a huge chess game and they were the pawns. The Army knew it couldn't send jarheads into the Balkans to buy AK-47s from Serbian and Croatian and Albanian gunrunners. The chances of corruption and scandal were far too high. A bureaucracy like the Pentagon wasn't capable of dealing with the many and varied demands of acquiring millions of dollars' worth of surplus munitions—like paying off politicians or petty officials or killers. Arms dealing was an in-

---

* Colby Goodman, "Dealing with Arms Intermediaries: The Pentagon's Missing Controls on Contractors Engaged in Arms Transfers" (Amnesty International, 2009).

herently dirty business, infused with Swiss bank accounts, prostitutes, double-dealing, and the willingness to do anything to get the job done—legal or illegal. American soldiers wouldn't have a clue how to navigate such treacherous waters.

The US government needed companies like AEY to get to men like Thomet. Like the others bidding on contracts on FedBizOpps, Diveroli and Packouz were being used by the Army. Likewise, Thomet was using Diveroli and Packouz as a conduit for dealing with the Pentagon. For all Diveroli's bravado, in truth the two young men were the monkeys in the middle. Or the fall guys, should things go wrong.

David Packouz understood none of this as Thomet's beautiful young assistant handed him a glass of Veuve Clicquot in Paris. Packouz kept silent as Thomet suggested to Diveroli that AEY should diversify and start selling Balkan AK-47 ammo in the huge American domestic market. Gun nuts all over the United States loved firing AK-47s and were willing to pay well for the thrill.

On the surface, Thomet's idea sounded perfectly reasonable. But it, too, contained an element of deception. The Army was running the procurement process in Baghdad, but the State Department was still in charge of the importation of arms into the United States. Thomet had to know there was a real probability that he was on the State watch list. Shipping ammo to the United States under his company's name could put his goods at risk. But if Diveroli bought the rounds and they came into America under AEY's name, there would be no reason to stop the shipment. None of this was spoken. Thomet's manipulative powers could be glimpsed in the way Diveroli was convinced he was the mastermind of the deal—not the other way around.

"Even when he was dealing with someone as obviously sophisticated and experienced as Henri Thomet, Diveroli always thought he was smarter and tougher than the other guy," Packouz said. "He told me he wanted to cut Thomet out of the deals he was doing. He wanted to buy directly from the contacts Thomet had so he could get more profit for himself."

Walking the show later that day, Diveroli noticed the booth for a company called Yugoimport. He recognized the name from some of the deals he'd done with Thomet. The company was the state military exporter for the Serbian government. Diveroli approached the men in the booth—burly, Balkan tough guys in their forties and fifties, with gray hair. Diveroli was twenty years old. But he showed them his Iraq contracts and they recognized the name AEY. Suddenly he was "Mr. Diveroli." They sent a woman to fetch coffee and invited Diveroli and Packouz into a private room in the back of their booth.

"Diveroli asked if they had an exclusive relationship with Thomet," Packouz recalled. "They said no—no, no, no. Arms dealing really was cutthroat. Literally. Diveroli didn't care about any personal relationships or loyalty. If he could fuck Thomet, he would. Diveroli really was ruthless—like I imagined Thomet to be."

Diveroli now had more in common with Thomet than he knew. On June 26, Diveroli flew back to Miami. When he arrived at the airport, he was stopped by customs. His luggage and documents were searched by law enforcement. The agents had no particular reason to seize Diveroli's personal effects; they were looking for anything suspicious— documents, contracts, business cards. Diveroli had no idea at the time, but the reason he'd been detained at the airport was that his name was on the State Department's watch list, like Thomet's. Because the list was classified, he had no way of knowing he was the subject of a federal criminal investigation. In more ways than he realized, Diveroli really was an international arms dealer, just as he'd dreamed—even if he was a particularly naive one.

Diveroli was oblivious of—or indifferent to—the increasing peril. He was making millions of dollars, but the riches only fueled his ambition to make more. Back in Miami, Diveroli was finding it impossible to keep up with himself. He'd win Iraq contracts for helmets and AK-

47s, but instead of focusing on fulfilling the orders he'd won, he'd race like a maniac back to FedBizOpps to find other deals to bid on. Deals mounted on deals as Diveroli became responsible for a significant amount of matériel arriving at the airport in Baghdad—and thus an ever larger part of the war effort.

The Pentagon didn't know that a young and unlikely arms dealer was playing such a prominent role. Simply coping with the reality on the ground in Iraq during the summer of 2006 was more than the US military could handle. In Baghdad, beheadings and massacres were occurring daily. The bombing of the Al-Askari Mosque fomented yet more violence and resulted in more than a thousand deaths. The launch of Operation Together Forward failed to lessen the level of violence in Sadr City, the Shiite quarter of the city. Then a fourteen-year-old girl was gang-raped by American soldiers, her parents and six-year-old sister murdered before the girl's body was set on fire—a crime that only increased the desire of the vast majority of Iraqis for the invaders to leave. In those desperate days, the Army had no ability to monitor contractors—or, often, even to know if contracts had been fulfilled at all.

Logistical problems were inevitable for any company doing what Diveroli was doing in Iraq, let alone a tiny start-up like AEY. Packouz was busy looking for his own deals, and he wasn't being paid to work on the ones Diveroli won; their agreement stipulated that Packouz was only paid on contracts he found and won. So in effect Diveroli was single-handedly managing the delivery of Glocks from Italy, AK-47s from Bosnia, and helmets from Korea—not to mention the many other deals he pursued with lunatic enthusiasm.

Overburdened and understaffed, Diveroli had defaulted on seven contracts in Iraq out of the dozens he'd won. The record wasn't stellar, but it also wasn't terrible, at least compared with that of the other con-tractors, who were also routinely facing logistical nightmares finding surplus nonstandard weapons and chartering flights into Baghdad. Lo-cating airlines and pilots willing to dare to land in Iraq was a challenge, a reality Viktor Bout exploited while the US government looked the other way.

Despite an increase in expenditures in Iraq of more than 600 percent in 2006, the Pentagon continued to decrease the number of personnel assigned to supervise private contracting. Billions were being squandered on outsourcing, it was widely understood, but next to nothing was being done about it as the war consumed all the attention and energy of the US military.

But AEY wouldn't benefit from such lenient treatment. For some reason the company seemed to receive the special ire of the American officers in Baghdad. Why Diveroli had been singled out remained a mystery until Thomet explained it one day on the phone. Thomet didn't only sell to AEY; he often did business with Diveroli's competitors as well. Thomet was familiar with how rival companies were setting out to destroy the competition. He revealed that AEY's competitors had sent executives to Baghdad to lavish money on the American officers responsible for awarding the contracts, buying drinks and dinner in the Green Zone as they whispered rumors about Diveroli's being a coke dealer and an illegal gunrunner. Thomet said that AEY was systematically being slandered by its competitors in Baghdad, as a way to destroy the business.

Diveroli could do nothing, short of traveling to Baghdad—and he had no intention of doing that. To help cope with the logistics of all the deals he'd already won, Diveroli decided he needed administrative assistance. When his aunt heard that her nephew was looking to hire someone, she offered to help. Diveroli's father's sister was older than the dudes and friendly at first, but she soon came to disapprove of Packouz and the way the two buddies smoked dope all day. Like her nephew, Diveroli's aunt was strong-willed and outspoken. She and Diveroli were soon regularly having screaming arguments. While Diveroli told her to shut up, she shouted that he was out of control—his ambitions, his appetites, his business. She talked openly about Diveroli on the phone with his mother as if he weren't present.

"Mark my words," she told Diveroli's mother repeatedly, "your son is going to crash and burn."

"Shut up," Diveroli shouted back, the cold-blooded arms dealer turning into a pissed-off teenager. "You don't know what you're talking about. I made millions last year."

"Crash and burn. Mark my words—crash and burn."

Chapter Four

HELLO! IS THIS UKRSPETEKSPORT?

In 2006, Operation Mountain Thrust began in the south of Afghanistan. The intention was to confront the resurgent Taliban in Helmand Province and elsewhere. Thousands of American, Canadian, and British troops fought alongside the Afghan National Army, encountering a well-coordinated, disciplined, and deadly enemy in the Taliban. Despite the disparity in firepower, and the heavy aerial bombing, the Taliban inflicted large casualties on the foreigners. Worse, the death of more than one thousand Taliban fighters seemingly did nothing to harm their morale or diminish the apparently limitless number of jihadis willing to fight the infidels. According to the Army's statistics, by the middle of 2006 the number of improvised explosive devices being deployed by the Taliban had more than doubled, direct attacks on American and Afghan soldiers had tripled, and suicide attacks had quintupled. Using sanctuaries in Pakistan, the Taliban and the Haqqani Network had increased their territorial holdings fourfold, according to classified intelligence estimates. As in Iraq, another war that had been prematurely imagined as a great and glorious victory was turning into a strategic disaster.

Something had to be done to turn the war around, the Bush administration decided. The United States had ceded "control" of the south of Afghanistan to the Canadians, but the level of violence only increased as the Taliban won battles for key territories. New thinking was required, it was decided, as the United States entered into a new compact to take control of military operations in Afghanistan. For years, the multinational alliance in Afghanistan had tried to equip and train hapless Afghans, but the effort had been a near-total failure. Corruption, narcotics, poor training, substandard equipment, terrible morale, and tribal animosity, not to mention language, cultural, and religious barriers, had made the Afghan problems as intractable as those in Iraq. With the United States focused on the surge in Iraq, transferring security arrangements to the Afghans had become the top priority—if it was even possible.

One of the most pressing issues for the Afghan security forces was a lack of ammunition. Like the Iraqis, the Afghans were used to nonstandard, Soviet Bloc weapons. Many formerly Communist countries were fighting alongside the Americans in Afghanistan—Bulgaria, Hungary, Lithuania, Poland, Romania, and Albania, to name a few. These countries all had large stockpiles of nonstandard ammo they could supply. Many were eager to assist the United States in any way they could. Like the Albanian government. The tiny Muslim nation, wedged between Italy and Greece on the Adriatic Sea, was one of the most pro-American countries on the planet. The formerly Communist country was preparing to join NATO at the time and had to get rid of decades' worth of surplus ammunition, most of it donated in the 1960s by its then close ally China. The Albanians had offered to *give* the Americans millions of rounds of ammunition for free in Iraq. Surely the same offer would stand for Afghanistan.

But there was a problem. Under the policies and procedures that ruled the US military, agreements could not be entered into directly with foreign allies to supply munitions—no matter the strategic necessity. America couldn't simply ask the Albanians for their ammunition, even if it was the ideal solution. The Army had to follow its own procurement procedure—however dysfunctional it might be. The letter of the law had to be followed, even if it made no sense in a time of war.

There was one huge difference in Afghanistan, however. The Bush administration appeared to have learned the hard logistical lessons of Iraq. Posting thousands of small contracts online had led to widespread chaos and fraud in Iraq. This time, the Pentagon wasn't going to be foolhardy enough to use FedBizOpps to buy third-rate surplus from the Balkans via dodgy outfits like AEY; the practice of awarding contracts to the lowest bidder in an online lottery, thus virtually ensuring the lowest-possible-quality goods, was obviously flawed, as the unfolding disaster in Baghdad proved. This time the Americans would buy directly from one source, not use a daisy chain of brokers like Efraim Diveroli and his competitors. The military wouldn't buy cheap surplus from Balkan bunkers—this time brand-new ammunition would be acquired.

So on May 22, 2006, an article appeared in the *London Telegraph* headlined "US Sets Up £215M Deal for Afghan Arms." The defense correspondent for the *Telegraph* reported that American officials were going to purchase a "prodigious quantity" of ammunition from the Russian government's military-export company, Rosoboron. The US Army would acquire the rounds on behalf of the Afghan security forces:

"Pentagon chiefs have asked the Russian arms supplier for a quote on a vast amount of ordnance, including more than 78 million rounds of AK-47 ammunition, 100,000 rocket-propelled grenades and 12,000 tank shells," the *Telegraph* reported.

If true, the story had heady implications. After decades of hostility between America and the Soviet Union, the international equation was changing in new and unexpected ways. It appeared that the Cold War enemies were on a path toward becoming allies against the shared threat of Islamic extremism. The historical ironies of two longtime superpower enemies coming together in Afghanistan made it seem as if the reported transaction had to be a prank; the Soviet Union had been defeated in Afghanistan in the 1980s, in large measure because of a covert American operation to arm the mujahideen fighting the Communist invaders. Now the Americans were asking for Russian help as they faced defeat in the same mountains.

"Defense specialists said Russian arms chiefs at first 'fell about laughing' because they thought the order was a joke when it arrived this month," the *Telegraph* reported.

But it wasn't a stunt. Under the new paradigm, the Russians would supply brand-new matériel that would give the Afghans an advantage against the Taliban and their ancient Soviet surplus ordnance.

"This is completely refitting the Afghan army for the long term and it should stop a resurgence of the Taliban in its tracks," a British arms expert was quoted as saying. "This deal makes sense if we are going to hand over military control to them."

One small caveat was mentioned: no actual contract existed with the Russians. The US Army was only asking for a quote. But that appeared to be just a formality. No other company in the world was more capable of providing so much high-quality Eastern Bloc munitions, and Rosoboron's prices were well known in the marketplace. Burying old grievances to forge a new future with the Russians looked to be a historic masterstroke.

However, yet another geopolitical goal trumped the need to arm the Afghans. Years earlier, the United States had imposed an arms embargo on Iran, supposedly to stop the Iranians from obtaining nuclear weapons. But the Iranian ban had reached far beyond its original intentions—all the way into the territory of unintended consequences.

Soon after the story about the Afghan contract appeared, Rosoboron agreed to repair and upgrade Iran's long-range strike-force aircraft. The deal had nothing to do with Iran's suspected program to manufacture weapons of mass destruction. But that didn't matter to the Bush administration. The Iranian deal meant that the Russians had forfeited the opportunity to bid on the Afghan ammo contract. Indeed, the Russians were now banned from any arms deals with the US government.

As a result of the Iran embargo, the US government would have to do the same thing in Afghanistan that it had done in Iraq. The Pentagon wouldn't pursue the obvious logistical solution to its problems for reasons that could be described as political but were better understood as ideological and confrontational. Rosoboron was out. FedBizOpps was in. Once again, Diveroli and Packouz and the other denizens of the federal arms-contracting world would search Eastern Europe for the cheapest surplus ammo they could find, a supply that was severely diminished after years of the fight against the insurgency in Iraq.

Thus, in one fell swoop the attempt to supply ammunition to the Afghan army became infinitely more difficult. Worse, according to a report in the *Washington Post*, the Russians considered the American ban tantamount to a declaration of war. The Russian quasi-governmental company Rosoboron was run by a former KGB agent who was a close personal associate of Vladimir Putin's; the company was a central part of the country's corporate oligarchy. The Russians retained many ways to express their displeasure and hinder American efforts in Afghanistan. To reach Kabul, suppliers such as AEY would need to obtain permission to fly over many countries that were formerly part of the Soviet Union—like Kyrgyzstan, Turkmenistan, and Kazakhstan. These nations all remained in the Russian sphere of influence. In due course, Putin would have his revenge.

So it came to pass that on the evening of July 28, 2006, David Packouz was driving his ancient Mazda Protégé along Interstate 195 in Miami on his way to dinner with his girlfriend. Normally he would've sparked a bowl at the end of another day on the job, but he tried to stay straight for his pregnant girlfriend.

Packouz had now been working with Diveroli for more than six months. He'd won a couple of small contracts and he'd learned a lot—how to calculate profit margins, how to source obscure Communist weapons, how to maneuver on FedBizOpps. But he'd yet to make any real money, and his patience was beginning to wear thin. Dealing with Diveroli was stressful and exhausting. Packouz was starting to wonder if he should go back to school and finish his degree.

As Packouz turned off the freeway, his cell phone rang. It was Diveroli. He was excited—really excited, Packouz recalled.

"Dude, I've found the perfect contract for us," Diveroli said. "It's enormous—far, far bigger than anything we've done before. Hundreds of millions of dollars. But it's right up our alley."

"What is it, dude?"

"An Afghanistan contract. It's all ammo—no weapons. It's all Russian caliber, so we've got the past performance to bid on this thing. But here's the best part. There's no age limit. Seriously. We can get Thomet to go through every old ammo dump in Eastern Europe and get rock-bottom prices."

"Wow!" said Packouz. "Sounds perfect."

"The solicitation only says that the ammo has to be *serviceable without qualification*. In my book, that means it goes bang and goes out the barrel."

"You sure there's no official definition of *serviceable without qualification*?"

"I looked. If there were specific quality requirements, it would have been posted in the solicitation. They say *serviceable without qualification* when they're telling us not to deliver shit. That means no rust, no defective rounds. The ammo has to be in generally good condition."

"Why wouldn't the Army be more specific?"

"The United States government wants to arm the Afghan army," Diveroli said. "But they want to do it as cheaply as possible. I guess the US Army isn't too worried about Afghan soldiers on the front lines."

"Well, surplus is our specialty."

"I need you at the office immediately."

"I'm on my way to have dinner with my girlfriend."

"Who gives a shit? You want to yakety-yak with your bitch, or you want to get rich?"

"Chill, dude."

The next morning they met at Diveroli's girlfriend's apartment to parse the forty-four-page document posted on FedBizOpps titled "A Solicitation for Nonstandard Ammunition." The contract looked like any other contract for screwdrivers or forklifts. It had blank spaces for names and telephone numbers and squares to be filled out for more detailed information. But the scope of the solicitation was astounding. Contracts on FedBizOpps were frequently worth millions of dollars for significant amounts of matériel. But this request for proposal—or RFP—was worth hundreds of millions of dollars and had vast geopolitical implications. The RFP called for 100 million rounds of ammunition for AK-47s—and that was just the start. Then there was the list of other munitions—millions of rounds for SVD Dragunov sniper rifles, thousands of GP-30 grenades, huge amounts of 82 mm mortars, aviation rockets, on and on it went.

One firm fixed-price award, on an all-or-none basis, will be made as a result of this solicitation, the tender offer said.

This meant that the contract was winner take all. One company would be entrusted with the epic responsibility of acquiring and shipping tons of ammunition to the mountains of Afghanistan. But who should bear such a heavy burden? Who could be relied upon to carry out a key component of America's foreign policy? Who would win the contract?

Even though it was early in the morning, Packouz could see Diveroli was already stoned and scatterbrained.

"It's going to be a lot of work to source all these items," Diveroli said. "Frankly, I don't have time to do it myself. I got to deliver on the Iraq contracts. I can get quotes from my regular guys, like Thomet. But you've got to be the guy scouring the Internet for new sources. You can't leave any stone unturned."

"Yes, sir, Mr. Diveroli," Packouz said mockingly.

"I'm serious. This is your shot. The contract is going to be worth at least a few hundred million. This is going to make us both filthy fucking rich."

Diveroli wanted to talk terms. With his trademark 9 percent margin, the profit on the contract could be as much as $30–$40 million. AEY was unlikely to win the deal, but the sums were so huge they needed to agree up front how they'd split the winnings. Their prior deal was to split profits fifty-fifty. But the Afghan deal was totally different, Diveroli said. There would be financing costs, plus a lot more risk. Diveroli proposed that if they won the contract Packouz would get 25 percent of the profits for any sales that came through sources he found online or through his own research. Diveroli would take 75 percent because he was providing the financing for the deal. It was a new structure but, given the size of the solicitation, a quarter of the profits would still be millions. Packouz readily agreed.

"Do Google searches and find companies that aren't listed in the usual places," Diveroli said. "Find the little companies in the Balkans and all over the former Soviet Union. E-mail 'em, fax 'em. Fly over there and give 'em a fucking blow job if you have to. You're good at drafting official-sounding letters, so put that brain of yours to work. Just get their pricing, and make us some money."

"I'm on it," Packouz said, pushing aside thoughts of returning to school—and his uneasiness about being in business with Diveroli.

"Now, you want to hit this bong or what?" Diveroli asked.

For the next six weeks, Packouz was up all night, scouring the Web to find companies that sold Soviet Bloc ammunition. He slept on Diveroli's couch, surviving on weed and adrenaline. Packouz discovered that the business mentality in Eastern Europe was less than desirable. Instead of trying to provide helpful service to a potential customer who might buy millions of dollars' worth of goods, the officials he contacted treated him like a pest.

To gain their attention, Packouz told the companies that AEY already had won the contract with the Pentagon. To be taken seriously, he considered the lie a necessity. He also faxed AEY's firearms license from the ATF, even though it had nothing to do with international arms dealing—it looked official, and he hoped it would impress the Eastern Europeans. Then he'd follow up with a phone call.

"Hello! Is this Ukrspeteksport?" a typical call from Packouz would begin, this one to Ukraine.

"Da" would come the reply.

"Do you speak English"

Unintelligible.

"English, English, USA, USA," Packouz would say slowly, insistently.

"One moment."

Mumbled Ukrainian conversation could be heard in the background. Slam: the phone would be placed on a desk. Fifteen minutes would go by.

"Hello" would come a voice.

"Do you speak English?"

"English? One moment."

Another ten minutes would elapse.

"What do you want?" a man would finally ask.

"I want to buy ammunition. I sent you a fax requesting a price. I haven't heard back from your company."

"What kind ammunition?"

"Automatica Kalashnikova," Packouz would say, using the Russian pronunciation.

"Ah, good. Yes, very good. You buy?"

"Yes. Did you receive my fax?"

"You send fax?"

"Yes."

"Okay, I check."

Another five minutes.

"We get no fax," the man would say.

"I'll send it again now. Please don't hang up."

Packouz would resend the fax. "Did you receive it?"

"One moment please."

Fifteen minutes.

"We get fax. You buy this ammunition?"

"Yes. For United States government, for a contract in Afghanistan."

"Okay. I show my deputy director."

"Yes! Please show the deputy director. My contact information is on the fax."

"Okay. Good-bye."

"Wait, wait! What's your name?"

Click.

Weeks would pass and no prices would appear. Packouz would call again, this time sure to obtain a name at the beginning so he would have a contact to ask for when he inevitably had to call again and again.

"The first prices I got were ridiculously high," Packouz said. "They insisted on meeting for drinks in Kiev or Sofia in order to have any discussions about lowering prices. I didn't have the time or money to fly over to meet every shady arms dealer I was contacting. So I just kept moving along, hoping to find suppliers who were more business-friendly."

Packouz's efforts paid off. Over time, he accumulated an impressive collection of quotes from different countries in Eastern Europe. The best prices were for large-caliber items like grenades and mortar rounds that he sourced from a Bulgarian company. Packouz and Diveroli agreed that their prices were competitive—or at least it seemed so.

"We knew the big boys were also chasing prices," Packouz said. "Giant companies like General Dynamics were going to bid on the deal. There were also other little companies like ours. We knew they had to be getting quotes from many of the same companies we were using.

"I knew actually winning the contract was a long shot. I didn't talk about bidding on it with anyone else. I didn't want to talk about pie-in-the-sky things. I thought we maybe had a chance. We had delivered this stuff before. And the contract was so vaguely worded. There was so much leeway in the solicitation."

Packouz and Diveroli figured they could buy old ammo, as long as it wasn't rusty or obviously exposed to the elements. The rounds had to look okay to pass muster by the receiving officer when they arrived on the tarmac in Kabul.

"If it looked like shit, the Army could refuse to accept it," Packouz recalled. "That was all we cared about. The Army just wanted to get as much ammo into Afghanistan as quickly as they could. Our job was to accommodate them. It wasn't like the ammo was for American soldiers. The Pentagon was buying ammo for Afghan soldiers. It seemed like the Army didn't really care about quality or reliability—just speed and price."

While Packouz spent all his waking hours hunting for suppliers, Diveroli continued to win other contracts. He didn't care how the Americans were doing in Iraq or Afghanistan, as long as the contracts kept appearing online—and those only increased as the United States kept trying to solve its troubles by outsourcing.

Despite Diveroli's indifference to politics, it had a way of intruding in the work of an arms dealer. Like the survey he received in an e-mail from the Army in the fall of 2006. The military wanted to know if AEY had sourced any weapons or ammunition or other war-related equipment from China or Chinese military companies?

Unaware of the purpose of the question, Diveroli replied that he hadn't purchased matériel from the Chinese. Unwittingly, he wasn't being entirely accurate. The year before, Diveroli had purchased $300,000 worth of old AK-47 ammunition from an Albanian company for a small FedBizOpps contract. The ammo had been manufactured in China in the 1960s and then shipped to Albania, where it had sat for decades in caves in the mountains outside Tirana. Henri Thomet had brokered the deal, failing to tell Diveroli that the rounds had actually been made in China. At the time, it was irrelevant. The important thing was that the ammo got to the Special Forces in Germany for them to use to train with Kalashnikovs. The deal had gone so well that the Army had written AEY a thank-you letter.

But the geopolitical equation had changed again. In 1989, a ban on selling arms to China had been imposed in the aftermath of the Tiananmen Square crackdown on pro-democracy student protesters in Beijing. The embargo against selling weapons to China had been challenged in 2004, when France and many other European countries advocated lifting the "anachronistic" ban.* The Americans had maintained the ban, justifying the move as a way to protect against the transfer of high-technology weapons. But the reelection of George W. Bush at the end of 2004 had emboldened a faction in the military-industrial complex to lobby for a more belligerent policy toward China. Neoconservatives, triumphant from the campaign, believed China had to be treated as an enemy, even though it had become America's largest trading partner. "How We Would Fight China" was the cover story in the *Atlantic* by the influential military writer Robert Kaplan. "The American military contest with China in the Pacific will define the 21st century," Kaplan wrote. The accumulation of wealth in China, and the concentration of that money in the hands of a small elite, convinced American hawks that any military or territorial ambitions the country held needed to be squashed—by coercion, if necessary.

The State Department wanted to pursue a more balanced and conciliatory policy, but Defense used bare-knuckle tactics to try to impose an alarmist view of China's rise. The infighting delayed the release of the annual report to Congress on the military power of China. During the internal dispute, Secretary Rumsfeld issued a "sharp rebuke" to China about its increased military spending—even though the *increase* in American military spending from 2001 to 2003 in the United States was more than the entire military budget of China.**

---

* Leaked cables in 2011 would reveal the fragility of the ban on China: http://euobserver.com/china/32658.

** William D. Hartung, *Prophets of War* (Nation, 2011), 7.

By the time Packouz and Diveroli were sourcing the Afghanistan contract in 2006, the hard-line forces in the Pentagon had won the day. The Russians had just been banned from selling to the military for ideological reasons—in that case, American policy toward Iran. China was likewise selling arms to Iran. So now it was China's turn: the National Defense Authorization Act of 2006 included a new ban on Chinese arms. The 1989 ban that had restricted *selling* weapons to China was no longer enough; this ban made it against the law for the US government to *buy* weapons from the Chinese. The original intention of the 1989 embargo was to stop arms deals with China that might involve the acquisition of sophisticated Western technology and systems. Now the intention was purely punitive: the Chinese wouldn't be able to enrich themselves by selling arms to the Pentagon.

As the law was drafted, it took a strange, even perverse, turn. Instead of referring to weapons of mass destruction or high-tech secrets, it was now stated that the federal government couldn't acquire *any* munitions, "directly or indirectly," from a "Communist Chinese military company."

The ban apparently included Chinese-made Kalashnikovs, heavy machine guns, grenade launchers—the kinds of arms the Army urgently needed in Iraq and Afghanistan. The ban also included ammunition for those weapons. At least that was what was said in an e-mail the Army sent to the dudes. The notice came in the middle of the bidding for the Afghan contract. AEY and its competitors were scouring the globe, looking for nonstandard ammo to get to Kabul. The e-mail from the procurement office in Rock Island, Illinois, said that none of the munitions could come from China—period.

Earlier in the process, the Army had specifically been asked by one of AEY's competitors if Chinese ammunition qualified for the contract. The Army had replied that the solicitation didn't rule out China, provided the munitions met the stated technical specifications. For all the Army knew, or cared, that company had developed its bidding strategy based on Chinese ammunition. But fairness had nothing to do with the process. Nor did the rule of law—not when the government decided the law. One day Chinese munitions were allowed; the next they weren't.

Sitting in Miami Beach, the dudes didn't know or care about any of these fine legal questions. They read the Army e-mails and shrugged—at least the rule explained the earlier e-mail they'd received about acquiring Chinese munitions. As it happened, Packouz *had* sought a couple of quotes from Chinese companies, but nothing had come of the queries. Packouz and Diveroli quickly moved on. Russia was out. Now China was out. Whatever. Packouz amended his standard-form e-mail to Henri Thomet and other potential suppliers to state that Chinese ammunition was now unacceptable.

As the weeks passed and the deadline loomed, Packouz continued to search for sources for huge quantities of twelve-gauge slugs, GP-30 impact grenades, 82 mm mortar rounds, 57 mm rockets—an entire arsenal. But what most concerned the pair was the single largest component of the solicitation—100 million rounds of 7.62x39 mm and 7.62x54 mm AK-47 ammunition. The Kalashnikov ammo order wasn't the biggest element in terms of dollars—grenades and RPGs were much more expensive and represented a larger portion of the contract, moneywise. But in terms of sourcing and transportation, 100 million rounds of AK-47 ammo was the greatest logistical challenge. The small-arms ammo was also crucial to how the war would actually be fought on the ground. Soldiers and police officers in Afghanistan relied on nothing more than their personal AK-47. They needed ammo in huge volumes, because the Afghans lacked fire discipline and were notorious for shooting at anything that moved. "Spray and pray" was the best way to describe how the Kalashnikovs were used in combat by the Afghans, according to the American trainers embedded with the units.

Hunting for quotes, Packouz got low prices on surplus AK-47 rounds from suppliers in Hungary and Bulgaria. But none could satisfy the entire order of 100 million rounds because of a worldwide shortage of the ammunition. Ironically, the US military's insatiable demand for AK-47 ammo for Iraq had drained caches in Eastern Europe—at the very moment demand in Afghanistan was at its greatest.

The result was skyrocketing prices. New rounds were selling for as much as thirty-five cents each. For decades, new AK-47 ammo had sold for around ten cents, with even the highest-quality rounds going for less than twenty cents. With both Russia and China banned from selling to the US government, the cost of supplying new ammo would be prohibitive, the dudes knew.

Old, surplus cartridges could be had much cheaper—the cheaper and older, the better. But finding such a huge stockpile seemed impossible. AEY would have to laboriously piece together different sources—10 million rounds from one supplier, 5 million from another. How could the tiny company hire enough staff in time to deal with the logistical problems of managing so many suppliers and air-freight companies? AEY's bid had to be submitted within weeks.

As ever, Henri Thomet had a brilliant answer. Thomet said he could get AEY the entire order in surplus ammo from one source. Even better, Thomet's price was four cents a round—barely *one-tenth* the cost of new AK-47 rounds. If the ammo was good enough quality—if it was serviceable without qualification; if it went bang and traveled out of the barrel—it was possible that AEY would be able to seriously underbid the competition.

Thomet's supplier for all of the 100 million rounds was MEICO, the Military Export Import Company, the Albanian government's arms-dealing company. The dudes knew about MEICO. The year before, AEY had brokered a deal with MEICO for a relatively small amount of AK-47 ammo for American Special Forces stationed in Germany.

Explaining how he was able to get such a great price, Thomet said that he was extremely well connected in Albania, being friendly with the prime minister, as well as the defense minister and the official in charge of MEICO. Thomet had "bound" the ammo in Albania—he was the exclusive agent for one of the biggest stockpiles on the planet. That meant that Thomet could give AEY an exclusive, which was another fantastic advantage over the other bidders.

The structure Thomet proposed was classic for shady arms deals. His shell company in Cyprus, Evdin, would purchase the ammo from MEICO, instead of AEY, to ensure that Thomet wasn't cut out of the deal. At least, that was the express rationale. But it also meant that Thomet didn't have to disclose the real price he was paying MEICO for the ammo, so Diveroli wouldn't know Thomet's true profit margin. Likewise, Diveroli wouldn't disclose to Thomet the price he was going to charge the Pentagon.

In reality, Thomet was paying the Albanians 2.2 cents per round, or barely half of what AEY was paying. An obvious implication for such a huge gap between the price Thomet was paying the Albanians and what he was charging AEY—nearly double the amount—was that money from Evdin could be used to pay kickbacks and bribes to Albanian military officers and politicians. Doing business in notoriously corrupt countries like Albania almost inevitably included bribes and kickbacks. Thomet could handle this matter discreetly, which was especially important at that moment, as Albania was slated to be admitted to NATO in 2007 and scandal had to be avoided at all costs. Evdin also provided a degree of insulation for AEY: the dudes wouldn't have to directly grease palms in Albania, which would violate foreign-corrupt-practices laws in the United States. AEY's involvement, in turn, provided a layer of protection for the Pentagon—though Packouz and Diveroli didn't fathom that they might be part of a much larger game.

To calculate its final bid, AEY needed to figure out the cost of transportation—a particularly hard number to determine because of changes in the price of oil. Often the cost of flying weapons to a war zone was greater than the price of the arms themselves. Delivery of the AK-47 ammo from Albania was going to require dozens of flights, along with scores of flights from Hungary and Bulgaria, where AEY had sourced other munitions. Finding freight airlines, obtaining the necessary overflight permissions, getting proper end-user certificates, complying with regulations on moving hazardous materials like ammunition—the logistics presented an immense challenge.

Thomet had an answer for that, too. To tend to the logistics of flying a mountain of ammunition to Afghanistan, Thomet had teamed up with a veteran Israeli soldier named Sammy Avivi—a decorated war veteran who'd been injured in combat multiple times.* To enable AEY to bid on the Afghan deal, Avivi was put in charge of coming up with a price for airfreight. After weeks of research, Avivi said it would cost $63,000 for every flight from Tirana to Kabul. This seemed like another good price—although the dudes had no way of knowing what quotes their competitors were getting.

Sitting in AEY's tiny office, Packouz and Diveroli put the airfreight and cost of the AK-47 ammo into a spreadsheet they called the Final Afghan Price Matrix. They'd priced out all of the elements—howitzer shells, Mossberg riot-shotgun ammo, grenades, T-62 tank rounds, and so on. But their numbers disguised the uncertainty lurking beneath the surface. Like Thomet's price for 122 mm HE shells. New, the shells cost $240, but Thomet said he could get 80,000 surplus shells for only $60 each. The cheaper shells were enough to cover what the contract required for the first year of the two-year deal. But Thomet didn't have a large enough cache to satisfy the demand for another 150,000 in the second year of the contract.

Trying to trim every dollar possible, Diveroli decided to use the lower price on the 120 mm shells for both years, reasoning that he could bid millions less for the overall contract that way. If he wasn't able to supply the shells in the second year at the lower price—well, they'd drive off that bridge when they got to it.

The deadline had arrived. The final number was Diveroli's decision.

---

* Avivi had been the military attaché to Israel's embassy in Switzerland. To gain access to Israel's lucrative arms business, Thomet recruited Avivi by giving him an expensive Land Rover and making payments that would later end in the war hero's conviction in an Israeli court.

He paced day and night, a cloud over his head as he smoked joint after joint, muttering, worrying, cursing.

Diveroli was conflicted about whether to use a 9 percent or a 10 percent profit margin. The difference between the two percentage points was around $3 million in profit. He figured everyone else was going to go with 10 percent. But he didn't know the prices the other bidders had been able to find.

"How could we be sure our prices were better than what others had been able to source?" Packouz recalled. "Diveroli was worried that another bidder had figured out his 9 percent trick and would use it, too. So maybe he should go with 8 percent. But then he might be leaving money on the table—God forbid!"

On the day the bid was due, Diveroli was frantic. He needed to make up his mind. He took a deep breath and decided to be aggressive. Eight percent it was. Fortune favors the brave. He wrote the number in: $290,544,398.

Time was up. The final bid had to be submitted by mail, postmarked to show it had been sent on time. The two friends leaped into Diveroli's car and sped through the streets of Miami Beach, making it to the post office with only minutes to spare.

Packouz and Diveroli didn't spend the weeks that followed worrying about the Afghanistan contract. Fretting about the outcome was pointless, Diveroli explained, as he started searching for new solicitations the next day. Packouz was exhausted by the work he'd put into the bid. But he could see that his efforts were paying off. He'd developed contacts with arms manufacturers all over the former Communist world. He was beginning to truly grasp Diveroli's business model—how it was possible to be daring on FedBizOpps.

Diveroli and Packouz held AEY's annual board of directors meeting as the end of 2006 neared—an event consisting of the two of them sitting at a desk together. The minutes recorded their desire to continue to pursue "major contracts," like the Afghanistan deal. The company would move to a larger office, but they would keep staffing to a minimum, and, instead, "hire independent contractors and consultants to work on assignments for a limited duration, thus keeping costs down and profits up."

The pair had cause to be optimistic. The early signs on the Afghanistan solicitation were promising, if somewhat mixed. AEY was clearly in the running, but the Army was suspicious about AEY's pricing on the 122 mm HE shells. Diveroli had deliberately underpriced the shells to present an artificially low bid. The practice was known as "buying in" in the defense-contracting industry, shorthand for getting the government to sign a contract and then gradually altering the terms in your favor. Purposefully underpricing a contract and then encountering massive cost overruns was known as "gold plating" and was a routine way large companies rigged the system.

The Army sent an e-mail asking AEY to double-check the 122 mm shells quote as it seemed unreasonably low. Packouz and Diveroli freaked out: Did the Pentagon know what they'd done? They decided to revise the estimate to include the higher price for the second year.

"We should have used new production pricing for the second year since there is no assurance that surplus goods will still be available in a year's time," AEY wrote. "Our revised pricing is included. We could withdraw our bid, or continue forward as revised. This would be your call, if the bid is still interesting to you."

The new number was $298,004,398—an increase of $8 million.

The sly deception worked. In the weeks that followed, the Army had a series of picayune questions and concerns. The dudes sent a letter listing the suppliers they'd worked with—an impressive array of munitions companies in the former Yugoslavia and Romania and Bulgaria and Albania. They said they couldn't disclose the precise nature of the transactions they'd completed because of nondisclosure agreements. "Confidentiality is a common inclusion in most contracts of this kind," they wrote. "We wish to express our confidence that with our resources and expertise, in addition to our valued suppliers, and the strong relationships we have with these companies, we can fulfill all aspects of this ammunition tender in a seamless and timely manner."

Two months had passed and waiting was now excruciating. Packouz tried not to think about the fortune he stood to make from the Afghan deal. If they won the contract, he figured he'd make $8 million personally. The money was more than enough to enable him to record the album of songs he was completing. He'd be able to hire top session musicians and a high-end producer. The record would be slick, professional, sure to attract the attention of a major label. Packouz was going to back his dream by investing $1 million of his own money in promotion. Within a year or two, he'd be rich and he'd be famous.

Trying not to obsess over the outcome, Packouz and Diveroli attended a trade show in Florida for companies specializing in electronic surveillance. Walking the aisles, they ran into a senior procurement executive for General Dynamics, the giant arms company. Joe Pileggi was middle-aged, stocky, with close-cropped, graying black hair. Despite the vast disparity in size with AEY, General Dynamics was a rival for the Afghan contract, the dudes knew, which should have made both sides wary. But Pileggi was friendly, acting as if they were colleagues, not brutal competitors. Pileggi asked if they had a minute to talk. They all took a booth in the food court.

"You guys sure seem pretty busy," Pileggi said, as Packouz recounted.

"We work hard," Diveroli said.

"We're kinda like you guys," Pileggi said. "General Dynamics is huge, but we've only got twenty-five guys in our department. We do foreign sourcing and logistics. But we have the General Dynamics name behind us, which helps a lot."

"We're just two guys," Diveroli said, staring blankly.

Everyone else at the trade show was middle-aged, nearly all ex-military or law enforcement, and in that circumstance Diveroli and Packouz looked comically out of place.

"You're making quite a splash in the industry. A lot of guys at the office won't believe how young you guys are when I tell them."

"We're old at heart," said Diveroli. "How can we help you, sir?"

"I know we bid on some of the same contracts. But that doesn't mean we can't do business."

"What do you got, what do you want?" Diveroli asked.

"Small ammo," Pileggi said. "Large-caliber munitions. Let's compare prices. Maybe we'll work something out."

"So I know you guys bid on the Afghan contract," Diveroli said, a sneaky grin forming on his face. "How you feeling about that?"

"We worked hard on that. Lots of man-hours. Tight margins—pretty damn tight, I'll tell you. So we're fairly confident. I've got to admit, it would kill me if we lost a contract that big. We really gave it our all."

"Yeah, us, too," Diveroli said. "Now if you'll excuse us, we've got another meeting."

The pair left abruptly.

"Another meeting?" Packouz asked.

"He's just wasting our time," Diveroli said. "He was fishing for information on what we bid on the Afghan deal—trying to hear our prices. How obvious can you get? Fuck him. He thinks he's hot shit because he works for General fucking Dynamics. But you see how he's scared shitless of us? He knows we're going to eat them alive."

"We're going to eat General Dynamics alive?" Packouz asked, incredulous.

"You and me, buddy, we're going places," Diveroli said, strutting past a booth displaying high-tech surveillance cameras.

December 20, 2006, was Efraim Diveroli's twenty-first birthday. The gunrunner was finally old enough to legally drink alcohol. Of course, he'd been sneaking into bars for years, always equipped with excellent fake ID. But now that he was of age the dudes decided to hit the clubs to celebrate legitimately. Diveroli's apartment building had valet parking, but he was on poor terms with the man tasked with fetching cars. When they reached the parking lot, Diveroli decided he wanted to get his car himself, instead of dealing with the middle-aged Cuban valet, who obviously didn't like Diveroli and his brash manners. Diveroli had already snorted a few lines of coke, so he was feeling feisty. He sneaked into the valet's cubby and snatched his keys. As he turned to leave, he saw the valet coming toward him at a run.

"Get out of there!" the valet shouted.

"I just want my keys," Diveroli said.

"You can't go in there," the valet yelled, trying to grab the keys back.

Diveroli and the valet began to argue. A security guard on duty came over, drawn by the screaming. When Diveroli looked away for a second, the valet punched him in the head. Diveroli turned and the valet punched him again as the pair began to wrestle and choke each other. Packouz instinctively grabbed the valet. The security guard pulled Diveroli off the valet.

Panting and bent over to catch his breath, Diveroli was a mess, his shirt torn apart, his face swollen. "I'm calling the cops," he screamed at the valet. "I'm getting you arrested. I'm getting you deported."

Diveroli and Packouz went back up to Diveroli's apartment and called the police. Diveroli said he'd been attacked and wanted to press charges. Hanging up, he remembered that he was carrying a packet of cocaine for the night's festivities. He told Packouz he couldn't have the drug on him when he talked to the police. He asked Packouz to hold the coke.

"I was stupid enough to take it," Packouz recalled. "I stuck it in my sock to be safe. When we got downstairs, there were three cruisers with their lights on in front of the building. They came over and put us both under arrest. We couldn't believe it."

The Miami Beach police began to question Diveroli and Packouz. When they took Diveroli's wallet, they discovered that he was carrying fake ID showing that he was older than his true age. Diveroli, eager to disassociate himself from the ID, told the police he was officially twenty-one years old, so it was no longer relevant. The police thought otherwise. Instead of filing a victim statement, as he'd anticipated, Diveroli was charged with carrying a false identification. Both Packouz and Diveroli were also placed under arrest for the altercation with the valet. Driving in the cruiser to the police station, Packouz remembered he had Diveroli's cocaine in his sock.

Packouz and Diveroli were put in different holding cells. When Packouz was searched, the officer told him to take off his shoes and socks but failed to notice the baggie of cocaine—a complete fluke.

"I was scared shitless," Packouz recalled. "It was a miracle, but he didn't find the baggie crumpled up inside my sock."

Afterward, Diveroli didn't apologize to Packouz about the fight or the cocaine. He was angry at the valet and the security guard and the police, as if he were the victim, ignoring what Packouz had been through.

"I didn't bother telling him how I felt—how I could have been caught with his coke," Packouz said. "I knew he didn't care. I knew I was being forewarned. Things could go wrong very quickly with Efraim. But I was blinded by the possibility of getting rich. I was waiting to see if the Afghanistan contract came through. I'd been bitten by the money bug. I had it bad."

Chapter Five

TASK ORDER 001

On January 26, 2007, David Packouz was parking his Mazda Protégé in the lot of his dive apartment building when his cell phone rang.

"Dude, I have good news and I have bad news," Efraim Diveroli said. "What do you want first?"

"What's the bad news?"

"Our first order is only for $680,000."

"So we won the contract?" Packouz asked in disbelief.

"Fuck yeah."

An upscale Italian restaurant in South Beach was the site for their celebration. Multiple bottles of Cristal were consumed as they toasted their incredible good fortune. The two friends, already stoned from the joint they'd smoked on the way to dinner, were now responsible for one of the central elements of the Bush administration's foreign policy. Packouz's cell phone rang: a massage client wanting to make an appointment. Packouz told her he'd retired as a masseur. As they ate, they passed Diveroli's plastic cocaine bullet back and forth under the table, using their linen napkins to pretend to blow their noses as they wiped away the residual white powder.

"You and me, buddy," Diveroli said. "You and me are going to take over this industry. I see AEY being a ten-billion-dollar company in a few years. Those fat cats in boardrooms running Fortune 500 companies are worried about their stock price. They have no idea what's about to hit them."

"General Dynamics isn't going to be too happy right now," Packouz agreed.

Diveroli grinned at the thought of two dozen corporate employees twisting in the wind while two kids outwitted them. They both knew many hurdles had to be overcome. The first was confirming that AEY had really won the entire contract. The year before, when Diveroli had "won" a contract in Iraq supposedly worth $50 million, he'd gone on a jag rejoicing in his triumph. But the next day he'd discovered he was only one of five companies that had qualified to bid on scores of much smaller contracts that were being put out for mini-competes. He'd done well in the mini-competes, frequently beating the larger companies he was vying with. But the experience had taught him not to get too excited too quickly.

Then there was the size of the first task order. More than $600,000 in grenades was a big sum, it might seem. But in the context of a $298 million contract it was suspiciously small. Was the government testing AEY? Was the order for grenades a way for the Army to see if AEY could actually deliver? The spring fighting season was looming, with the US deploying a small number of forces to counter the anticipated spring offensive from the Taliban, but the surge of troops into Iraq had made arming the Afghans even more crucial. In the headlines, a new candidate for president named Barack Obama was claiming that the Bush administration had failed to pay sufficient attention to Afghanistan— a contention underscored by daily reports of bombings, skirmishes, and casualties in the rapidly deteriorating offensive against the Taliban called Operation Mountain Fury.

Arranging a line of coke on the dashboard of his new Audi in the parking lot after dinner, AEY's president reminded his colleague of their precarious position. "You've got the bitch's panties off," Diveroli said, affecting his best movie-star swagger. "But you haven't fucked her yet."

The days that followed were euphoric—and terrifying. The fear that they'd make a mistake and lose the contract crowded their thoughts, just as the calculation of their coming riches quickened their pulses. The notion that they'd do something to blow the deal wasn't fanciful. For all their precocious skills, the dudes were prone to be precisely that: dudes. This propensity was on display in the e-mail Packouz drafted to the Pentagon's defense attaché in Skopje, Macedonia. It was part of a larger effort to enlist the assistance of American soldiers stationed in countries throughout the former Communist Bloc. Packouz reasoned that American-embassy officials in countries that were now friendly with the United States would know details about these countries' stockpiles of surplus ammunition.

Like some others, Colonel Chris Benya had agreed to help AEY source ammo in Macedonia; assisting the company was effectively assisting the US military, after all. Packouz imagined himself to be efficiently conducting business as he sent Benya an e-mail outlining the ammo AEY wanted to acquire; finance would be provided by the "Banc of America," Packouz wrote. The message looked amateurish to Benya—maybe even fraudulent.

"I was contacted today by David Packouz of AEY," Benya wrote to the Army's procurement representative in Rock Island, Illinois—the agency in charge of AEY's contract. "There are many alarm bells going off based on what he sent. The attached documents had many errors, including misspelling 'Banc of America' on the letterhead and the use of different typesets on the alleged contract. I also found it strange that the company does not have a corporate e-mail address and seems to use Gmail. Bottom line is none of this seems to add up."

Packouz had the spelling correct, but Benya was right: giving two stoners from Miami Beach the contract to supply ammunition to the Afghan National Army didn't add up.

But Benya's suspicions didn't give anyone in the Army pause. "The contract with AEY is legitimate," replied Rock Island.

If the Army had done even rudimentary due diligence on AEY, the company would've been ruled out of contention long ago. Although the dudes didn't know it, AEY and Diveroli had been placed on the

State Department's watch list a year earlier, when he'd flown back from an arms show in Paris. But the entry didn't mean that AEY had done anything against the law.

"There appear to be several suspicious characteristics of this company," the State Department's classified profile of AEY reported, "including the fact that Diveroli is only twenty-one years old and has brokered or completed several multimillion-dollar deals involving fully and semi-automatic rifles. Future license applications involving Diveroli and/or his company should be carefully scrutinized."

But the Army didn't consult the watch list, because it didn't have to—by design. Then there were the accounting practices of AEY. If the Army had inquired, it would have been discovered that the dudes essentially had no bookkeeping or record-keeping systems. From the beginning, Diveroli had operated by the seat of his pants. When checks came in, he put the money in AEY's various accounts—the locations and amounts in these accounts were top secret. When he spent money—on office supplies, on weed, on body shots at hot spots like Skybar or B.E.D.—he spent AEY's money. The company had no protocols to ensure it was keeping its affairs in order. The possibility of attracting the attention of the Internal Revenue Service terrified Diveroli, Packouz could see.

Before AEY had been awarded the contract, it had been audited by the Army to make sure it had the financial wherewithal to sustain the contract on the government's net-thirty-day terms. Reams of documents had been produced by Diveroli and Packouz, many of them exaggerated to show that AEY had far more money than it actually did. None of the ledger high jinks had been detected.

AEY's patchy record of performance in Iraq hadn't alerted the Army either. Night-vision goggles, mounts for gun scopes, ammunition— AEY's goods had sometimes been of poor quality or been delivered late, or Diveroli had used bait-and-switch tactics, substituting an inferior brand for the one the contract specified. The "source selection team" assessing AEY's abilities had determined that the company should be rated "unsatisfactory." This should have ruled AEY out of the running. But days before the contract was awarded the official who oversaw the contract had changed the rating to "good." The official hadn't bothered to closely examine AEY's past performance, not through negligence but because the system didn't require tiresome attention to detail. The contract was being run from the offices of the Sustainment Command in Illinois, a million miles from the war. American and Afghan soldiers in the war zone would have to live with the consequences of a decision made in a distant armory.

The process was not only emblematic of the entire procurement procedure, but also the war itself. Somehow the US government was simultaneously squandering billions and shortchanging the war in Afghanistan. AEY had won the contract because it had the lowest price, although two other bidders were within 2 percent of the total evaluated price AEY came up with. Price was only one criterion the Army was supposed to consider. The only competitor with an overall rating higher than AEY's had bid 80 percent more than AEY—more than $500 million. The Army had seen no reason to pay such a vast premium, given that AEY's evaluation was only slightly lower.

"Our competitors had bloated budgets and big staffs," Packouz recalled. "We were lean and mean. The Army wanted to do Afghanistan on the cheap, and we were the cheapest."

But Diveroli wasn't content with his generous profit margins, which promised to make AEY at least $30 million. All of the ammunition AEY was buying had to be paid for up front, and the government wouldn't pay the dudes until thirty days after delivery of each shipment. Because of the size of the contract, Diveroli would have to commit all of his money and also borrow millions from the Utah businessman Ralph Merrill. To finance the deal they'd also likely need to get a loan from a bank. So Diveroli decided the company should apply for "progress payments," which would enable AEY to be paid more quickly by the government—and thus avoid onerous financing costs. To receive these preferential terms from the Army, the company had to undergo a financial inspection. Diveroli decided to risk this further scrutiny.

To prepare, Diveroli and Packouz wrote biographies of themselves to provide to the Army's officials. Packouz was modest. Diveroli less so. "Efraim has built a stellar reputation for very competitive, on-time, smooth, and successful deliveries," Diveroli said of himself. "Efraim has proven himself to be a professional, savvy, and knowledgeable businessman, with legendary skills in negotiation and business strategy. His passion and skill have enabled him to build AEY into a multimillion-dollar defense-contracting firm of worldwide renown. He plans to continue building AEY into a lasting and respected institution."

The reality was less grand. AEY's books were a mess, as Ralph Merrill knew, and the Army would be sending a team to Florida to examine AEY's records. To help the dudes, Merrill sent his personal accountant from Salt Lake City to Miami to introduce them to elementary bookkeeping software in an attempt to make AEY's accounts presentable.

On the day of the inspection, Packouz and Diveroli made it a point not to smoke a joint first thing in the morning, as was their custom. They wanted to be sharp. Both dressed in their best button-down shirts and business shoes as they nervously braced for the encounter.

They needn't have worried. The Army's team consisted of half a dozen matronly women dressed in frumpy skirts and sensible shoes. To Packouz they looked like grandmothers, not fierce auditors. Diveroli was a master at ingratiating himself with older women as a goofy but lovable kid.

"If it wasn't absolutely illegal," Diveroli announced, surveying the conference room, "I would love to buy you all diamonds."

The women smiled. Formalities were attended to. The women said that the ammo AEY was acquiring had to be safe, it had to work, and it had to be delivered on time. No problem, Diveroli assured them. Diveroli said AEY would send a representative to each country to see that the ammo had been stored and preserved properly, particularly against moisture damage. AEY would test-fire the ammo to make sure it worked.

While Diveroli charmed the women, Packouz sat silently—a bald-headed, blue-eyed specter.

"What does David do?" one of the women finally asked. "What's his role?"

"David is our international man of mystery," Diveroli said. "He's the guy who makes the magic happen for us in some pretty unmagical places. If you need to move some kind of product"—Diveroli didn't specify arms, but the euphemism for arms was understood—"from one godforsaken country to another godforsaken country, David is your man."

Packouz remained poker-faced. As the meeting adjourned, the dudes were triumphant. Rolling a spliff in Diveroli's car, they agreed they'd aced the test.

Days later, bad news arrived. If AEY was to receive progress payments, the Army wanted to see the company's tax returns. For Diveroli, this was verboten. No subject was more sensitive to the young gunrunner than taxes and his relations with the IRS—or, as he referred to the agency, "the three-letter word."

Finance would have to be done conventionally. Diveroli had to risk his own money, as well as take a loan from Ralph Merrill. AEY also established a "factoring agreement" with Wells Fargo. Instead of waiting for payment from the government, AEY would sell its receivables to Wells Fargo at a discount. AEY would get paid quickly enough to satisfy its suppliers, and in return the bank clipped a piece of the profit from the deal. The arrangement wasn't ideal, but it provided a steady and reliable source of funds—as long as Diveroli was content with the profit margin, an issue that continued to be his Achilles' heel.

It was now February, time to perform—time to enter into contracts with suppliers and start the deliveries. The quotes they'd used for the bid were still available. But now that they'd actually won the contract—instead of lying about having won the deal to get good quotes—Diveroli and Packouz were sure they could command better prices than the ones they'd used for the bid.

The first delivery was slated to be 40 mm underbarrel grenades designed to attach to a Soviet Bloc rifle. For the bid, AEY had used prices from Yugoimport, one of Thomet's Serbian connections. Now Diveroli wanted to cut Thomet out—or get the Serbs to lower their price. Working the Internet, Packouz found a company named Arcus, in Bulgaria, that was willing to sell the grenades at fifty cents less per unit than Yugoimport. The difference meant nearly a million dollars more in profit.

Diveroli e-mailed the Serbs, describing the lower price from the Bulgarians and demanding they meet or beat it. The Serbs were not pleased. The Serbian tough guy who ran the company had, understandably, assumed that the quote he'd offered would be honored. But the dudes had no intention of doing anything other than making the most money possible. The Serb called as soon as he received AEY's demand.

"You buy from us," the Serb told Diveroli. "We do business long time. We good partners."

"I'd love to buy from you," Diveroli replied, inviting Packouz to listen on the speakerphone as he often did, relishing the chance to perform for his friend. "But my hands are tied. I got a better price."

"Price is already too low. You buy from us."

"Listen, baby, we may have had sex, but we're not married. I don't run a charity. You either come down on price or we gotta buy somewhere else."

Diveroli hung up and said to Packouz, "Can you believe that fucker? Who does he think he is? Does he think he can push us around? This is the USA. Nobody fucks with us. Get the Bulgarians on the line and let's close this deal."

Packouz dialed the director of the arms company in Sofia—a man who spoke good English. Diveroli wasn't satisfied taking the lower price from the Bulgarians. He wanted to squeeze even more from the deal.

"Buddy, you and me, we're going to do some big business," Diveroli began. "We got a really bright future. Just one little thing. You gotta come down a little on price."

"But we're already lowest on market," said the Bulgarian.

"I know that and I appreciate it. But I need a price that's a dollar apiece lower."

"Impossible. My board will never accept."

"I'm counting on you to use your world-class powers of persuasion. I know this is rough, but it's the only way. We got some bad quotes from some people who now can't deliver. If we don't deliver, the American government will cancel the whole contract and then the party's over. Everybody loses."

"How can I convince my board this is the truth?" the Arcus executive asked, implying that Diveroli was lying.

"I know you're about to pull down your pants and you gotta make sure you're not about to get fucked. I'm willing to pull my pants down here. I'm going to go against my company policy just this one time. I'm going to show you my government contract. The price the Army is paying me is on the contract. If I send you those documents, do you think the board will go to nineteen bucks a grenade?"

There was a long pause. "It is possible."

"I will send the documents over right away," Diveroli said, trying to contain his glee. Hanging up, he grinned and started to jump up and down, then fell to the floor and kicked his legs in the air in joy. "Who's the fucking man!" Diveroli bellowed. "Who just negotiated one point one million dollars in extra profit in one phone call?"

Giddy, Diveroli leaped up and high-fived Packouz. "Now you're going to modify the contract and put in a fake price that the government is paying us," Diveroli instructed Packouz. "Put it like we're only making three percent profit on the deal. But make sure the fake documents are fucking beautiful. We got millions riding on this."

"Yes, sir," said Packouz, awed by Diveroli's gift for dissembling. "We're going to have a twenty-five-percent profit margin on a twenty-six-million-dollar deal. Holy fuck, dude!"

"Stick with me, buddy. You and me, we're going places."

David Packouz felt his life changing quickly and in exciting ways. He tried not to calculate the money he was going to make, but it was hard to resist the temptation to imagine the life he'd soon be leading. He was going to be a millionaire many times over. But as his girlfriend's pregnancy progressed, she began to despair of Packouz's growing obsession with money. They'd finally broken up after weeks of fighting over his work schedule. She told him that he'd lost track of what mattered in life. Packouz believed he was building a secure financial future for his daughter—which had to take precedence over everything else, even his hope of becoming a rock star.

On February 9, 2007, his daughter, Amabelle, was born.

"I knew I had to get even more serious about business," Packouz recalled. "It wasn't a game anymore. I was a father now."

Diveroli decided that Packouz would be primarily responsible for fulfilling the Afghan contract. Diveroli determined that the best use of his time was to search for even more contracts to bid on. Diveroli told his friend not to "waste" time babysitting his newborn daughter. "You got your whole life to spend with your kid," Diveroli said. "Right now, we've got to make money."

To help with the administration, AEY hired an office manager as well as two young Latina office assistants they'd found on Craigslist. But essentially Packouz was on his own with the Afghanistan deal, apart from Diveroli's overbearing oversight and occasional troubleshooting. An undertaking like this would command dozens of skilled and experienced employees at a company like General Dynamics.

To find new sources for the Afghan deal, in mid-February Packouz flew to Abu Dhabi for IDEX, a munitions trade show in the Middle East that billed itself as the "most strategically important defense exhibition in the world." He was carrying business cards with his new title: Vice

President. To prepare for the trip, Packouz had purchased a silver aluminum briefcase and a pair of wraparound reflective sunglasses, to better look the part of a badass gunrunner.

On the plane Packouz met Jorge,* a young man from Guatemala who was attending the show on behalf of his family's business, which supplied rich ranchers with the weapons to enforce their dictatorial rule over that country.

In Abu Dhabi, Packouz and Jorge went directly to the convention center, a gleaming new facility in the desert. IDEX was the largest arms show on the planet, bigger even than Eurosatory; the vast facilities accommodated fighter jets, tanks—every war machine imaginable. The opening reception was like the bar scene in the first *Star Wars*, it seemed to Packouz, a congregation of all manner of killer and conniver in the universe: sweaty Filipino generals, vain, ribbon-wearing Brazilian colonels, dim-witted upper-crust British officers. Then there were the weapons: armored vehicles, unmanned drone aircraft, precision-strike bunker busters. There were seminars and live-fire shows in front of the grandstand outside the pavilion, with mobile missile launchers and amphibious tanks emerging from the water.

Walking the show, Packouz no longer felt like a kid tourist gawking at the exhibits. The twenty-five-year-old with the silver briefcase may not have looked the part, but he had good reason to feel the strut of a gunrunner enter his stride.

"I was probably one of the biggest private arms dealers on the planet," Packouz recalled. "It was bizarre. It was like Efraim had put me into the movie he was starring in. It was an out-of-body experience—strange but exhilarating."

To help Packouz get oriented, Diveroli had given him the contact information for a Ukrainian arms broker named Vidak.** The youthful

---

* Not his real name.
** Not his real name.

Packouz, the slick Jorge, and the heavyset Vidak stationed themselves near the bar for a cocktail reception. The emirate was a Muslim country, but booze was plentiful. As they surveyed the sheikhs and generalissimos, Jorge and Vidak fell into an in-depth debate about where the best prostitutes could be found—Thailand or Ukraine? Judging by the beautiful, gaudily dressed young women working the all-male crowd, Abu Dhabi had plenty of hookers, too.

The next morning, Packouz woke in his hotel room so hungover he could barely lift his head. Something about drinking in the desert air made it doubly punishing, he was learning. But Packouz knew he needed to seize the day, regardless. At the show, he met up with Jorge, who told him about the three Chinese hookers he'd hired the night before. They were cheap, Jorge said. Why not have three?

China was on Packouz's mind for other reasons. The dudes had been informed that they couldn't source any of the weapons from China. But the ban was an obstacle to be overcome, they'd decided. As Packouz walked the show, an e-mail from Diveroli arrived, the whole message written in uppercase: "MAKE GOOD CONNECTIONS WITH CHINESE AND EXPLORE ALL LEGAL POSSIBILITIES."

The idea of buying Chinese ammo to ship to Afghanistan made perfect sense. As China was a neighbor, it would mean avoiding having to fly over a bunch of Eastern European countries, greatly simplifying logistics. Chinese ammunition had been purchased by the United States in the 1980s to arm Islamic insurgents in Afghanistan fighting the Soviet Union. The covert operation, famously depicted in *Charlie Wilson's War*, was a strategic triumph and a prime example of the kind of sly intelligence that once ruled American procurement policy—and won wars.* "Just the thought of using Chinese Communist guns to kill Russians—just the irony of it," one of the CIA agents who worked the case recalled. "Getting two guys on the same side

---

* At least until Osama bin Laden and other jihadis who'd fought in Afghanistan turned on the United States and staged the attacks of September 11, 2001.

fucking each other makes it easier for you to fuck both of them, and aside from just the general idea of fucking each other, their equipment was good—top-notch—and it was cheap."*

Packouz made his way to the booth for the Chinese arms company Norinco. The Chinese were proudly displaying their new eight-wheeled combat vehicle. Packouz handed a Chinese official his list of munitions for the Afghans. The man inspected the contract with interest. Norinco could supply nearly everything AEY was after and at competitive prices, the official said. For years, China had shipped vast quantities of AK-47 ammunition to the United States for the domestic market. Now the country was staking out a claim as the low-cost alternative to both American and Soviet Bloc weapons—and low cost interested the dudes above all else.

As Packouz inquired about terms, he recalled, the Chinese delegate seemed to have a vague inkling about a new American ban on certain weapons systems they produced. But he was shocked when Packouz explained that it appeared the ban applied to the purchase of *all* Chinese munitions. For the US government and its contractors, doing business with a "Chinese military company" was now illegal, Packouz said.

"Do you know if your company is considered a 'military' company?" Packouz asked the Norinco executive.

"Military company?" he asked. "We manufacture military equipment, so of course we military company."

"Is it a private company or a state company?"

"In China ownership not so simple. It sometime secret who own company. Could be advantage to be public or be private. This information not public."

"I can't buy from you if you're a government company," Packouz said.

---

* George Crile, *Charlie Wilson's War: The Extraordinary Story of How the Wildest Man in Congress and a Rogue CIA Agent Changed the History of Our Times* (Grove Press, 2007), 268–69.

"This not fair! In China, company can be private one day, state-controlled the next. What difference it make?"

"We have to follow American law."

"But it make no sense for China-type business."

Packouz sighed and took the Chinese catalogs and moved on. He didn't possess a law degree, or a diploma from the Pentagon's Defense Acquisition University. His training reading the Talmud or learning massage hadn't prepared him to parse poorly defined terms in obscure defense regulations.

The Russian pavilion was nearby. With an exhibit covering more than an acre, the Russian company Rosoboron was selling everything from the latest iteration of the Kalashnikov to the Antey-2500 long-range surface-to-air missile and a line of non-nuclear submarines. When Packouz approached one of the hard-looking military types manning the exhibit, the Russian didn't want to talk to a kid muttering about buying 100 million rounds of AK-47 ammo. Packouz showed the Russians the contract and asked to meet his boss. The man waved him off.

Packouz persisted and persisted, circling back to the Russian exhibit every day. Finally, on the fourth day of IDEX, as the show was drawing to a close, he was granted an audience with a deputy director of Rosoboron. The Russian was overweight, in his sixties, with thick, square glasses and a five-o'clock shadow. To Packouz, he looked like a KGB villain from a James Bond movie. He listened as Packouz spun his tale about the giant Afghanistan deal, eyebrows raised skeptically. What Packouz was saying sounded insane. It didn't seem plausible that the US Army would rely on an overeager naïf to supply hundreds of millions of dollars' worth of ammunition to Afghanistan. The Russians had been about to bid on the contract when the Pentagon suddenly and arbitrarily announced its ban. Standing before the Russian was a kid who plainly was unqualified to handle such a momentous contract. Was this a joke?

The Russian kept surveying the exhibition center, looking to see if he was being videotaped or watched—if he was the subject of a prank, or a sting.

Exasperated, Packouz handed over the list of ammo and the quantities. The director appraised the list and looked at Packouz skeptically.

"I'm serious," Packouz insisted. "My company has the whole contract."

"We have very good interest in this business," the Russian finally said. "You know we are only company in world who can provide everything."

"I'm aware of that. That's why we want to do business with you."

"*Da*. But as you know, there is problem. State Department has blacklist us. I don't understand your government. One month is okay to do business. Next month is not okay. This is very political. Pentagon want leverage with Kremlin to get better price."

"We can't do business with you *directly*," Packouz said. "But what if you sold the ammunition to another company, then we bought it from them? If you can help us do business with another Russian company, then we can buy from them. As long as they aren't a government business."

"Let me talk to my people," the Russian said, taking one of Packouz's freshly printed cards.

Packouz would never again hear from the Russian—the significance of which would only be revealed in time.

/////

Task Order 002 arrived at AEY's headquarters in Miami on March 9, 2007: 1.1 million GP-30 grenades, nearly 100 million rounds of AK-47 ammo, and on and on. The total value was $48,717,652.70. There was no doubt anymore: AEY really had won the contract. The dudes really were the sole suppliers for the Afghan National Army and police. It was one thing for Diveroli to win scores of small contracts in Iraq, but an entirely different matter for the Pentagon to entrust a significant portion of the fate of a nation to a couple of young stoners—no matter how smart and adept they were.

Packouz's sense of elation was overwhelming. He decided it was time to upgrade his life. He was sick of living like a penniless masseur.

Packouz had yet to receive a dime from Diveroli, but he sold his beater Mazda and bought a late-model blue Audi A4. He moved from his tiny efficiency studio into a nice one-bedroom in the Flamingo—the swinging South Beach condo where he'd long given massages to the residents and met the mother of his child. Diveroli had moved there a few months earlier. Packouz's new pad overlooked the pool, where attractive young women could be seen lounging in the hot tub at all hours. Their dope dealer, Raoul, also lived in the building, providing unbeatable convenience.

Packouz went online and bought a Volcano vaporizer, a smoke-free pot-smoking device that heated the marijuana and turned the cannabis oil into a vapor. The Volcano meant he didn't have to actually smoke the pot, avoiding toxins and carcinogens. With the amount of weed he was consuming, Packouz considered it an important investment in his health. The stainless-steel device took pride of place on his new living-room table—the crisp, clean high a manifestation of his state of mind.

The Flamingo was a constant party, Packouz discovered, a swirling, sexually supercharged South Beach scene. The marketing slogan for the building was "South Beach revolves around us," and it was true: at all hours of the day, people were drinking, dancing, making out in the Jacuzzi.

"Sometimes more than just making out," Packouz recalled. "Outside my balcony there were always a few women sunbathing topless."

Packouz and Diveroli went to a lot of parties in the building. Most of the other tenants worked in fashion, if they were women; the men tended to be young stockbrokers and lawyers. When people asked what the pair did for a living, they would talk about being international arms dealers. They'd say that they were responsible for all the bullets in the Afghan war.

"They'd think we were lying, but it was the truth," Packouz said. "It was heaven. It was wild. We felt like we were on top of the world."

The pair would often toke up and go to the American Gun Range, the only firing range in Miami that would let them fire the automatic Uzis and MP5s Diveroli had collected.

"When we let go with our machine guns," Packouz recalled, "all the shooters would stop and look at us like, 'What the fuck was that?' Everyone else had pistols going *pop pop*. Diveroli's MP5 would go *tututu-tutu*, like a dog's bark. We loved it."

With the business growing so radically, Diveroli began to approach the other kids in their posse to recruit them to work for AEY. One of the first he approached was Alex Podrizki, Packouz's best friend, who was then a student at college. Podrizki deflected Diveroli.

"I wasn't interested," Podrizki recalled. "After he'd come back from LA—after he told us that his uncle had fucked him out of a lot of money—Efraim changed. He was controlling, always trying to get everyone to work for him. He wasn't funny anymore. He tried to get me to work with him a few times but I said no."

It seemed to Packouz and Podrizki that Diveroli's greatest ambition—apart from vast riches, a private jet, and a reputation as a ruthless arms dealer—was to have all his friends working for him. It was partly a power trip, they thought, but it was also how Diveroli blended business and personal life into a monomaniacal vision.

Seeking more help around the office, Packouz and Diveroli put up an ad on Craigslist. A random assortment of applicants turned up for interviews: young Hispanic women, African-American men, Asian college students, Haitian and Cuban refugees without immigration papers. The interviews were unorthodox, with Diveroli offering an extended speech on what he expected from his employees:

"The most important thing is hard work. I'm not promising it's going to be easy. Look at me. I'm barely twenty-one years old and I'm a multi-fucking-millionaire. You know how I got this way? By hard fucking work, that's how. If you listen to me and do what I say, you'll make a lot of fucking money." Diveroli would pause and gesture at Packouz, talking on the phone. "Look at him. I brought him into the business a year ago, and now he's managing one of the largest small-arms munitions purchases in history. He's about to be very rich. That can be you. But you gotta do what he does. You gotta be faster, smarter, better than all the schmucks out there. It's a dog-eat-dog world. So are you going to be the alpha dog? Or are you going to be eaten?"

Most applicants sat dumbfounded. Some took the bait. Diveroli set them to work bidding on virtually every contract the Pentagon posted on FedBizOpps—everything from walkie-talkies to sniper sights—working entirely on commission. Instead of concentrating on the huge Afghan deal, and contenting himself with ensuring AEY did a stellar job and reaped millions in profits, Diveroli set out to win as many contracts as possible. But a pattern quickly emerged with the new hires. Most quit within days, repulsed by Diveroli's screaming and ranting and raving. New ads were put up on Craigslist and new recruits were brought in, the company lurching from crisis to crisis. Diveroli was creating a "boiler room" atmosphere at AEY, though instead of pushing worthless penny stocks for commission, the new staff was bidding on federal contracts. AEY was the epitome of what the Bush administration had aimed to achieve by using private contractors—or it was a parody of that policy.

Packouz tried to ignore the commotion as he concentrated solely on the Afghan contract. He was indeed smart, adaptable, a fast learner. He was also out of his league. He'd never actually delivered a major deal for the US military overseas. Now he was tasked with single-handedly attempting to oversee the entire Afghan contract.

Signs that AEY was going to hit trouble were evident before the first shipment of grenades left Bulgaria for Kabul. Henri Thomet had given the dudes a "delivered" price for the ammo he was going to supply. This included a quote for airfreight. To calculate its bid, AEY had used

Thomet's price of $63,000 for each flight. But that quote was now obviously totally unrealistic. In the early months of 2007, oil prices were going through the roof, in part because of the uncertainty of America's two faltering wars. When Packouz tried to charter flights, he discovered the real cost was more than $125,000 per flight.

"We're fucked," Diveroli wailed when Packouz told him the numbers. "We're fucked! These numbers are totally unfuckingacceptable. You better fucking fix this. Get that Swiss motherfucker on the phone."

When they tracked Thomet down, Diveroli insisted that he cover the difference between the price quoted and the current market cost. Thomet refused. A flurry of angry e-mails followed. Then Thomet vanished. For weeks he became impossible to reach. He didn't return Diveroli's e-mails or answer calls on his cell phone.

Diveroli and his ever-changing group of workers continued to bid on Iraq contracts, while Packouz chased the other parts of the Afghanistan contract. Weeks were passing—critical weeks, as AEY was expected to begin delivering in April and it was now March.

Time was of the essence because of the urgency of the demand for ammunition in the war zone. But there was also a bureaucratic reason for the hurried delivery schedule. The Afghan contract had been created by way of a little-known process called a "pseudo case." Employing the pseudo case meant that the Pentagon was using money preauthorized by Congress without any specifications for how it was to be spent. This lack of oversight applied to Congress as well as the press, as few beat reporters covered arcane matters like small-arms procurement policy. Money designated under a pseudo case had to be spent within a specific time—in this case, two years. Given the vast scale of munitions called for in the contract, the Army was pressuring AEY to perform—and to perform immediately—otherwise the money would be lost.

As the end of March loomed, Thomet still wouldn't answer his phone. Nor would he reply to e-mails. Diveroli and Packouz were panicking—yet again. Nearly two months had elapsed since they'd won the contract and deliveries were due. The Bulgarian grenades were sitting on pallets ready to go. AEY had to start making deliveries soon or risk losing the entire contract. Diveroli called his financier Ralph Merrill in Utah to plead with him to contact Thomet. Diveroli said that Thomet was treating him like a pesky kid—which, of course, he was.

Merrill agreed to try. He e-mailed Thomet and relayed Diveroli's complaints. Merrill was friendly with Thomet; they'd done business together long before Diveroli came along. Phone calls followed. From their conversations, Merrill could tell that Thomet was distracted by personal issues and wasn't paying close attention to business. Merrill urged Thomet to staff up, to hire enough people to handle the logistics of performing the Afghan contract. But Merrill realized that Thomet wasn't interested in doing the bidding of AEY. The Afghan deal was AEY's problem, not Thomet's.

Merrill shared his impressions with Diveroli. AEY might have to deliver the ammo on its own, without Thomet's promised assistance for the munitions he'd sourced. That included 100 million rounds of AK-47 ammo sitting in caves in Albania. Obviously AEY didn't have the experience to take on such a logistical nightmare. But what other choice did it have?

Every day the Army pushed for a date certain that the shipments would begin. Every day Diveroli kept trying to get Thomet on the phone. Day and night, night and day, Diveroli called and called.

Thomet finally picked up. He was infuriatingly calm, even patronizing. He had no sense of the pressure AEY was under. The entire contract was in jeopardy, and Thomet didn't seem to care. The skyrocketing airfreight prices weren't his concern, he said. How could he have predicted the oil shortage and huge price increases? Besides, Thomet said, the price he'd quoted Diveroli wasn't the final price—it was an estimate. Thomet was turning Diveroli's trick against him, refusing to be bound by understandings reached during bidding.

This only made the young man angrier. "You have to cover the difference," Diveroli insisted. "I'm going to lose money on the deal."

"You don't understand," Thomet explained. "The quotes I sent you were for three hundred flights. The first order for the grenades in Bulgaria is only for two flights. When you book a large number of flights, we do what's called a wet lease—that includes aircraft, crew, maintenance, insurance, all of it. A dry lease is for a short period of time. A wet lease is a long-term arrangement for a lot of flights. Everybody in the business knows the difference between wet and dry leases."

Diveroli and Packouz had never heard the terms before. But it didn't matter. Thomet was immovable. AEY had to be ready to charter dozens of flights to qualify for the cheaper rate. Diveroli decided the best solution was to play for time with the Army. The dudes needed to get the 100 million rounds of AK-47 ammo in Albania trucked to the airport, palletized, and loaded onto cargo planes. They needed to have enough shipments to qualify for a wet lease so as not to be murdered on airfreight.

The Army didn't care about AEY's profit margins—it expected the deliveries to be made as contracted. So Diveroli dissembled with the Army. He told the procurement officers in Rock Island that AEY couldn't ship because of delays in governments' issuing the export permits needed to move the ammo across national frontiers. It was a lie, but a necessary one to make the contract economically viable. Many administrative and logistical problems were besieging the dudes, but the main problem was AEY's profit—or the lack of it due to airfreight prices.

"Buddy, we're not donating this stuff to the government," Diveroli said.

At the same time, Packouz was furiously trying to obtain the necessary permissions to fly over the countries between the Balkans and Afghanistan. The Stans, as Packouz called the countries—Turkmenistan, Kazakhstan, Uzbekistan, Tajikistan. Packouz was rapidly learning how difficult it was to deal with the governments in countries from the former Communist Bloc. The bureaucrats in the Stans seemed to be deliberately delaying approval to make life difficult for AEY—and thereby the United States.

"I would call the American military attachés in the embassies in those countries and say I was working on a vital mission in the global war on terror," Packouz recalled. "I was careful to speak their language—'Yes, sir,' 'No, sir'—like I had maybe been in the military myself. Sometimes I would joke with them. It was the dead of winter where they were, so I figured it had to be freezing in the Caucasus. I'd ask what the weather was like in Ashgabat or Bishkek. Then I'd say that I was calling from sunny Miami Beach and tell them what the temperature was. I tried to put them at ease, to get them to my side.

"I told them that it seemed like it was impossible to get the right approvals, no matter how many strings I pulled. The American officers told me off the record that they believed the Russians were getting their neighbors to drag their feet. The Russians were supposed to have had the contract in the first place, but they'd been banned. So the Russians were getting revenge. Putin was fucking with us. Week after week was passing, and we were getting seriously behind."

In theory, AEY could have shared its woes with the Army—the oil prices, the flyover permissions, the evasive Swiss arms dealer, the Russian machinations. There were regulations that would have enabled the Army to increase the price for the Afghan contract. What was called an "equitable adjustment" made sense, as the changing circumstances were beyond AEY's control, most especially the hike in airfreight prices. But to tell the Army about the troubles risked AEY's losing the contract. To ask for a variance would be sending out a distress signal.

Worse, the dudes were convinced some elements in the government weren't happy that they'd won the contract. They knew that the arms-dealing establishment hadn't been thrilled when AEY underbid them. It seemed as if officials allied with General Dynamics and the other bidders on the Afghan contract might be undermining AEY. They were worried that false rumors were being spread about them—a fear that proved prescient.

Diveroli finally decided to call a purchasing officer named Kim Jones, at Rock Island, to gently inquire about the chance of a do-over.

"As a hypothetical question," Diveroli said, "suppose fuel prices suddenly went up. Is there a method for the government to adjust the price to reflect the situation?"

"This is a fixed-price contract," Ms. Jones explained. "Companies are expected to compensate for volatility in the market by purchasing fuel futures or signing a fixed-price contract with their transportation provider. Will you be having difficulty making the deliveries?"

"Oh, no, oh, no!" Diveroli replied. "That was just a hypothetical question. We are prepared and capable of making all deliveries. AEY will exceed your expectations."

Giving up, Diveroli called Thomet again.

"Prices are going to go even higher," Thomet said impatiently. "This is the way it is. Fuel is crazy. Many airlines are hedging with oil futures. Perhaps you should hedge."

Thomet hung up. Diveroli was downcast. If they paid the full airfreight, AEY wouldn't make any money on the deal. The dudes might actually lose money, at least on the AK-47 ammo in Albania. But hedging fuel would require AEY to invest in complex financial instruments. The company could buy a fixed or capped hedge, using a commodity swap or options or derivative side bets. Even the most sophisticated investors had to be wary when buying futures, especially in a market as volatile as oil was at that time. Diveroli's ninth-grade education had reached its outer limits.

"Are you going to hedge?" Packouz asked.

"Are you fucking kidding me?" Diveroli said defiantly. "I didn't get where I am by hedging my bets."

Airfreight was too expensive, but perhaps the ammo could be loaded on trains and sent to Kabul through the mountains of Central Asia, Packouz suggested. Or perhaps the ammo could be shipped by sea to Karachi, Pakistan, then carried north by truck to Kabul.

As the US government was learning daily, sending supplies to the mountains of Afghanistan was a logistical challenge of mindbending proportions. In the north of the country the main entry was through a narrow tunnel, built by the Soviets, in the Salang Pass. Trucks lined up to use the tunnel snaked for miles around the mountains. To the south, road transport in Pakistan was risky, with the real possibility that extremists would hijack the precious ammunition, causing yet another disaster.

"I'll try to look into Pakistan," Packouz said. "But this is high-value cargo. There are a lot of people in between the Balkans and Afghanistan who'd like to get their hands on all this ammo."

"We can get Blackwater's mercenaries to ride shotgun," Diveroli said, only half joking. "Or we could get Thomet to hire a bunch of those Special Forces soldiers from Eastern Europe that he knows. Those guys are sitting around unemployed. We could get them dirt cheap."

Diveroli wrote to the Army to again plead for time. "I would like to formally apologize for the recent delays in the delivery schedule that is expected of us," he wrote. He outlined the issues AEY had faced in the former Communist world. Obtaining overflight permission was still a problem, though it was being resolved. "Other solutions that we are exploring include mapping out alternate routes," he wrote. "On a good note, we would like to confirm that as soon as we receive these permits, hopefully no later than next week, we are scheduled to begin two to four flights per week out of Albania, Bulgaria, and Hungary. We hope you understand our position and know that we are ready, willing, and able to fully execute these Task Orders and the many more we will receive under this contract over the next two years."

Then Packouz had an idea. A brilliant idea. Maybe. It was certainly ingenious. The problem was weight—arms were heavy, especially the AK-47 ammo in Albania; a single crate of AK-47 ammo weighed sixty pounds. Even if they successfully stalled the Army long enough to qualify for a wet lease and lower airfreight rates, the weight would destroy their profit margin. But what if they repacked the ammo in Albania to reduce weight and increase profitability?

Henri Thomet had told the dudes that the cache of 100 million rounds of AK-47 ammo in Albania dated back to the 1960s. The cartridges were stored in heavy wooden crates. The crates were mounted on heavy wooden pallets. Inside the crates, the ammo was stored in heavy, old tins called sardine cans because they were opened with a key, like Spam. The ammo had been manufactured at a time when weapons were shipped by sea, not air, so little attention had been paid to weight.

The weight of the Albanian ammo was perhaps the only variable the dudes could control. Nothing could be done about the grenades in Bulgaria; they were new and already efficiently packed. But what if the old AK-47 ammo in Albania was taken out of the crates and placed in lighter cardboard boxes? What if the ammo was also taken out of the sardine cans and put in plastic bags? What if it was all loaded on much lighter, modern pallets?

The savings could be significant, Packouz said excitedly, reaching for a calculator. Dozens of flights would be required to ship 100 million rounds to Kabul. Cramming as much ammo as humanly possible on every flight was vital to making the Albanian contract profitable.

"We might be able to still make air transport work, even with the high oil prices," Packouz said, punching the numbers. "Thomet says the wood from each crate weighs around one kilogram—so just over two pounds. If we got rid of that much weight, we'd save a lot on the transport. I figure it would be just enough to break even on the deal."

"I don't work my fucking ass off to break even," Diveroli said.

"But I don't think Thomet's right about the amount of weight. I've seen crates that size. They weigh at least seven to ten pounds. With that much weight gone, we'd actually make money."

"How much?"

Packouz hit TOTAL on the calculator. "About ten percent."

"Let's do it."

Repacking was now the plan, which was obviously not going to be simple or straightforward. Albania was famously corrupt, for starters.

Neither of them spoke a word of Albanian. They had no contacts there, other than through Thomet, and he was totally unreliable. How could two dudes in South Beach arrange to have ancient ammo in wooden crates hauled from the mountains of Albania, repackaged, loaded aboard cargo airplanes, and then shipped to Kabul?

As Packouz tried to think, he received an e-mail from the Xinshidai Company in Beijing, a cruel reminder of the caprice so often involved in arms dealing. The Chinese company cheerfully said they would be more than happy to supply 100 million rounds of AK ammo, no problem. It was the ideal solution. The ammo would be new. The price was sure to be competitive. The quality would be at least as good as that of the old Albanian ammo. As next-door neighbors, the Chinese could fly directly to Kabul. All of the ridiculous logistical woes AEY faced would vanish.

Packouz shook his head in despair. He'd sent the Chinese company the request for a quote on the AK ammo months earlier, before the Pentagon had changed the rules and banned Chinese-made munitions. Packouz could see that Xinshidai was definitely a "Chinese military company," thus it had been disqualified. There was no sensible reason to stop a Chinese company from selling AK-47 ammo to the US Army, via a broker like AEY, certainly not when the urgency of the situation in Afghanistan was considered. But that was what the law said. Sighing, Packouz wrote to say AEY wasn't able to do the deal with the Chinese.

The reply from the Chinese only made him feel worse: "If the US lift the sanctions, we can provide the price and the products as soon as possible."

Diveroli had no time for irony. The Chinese and Russian bans were literally crippling the United States in Afghanistan—and that meant AEY. A global shortage of small-arms ammo existed in large measure because of America's spending spree in Iraq. The only real alternative left to the dudes remained 100 million rounds of ancient surplus ammo sitting in moldering wooden crates in Albania.

"We've got to get a motherfucker on the ground in Albania right away," Diveroli said. "We need a guy we can trust to check out how much these goddamn crates actually weigh. Then that guy can stay there and supervise the repacking job. I can't go because I've got to run the office. I need you here to take care of the government and run logistics on the Afghan deal."

"What about Alex," Packouz said, referring to their mutual friend Alex Podrizki. "He's a smart guy. He's multilingual. He's got international experience. He trained with the French armed forces, for God's sake. He's perfect for the job."

"I already talked to Alex about coming to work for AEY," Diveroli said. "He wasn't interested."

"I'll talk to him," Packouz said. "He's been looking for work."

"That's not a bad idea. Looks like Albania's going to be our problem child. We need someone to babysit that bitch."

Chapter Six

CIRCUMVENTION

What Alex Podrizki wanted from life was intangible—adventure, the chance to do good in the world, the courage to find his own path. For months Podrizki had listened with a mixture of amazement and alarm as his best friend, David Packouz, described his life as an arms dealer. Since Efraim Diveroli had started his business at the age of eighteen, Podrizki had quietly distanced himself as the young gunrunner's obsession with war profiteering grew in intensity, even as he'd grown concerned about Packouz's involvement. Like his two friends, Podrizki had rebelled against his Orthodox faith. But Podrizki wasn't motivated by money or material possessions, or other superficial rewards.

Politics was Podrizki's main interest. As a teenager, he'd given speeches, usually over a joint, to his posse of friends exhorting them to take up radical leftist causes. Podrizki also enjoyed pranks, like turning off the lights in the synagogue during prayers on the Sabbath, a major problem for Orthodox Jews, as they couldn't turn the lights back on and were forced to pray in the dark.

By the spring of 2007, Podrizki had graduated from college with a degree in international relations and defense studies, but he was living at home with his mother. Slim, with curly brown hair and an intelligent face, Podrizki was twenty-four, unemployed, and increasingly frustrated by his inability to find a job. He was also discouraged by the turn

American politics had taken with the invasion of Iraq and the reelection of George W. Bush—and appalled by Diveroli's campaign to cash in on the war.

"Efraim was viciously pro-war and ready to profit from it—but he didn't have the balls to go there himself," Podrizki recalled. "Like Dick Cheney with his five draft deferments in Vietnam, Efraim was happy to have others do the actual fighting and dying. To me, the invasion of Iraq was a naked, cynical grab for resources. It was obvious that Saddam Hussein had nothing to do with 9/11 and there were no weapons of mass destruction. I was only a kid and I could see that, so I was very disturbed by the overwhelming support the war was receiving. Before Iraq, I was planning on joining the Army, but the invasion changed everything for me. I went to a couple of antiwar protests in Miami, but it was frightening how small they were."

Like most of the dudes in their posse, Podrizki had been approached by Diveroli to come work for AEY. It was one of Diveroli's many quirks, like his coarse manners and his drug consumption. Podrizki had said no to Diveroli with a laugh.

But Podrizki was interested in traveling to a war zone, as a relief worker not a gunrunner. Fluent in French and Spanish, he'd spent a year as an English instructor for a paratrooper regiment in the south of France, which included basic military training. He'd tried to volunteer in Haiti, on a water-purification project, and he'd applied for an internship with the International Rescue Committee to work on its initiatives, like refugee resettlement, protecting children, and combating human trafficking. But his lack of foreign experience had held him back.

Broke and adrift, subsisting on bad part-time jobs, Podrizki made pocket money dealing small amounts of pot to tourists in Miami Beach. When Diveroli and Packouz decided the company needed a new office, AEY paid Podrizki $500 to find the space. But in the end Diveroli had decided to stay in their tiny space, where he had the lone office, a room he'd decorated with a bong on a side table and a giant poster of Nicolas Cage from *Lord of War* on the wall behind his desk—a gift from Packouz.

"I went to AEY's office to pick up my check," Podrizki recalled. "The vibe was awful. Diveroli was yelling at everyone, and everyone seemed really submissive. David was really stressed out. He was constantly telling me how miserable he was working with Efraim."

Despite the obvious dysfunction at AEY, when Packouz approached Podrizki with the idea of going overseas for the company, he didn't dismiss the idea. He'd have nothing to do with Diveroli, Packouz said. The company needed someone to travel to Albania, Bulgaria, and Hungary to be AEY's eyes and ears on the ground. Packouz said that he and Diveroli were having difficulty communicating with their suppliers and costs were running out of control, especially for a large amount of surplus ammunition AEY was buying in Albania that needed to be repacked. The ammo was packed in heavy wooden crates and aluminum cans and would have to be put into cardboard boxes and plastic bags to save money on airfreight. The idea was that Podrizki would fly to Albania and supervise the job.

Podrizki was intrigued.

"Mostly, I took the job because I didn't have anything else going on," Podrizki recalled. "I told David and Efraim that I wouldn't have anything to do with any deals involving Iraq. I was strictly going to work on the Afghan contract. My job was to get the Albanians to actually deliver the ammo and to make sure the quality was good. It sounded like an adventure to me—a chance to be on my own in a third-world country with a difficult assignment."

Podrizki's pay would be $1,100 per week, plus expenses. He was given the title Logistics Coordinator. Business cards were printed and a power of attorney was executed granting him the authority to conduct business in Albania on behalf of AEY.

"Before I left, the three of us met at Efraim's condo to talk the plan over," Podrizki said. "Efraim was much calmer than he'd been in the office. He wasn't so overbearing."

Diveroli fetched his pipe and packed a tight cone. The first shipment of $2 million worth of 7.62x39 mm ball and tracer rounds had already been paid for, Diveroli said—which wasn't true, an ominous beginning to the relationship; in fact, Diveroli was holding out on payment until the rounds were actually delivered, a ploy that was partly responsible for the delays.

Diveroli said Podrizki's first priority should be to get the Albanians to finally start trucking ammo to the airport in Tirana. Podrizki was given a copy of AEY's contract with Henri Thomet and Evdin. It showed AEY paying four cents each for the rounds. The Army was paying AEY eight cents a round.

"Don't show this contract to the Albanians," Packouz told Podrizki. "We don't want the Albanians to see our prices with Thomet."

According to the plan, Albania would be the first stop on Podrizki's trip. When he was done there, he'd travel on to manage AEY's deliveries from Bulgaria (grenades) and Hungary (more AK-47 ammo). He'd be gone two months in total, back in time to start graduate school in the fall, proudly burnishing his résumé with overseas experience.

Diveroli said that when Podrizki got to Tirana, he should inspect the ammo to make sure it was *serviceable without qualification*. Diveroli explained that the term meant it had to work—it had to go out of the barrel and go bang. Podrizki was experienced with weapons, so he was sure he could conduct a basic firing test.

"Don't tell anyone that you're an arms dealer," Diveroli advised Podrizki. "Tell them you import heavy equipment. When people hear about weapons, things get complicated."

The pipe was passed to the left, per decorum, followed by a shot of tequila.

On April 17, 2007, a bleary-eyed Alex Podrizki arrived in Tirana. He immediately learned that nothing was going to be straightforward in Albania. Struggling through the jostling crowd at Mother Teresa International Airport, he caught a cab and directed the driver to the two-star hotel in the city he'd booked. The driver nodded and they set off. After a few minutes, the cab turned into what appeared to be a village. The car stopped. Podrizki looked around in confusion as the driver insisted this was his destination in downtown Tirana. Handing over the agreed fare, Podrizki got out of the car reluctantly, protesting that he was in the wrong place. The cabbie feigned incomprehension and sped away, full fare in hand. Thus was Podrizki left in a cloud of dust in the middle of nowhere, chickens roaming the dirt road, old ladies dressed in black watching him suspiciously.

Finally catching another taxi to Tirana that afternoon, Podrizki arranged to meet Ylli Pinari, the Albanian official in charge of the ammo deal. Pinari was heavyset, short, with a five-o'clock shadow and dressed in a drab suit. MEICO was supposedly an autonomous commercial entity, but it was an instrument of the government and Pinari's office was located in the Ministry of Defense. Greeting Podrizki, Pinari was surprisingly friendly, Podrizki thought, given the nature of what he did for a living. Pinari also spoke excellent English, not an unusual attribute among Albania's ruling class; he possessed a green card from the years he'd lived in the United States, and like most every Albanian he was rabidly pro-American.

Podrizki raised the subject of the first 2 million rounds of AK-47 ammo: "When are you going to start delivery?"

"It's not so simple," Pinari said. "I need approval of the minister of defense and the officials at the airport. Let's go look at the ammunition now."

They got in Pinari's Mercedes and drove into the mountains outside Tirana. Podrizki could see little white pillbox bunkers scattered throughout the countryside—small, mushroomlike structures with a slightly comical appearance. The bunkers had been built all over Albania by the former Communist government, Pinari explained. For decades, hard-line leader Enver Hoxha had believed the country faced imminent attack from all directions. Russians, Americans, Yugoslavs—

all were going to assault Albania simultaneously. Total War was the name of Hoxha's defense strategy. Every man, woman, and child would become a resistance fighter. He'd planned for the Albanian people to engage in a brutal, endless war of attrition using the stockpiles of weapons and ammo he'd stashed in bunkers in every street and field and valley and mountain. More than a billion rounds of AK ammo had been amassed, making Albania by far the most heavily armed nation in the world. This was why Albania was the perfect supplier for AEY, Pinari said, smiling.

Up a remote switchback dirt road, past soldiers manning a checkpoint, Podrizki was led to a giant steel door, the entry to a vault built into the side of a mountain. Inside, a catacomb was filled with a vast supply of Albania's ammo. Standing on the threshold, Podrizki couldn't see the end of the tunnel; off to the left was another tunnel stretching into the distance. Somehow Podrizki had to figure out how to get Pinari to transport 100 million rounds of AK-47 ammo from bunkers like this to Tirana's airport and then on to Afghanistan, and it clearly wasn't going to be a simple task.

Podrizki walked into the cave. Some of the ammo crates had Albanian markings, some Russian, some Yugoslavian; most had Chinese. Podrizki paused in front of crates of British ordnance dating back to the Second World War. The ammo was in all kinds of calibers, from large-scale howitzer rounds to the AK-47 cartridges AEY was going to buy. The small-caliber ammo came from all over the former Communist world. But it was effectively identical: after the AK-47 had been invented in the 1940s, factories had been built in many nations to clone both the gun and the exceedingly durable and effective cartridges it used.

A crate of bullets was pulled down for Podrizki to inspect. Because ammunition was heavy, a single crate measuring only eighteen inches long, fourteen inches wide, and six inches deep weighed sixty pounds. The dimensions and heft were designed to enable an average soldier to handle one crate. Each box contained approximately fourteen hundred rounds. The lid was pried open. Podrizki found a placard stating that the ammo had been manufactured in 1964. The words were in English, the digits in Roman numerals. But next to the Western markings were Chinese characters indicating the date of production and the caliber of the rounds.

Podrizki looked underneath the placard and found the aluminum cans. Rusty and old, they were also marked in English and Chinese. A can was opened. The ammo had been packed in nitrogen to displace oxygen and humidity and prevent the steel jackets from rusting. Despite being more than forty years old, the ammo was in amazingly good condition. All ammunition degraded over time, but it wasn't unusual for AK-47 surplus to last for decades, provided it had been stored in a reasonable manner—as these rounds had.

Podrizki took out a handful of individual rounds and inspected them closely. The ammo really was good, it seemed to Podrizki, given the amount of time it had spent in the dank cave.

As Podrizki admired the ammo, a potential problem occurred to him. Packouz and Diveroli hadn't told Podrizki about the Chinese embargo before he left. Why would they? Podrizki was going to Albania, not China. But Podrizki was a student of international affairs. He was aware of the military rivalry between the United States and China and rising tensions.

Podrizki wondered if buying from the Albanians meant AEY was somehow buying from China. The ammo had been brought to Albania decades before the ban was imposed. Was the ammo Chinese or Albanian?

Podrizki perceived the problem in the blink of an eye. Anyone could see the ammo was literally "Chinese" by the markings on the crates. Podrizki figured he should at least ask what the deal was—because he was pretty sure it wasn't okay to trade in Chinese weapons.

"This is Chinese," Podrizki said to Pinari, holding up a round.

Pinari shrugged. "Is okay. We send the same ammunition to American Special Forces in Stuttgart in Germany last year. It was for them to train with. AEY did this deal. There was no problem."

Podrizki nodded. Perhaps Pinari was right. The ammo had been sitting in caves in Albania for decades, so it couldn't fairly be described as "Chinese." It was far more sensible to say the ammo was now "Albanian." And the reality was that the place of manufacture didn't change the quality of the rounds, or the urgency of getting the shipments to Afghanistan to fight the Taliban.

"Let me run this by my people in Miami," Podrizki said.

"Of course."

Podrizki thought Pinari was looking at him with pity, like he was a dumb kid with no idea what he was talking about. That much of the ammo in the cave had been manufactured in China would be obvious to anyone who knew the slightest thing about Albanian history. The country's alliance with China wasn't a footnote but one of the foundational facts of its strange past. In the 1950s, Albanian leader Hoxha had split from the Soviet Union, declaring the leader Nikita Khrushchev "defeatist." Albania had then formed a close friendship with China, at the time the sworn enemy of the Soviets. The unlikely alliance had resulted in Mao Tse-tung's sending thousands of tons of his country's surplus ammunition to Albania in the 1950s and 1960s—artillery pieces and surface-to-air missiles and tanks and armored vehicles. Pinari must have assumed that anyone in the arms industry would understand that if Albania was selling surplus ammunition, the likelihood was extremely high that some or all of it would be Chinese-manufactured.

Podrizki said he wanted to test the ammo to see if it was "serviceable." He said he needed to fire some rounds. An AK-47 was produced and he was taken to what passed for an Albanian shooting range: stones were placed on a nearby fence as targets. He loaded the magazine and let loose. The casings were steel, not brass, which made them of inferior quality and much cheaper. But as Podrizki unloaded the AK he could see that the ammo worked great.

Late that night, Podrizki called Packouz in Miami. It was April 20—4/20, or 420, the stoner nickname for marijuana, and an annual day for pot smokers to celebrate weed. The two dudes shared a joke, each wishing the other a happy "four twenty." Packouz was gently buzzed from a morning hit on the vaporizer.

"Hey, man, I inspected the stuff and it seems good," Podrizki said. "They've got a massive stockpile. All sorts of ordnance. Huge bunkers."

"How did the ammo look?" Packouz asked. "Any rust? The containers still sealed? You test some rounds?"

"Yeah. It all worked perfectly. No rust anywhere on the rounds. The vacuum seals are still intact. The ammo looked good."

"Great. That's a relief. Did you weigh the pallets?"

"I have to buy a proper scale. But they're around three and a half kilograms. So seven or eight pounds each. The tins weigh about two pounds."

"Excellent. That's significant weight we're going to get rid of."

"But, bro, you know the ammo is Chinese, right?"

"What are you talking about?" Packouz asked.

"The ammo is Chinese."

"How do you know it's Chinese?"

"There are Chinese markings all over the crates."

"You sure?"

"Yeah. It's definitely Chinese."

"Oh, fuck," said Packouz. "That's not good. What about on the metal tins? Any markings?"

"There were some, but I can't remember if they were Chinese. I'll have to get another look."

"This is what you've got to do. Tomorrow, you ask to see the ammo again. You take pictures from all angles—the crates, the tins, inside the tins. See if there is stencil paper inside the tins. We have to see what this looks like so we can decide what to do."

"Will do."

Packouz felt panic rising in his gut. He went back into the office and told Diveroli what he'd just learned.

"You got to be shitting me," Diveroli said, startled.

"I'm serious. There are Chinese markings on the boxes."

The entire contract was at stake, the pair instantly decided. Weeks of delays had pushed AEY to the outer limit of the schedule, so there wasn't time to find another supplier. Diveroli muttered that Henri Thomet hadn't mentioned the Albanian ammo was Chinese, a calculated and cunning omission, as he had to know that the ammo was "Chinese."

"Of course Thomet had quoted me 'Albanian' ammo," Diveroli recalled. "When I called him, he swore to me a hundred times that the Army had bought the same ammo before. He said the Army was buying Chinese-made AK-47 rifles from Albania from one of my competitors named Taos. He was brokering that deal. But he knew what was going on. He'd been dealing with Albania for years. He wanted to stick me in a position where I was locked into using him, and he did a great job at that."

Diveroli instructed Packouz to read the Afghanistan contract carefully to see what kinds of modifications they might be able to get from the Army. Diveroli said he'd try to figure out what could be done legally.

The next four hours were frantic. Packouz and Diveroli had never physically opened a crate of surplus AK-47 ammo, despite the deals AEY had done. So they had little understanding of how the rounds were packed. Their first idea was to simply paint over the Chinese markings on the crates. E-mails flew back and forth between Miami and Albania as they tried to find a solution.

The dudes were in the midst of a classic wartime snafu: the Army desperately needed ammunition that worked perfectly, but it couldn't buy the rounds, it appeared, because of a ban that self-evidently was never meant to apply to munitions shipped from China to Albania decades earlier. Faced with a situation in which the law seemed to defeat a necessary war purpose—for reasons that had nothing to do with the ban on Chinese munitions—the obvious solution for AEY would have been to tell the Army what was happening. They could explain to the Army that the ban shouldn't apply to the ammo. The rounds had been manufactured decades before the ban was imposed. It was ridiculous to retroactively outlaw ammo—and thus leave the Afghan armed forces without rounds for their guns.

The State Department's foreign-military-sales laws had a clause that dealt with exactly this scenario. The provision stated that if munitions had left their country of origin, after five years their nationality was transferred to the new country of their location. Under this rule, the ammo that had been in Albania for decades would now legally be "Albanian," not Chinese.

In a world of shifting alliances, the State Department's rule was a sensible policy. Once an implacable enemy of the West, Albania was now a close ally of the United States. The US Embassy in Tirana was deeply involved in helping the Albanians dispose of their surplus munitions through "demilitarization"—essentially taking the rounds apart. It was costly, dangerous, and cumbersome. Sending 100 million rounds of AK-47 ammo where they were so badly needed saved the expense and also helped an ally in Afghanistan.

But the Defense Federal Acquisition Regulation Supplement that governed AEY's contract had no such provision. Many of the Pentagon's regulations had been enacted quickly, under the strain of war. The Pentagon's haste in constructing its alternate procurement system meant that all of the consequences and implications of the new regime hadn't been considered. The law had no mechanism to change the place of origin and nationality of munitions.

Even so, if the Army had been informed, its lawyers could simply have found that MEICO wasn't a "Communist Chinese military company" so the ban didn't technically apply to the ammo in Albania. Moreover, there had been no such thing as a "Communist Chinese military company" when the ammunition had been manufactured. The ammunition had been made in the 1950s and 1960s by organizations called *machine-building industries*, the Chinese term for the entities running its military-industrial complex.*

If Diveroli had the wit to hire a topflight law firm, AEY could brandish a legal opinion marshaling compelling arguments that the ban didn't apply. If the matter had been thoroughly studied, AEY would have discovered that much of the "Chinese" ammo hadn't actually come from China. Many of the rounds had been manufactured in Albania but packaged in containers with Chinese markings. This oddity resulted from yet another obscure page of history. The ammo had been part of a much larger Chinese "gift" to Albania. As part of the alliance in the 1950s and 1960s, China had aimed to help industrialize the agrarian nation. The Chinese had built all kinds of facilities for the Albanians, from clothing manufacturers to steel foundries and arms factories. The Chinese had exported everything from the steel and brass for the cartridges to the wooden crates, paintbrushes, stencil machines, and headstamping equipment. Like a Hollywood movie-production team going to the jungles of Africa to shoot a film, bringing along everything from gaffer tape to Evian water, the Chinese had transported all the material they needed to Albania so they wouldn't have to rely on local materials.

Albanian laborers had put cartridges with Chinese headstamps in ammo cans with Chinese markings, layered in stencil paper with Chinese markings, then sealed the ammo in wooden crates stating that it had been manufactured in China. This ammunition looked exactly as if it had been made in China. Or nearly exactly. The dudes would have to have been world-class experts on Kalashnikov ammunition, which they most certainly weren't, to tell the difference.

---

* "A New Direction for China's Defense Industry" (Rand, 2005).

Trapping a small contractor like AEY in a maze of federal regulations like this was a well-founded fear of Congress when new laws and regulations were enacted. The Regulatory Flexibility Act required the Pentagon to study the impact any new regulations would have on small companies fulfilling federal contracts. This was to ensure that small companies weren't overburdened and put at a disadvantage by larger companies with legal departments and funds for fancy law firms. But the Pentagon claimed that no such study was required, because the ban applied only to Chinese military companies—not American companies.

The Pentagon was wrong about its own regulation. The ban had been drafted broadly, forbidding any acquisition "directly or *indirectly*," which could be taken to include AEY's purchase of Chinese-made ammunition from an Albanian company fifty years after the rounds were manufactured—an interpretation that would strain credulity and common sense.

But the dudes were the dudes. Podrizki and Diveroli and Packouz didn't grasp the legal niceties of the situation, or the political realities. The trio comprehended only what was directly in front of them: the ban, the Chinese markings, the need to deliver.

Unsure what to do next, Diveroli called Ralph Merrill in Utah. The older businessman had imported Chinese AK-47 ammunition to the United States for years. Instead of leveling with Merrill about the China problem, Diveroli dissembled and said the idea of changing the packaging came from the Albanians.

Over the next few hours, the deceptions within deceptions multiplied. AEY would either have to supply the Albanian ammo, or renege on the contract. The consequences of not delivering on such a large and vital contract would be harsh. In the language of FedBizOpps, it would result in a *termination for default*, not only costing AEY the Afghan deal but also severely undermining its ability to win contracts in the future. There was really no choice to make: AEY was dead if they didn't deliver.

First, the dudes decided they needed to be doubly sure the ammo really was "Chinese." The next morning, in Albania, Alex Podrizki went to check the rounds again and take pictures. He was escorted to another vault filled with ammo. He randomly opened ammo cans filled with a variety of Soviet Bloc ammo for different guns—AK-47s, Dragunov sniper rifles, SKS semiautomatics.

The Albanian soldiers accompanying Podrizki opened the locks on boxes with axes and smoked cigarettes while surrounded by tons of explosives—a remarkable lack of precaution. They grinned when Podrizki recoiled in fear: *Look at the stupid American kid*, he thought they were thinking.

But there was no doubt now: the ammunition was definitely "Chinese." Podrizki carefully took photographs, as instructed by Packouz—the crates, the tins, the stencil paper inside the tins. Then Podrizki went and fired the rounds. To him, all the fuss about the origin of the ammunition was a distraction. He was working for AEY and would do his best to follow instructions, but he believed he had a larger duty to fulfill—to the war effort in Afghanistan and the soldiers going into battle who lacked ammo for their guns. The rounds worked perfectly well, despite the place of origin.

"All I was interested in was serviceability," Podrizki recalled. "That was all I ever really gave a fuck about. What were the Afghan soldiers in the field going to take into battle? I was concerned about how things worked. I had trained as a soldier. I wanted to make sure that the ammo could be used to fight the Taliban."

Podrizki called AEY in Miami. This time he spoke to Diveroli.

"Diveroli told me that in the worst possible scenario it would be a civil matter, not criminal," Podrizki recalled. "Diveroli said he had lawyers looking into the matter. He said the ammo had been purchased by the Albanians before the embargo was imposed, so the law couldn't be applied retroactively. He said the weapons weren't coming from a Chinese company and the contract wasn't benefiting China in any way. He said the embargo only applied to certain kinds of weapons. It was about technology going *to* China, not ancient ammo in Albania. He had a bunch of explanations that made sense. I knew Efraim and David were going to make a lot of money out of the contract, so they had a motive to perform."

Diveroli wanted to know how many Albanian-made ammo there were, as opposed to the Chinese rounds. He instructed Podrizki to meet with Pinari immediately. The plan was to fulfill the first shipment of 2 million rounds with Albanian ammo, buying time to try to find another source. As they spoke, Packouz was checking with companies in Hungary and Bulgaria. The other countries had stockpiles of surplus ammo, and the pricing was competitive. But the question was timing. The earlier delays had put AEY under the gun. Getting approvals and end-user certificates was time-consuming. Precious weeks had passed, and the fighting season was in full swing in the Korangal Valley and other hot spots in Afghanistan. AEY had to move fast.

In Tirana, Podrizki presented the new plan to Pinari.

"We don't think the Chinese ammo is going to work for us," Podrizki said. "We need you to deliver only Albanian-made ammo."

"This is not feasible," Pinari replied. "Most of the ammunition close to the airport is Chinese. The Albanian-made ammunition is scattered all over the country. There is not enough to fill the order. It is too difficult and expensive to truck all this to Tirana."

The excuse sounded lame to Podrizki—because in fact it was. MEICO had Albanian-made rounds it could supply to AEY, but those rounds had brass casings, not the cheap steel casings AEY was buying. The brass-jacket rounds were being sold to another American company to be taken apart for scrap. Podrizki didn't think Pinari was being straight with him, but how could he compel a senior Albanian official to do what he wanted, or tell the truth?

Returning to his hotel room, Podrizki felt overwhelmed. Diveroli also wanted him to arrange to have airport fees waived, obtain export licenses, and oversee the repacking operation. Now, steps might have to be taken to remove the Chinese markings. It was all too much, especially in such an uncooperative country. Podrizki e-mailed Packouz that Pinari was failing to offer necessary practical and timely assistance—typical of Albania, he was learning.

"From the wrong side of the Iron Curtain," Podrizki ended his e-mail, trying to add a note of levity.

"We promised the government we'd deliver last week, so if we don't deliver this week we'll look horrendous," Packouz replied. He signed off, "From the luxurious leather couch in my South Beach condo."

To get approval for using cardboard packaging instead of the ancient wooden crates, Packouz sent an e-mail to Major Ronald Walck, in Kabul, titled "Packaging Issues." It was a minor masterpiece in the art of deception:

"During one of our inspections our team discovered that some of the metal cans the ammunition was stored in were in an unpredictable, poor, and worn condition due to many years of storage," Packouz wrote. As a result, AEY was going to have to repackage the AK-47 ammo in cardboard boxes. He attached photos Podrizki had taken showing that the actual rounds were in excellent condition. Every metal can was being opened, Packouz explained, to visually inspect every cartridge and ensure quality. He noted that extensive test-firing had been conducted by AEY's "team" in Albania. Packouz pointed out that the Army's Lake City Ammunition plant in Independence, Missouri, had long ago discarded wooden crates in favor of cardboard boxes, saving millions of dollars in airfreight and suffering no loss in quality for field duty.

"Since our contract does not specify any particular packaging, we want to confirm that this will not cause any issues," Packouz concluded. "Your prompt response would be appreciated."

Hours later Major Walck wrote back, "The ammunition in the

pictures looks good. I don't think there will be any problems with the cardboard boxes. If you band them to the pallets they should be fine."

"GOOD NEWS!!!" was the title of the e-mail Packouz sent to Podrizki in Albania. "The Army officer who will be signing for the goods has accepted loose-packed ammo in cardboard boxes!!! We must begin repacking IMMEDIATELY if we are going to make our deadline."

First thing Monday morning, Podrizki e-mailed Pinari, "We're already two weeks behind schedule and we risk losing the contract and being blacklisted by the Pentagon, thus preventing BOTH of our companies from ever again doing business with the US government. Once a company is blacklisted it is nearly impossible to regain legitimacy with the government. There are literally hundreds of companies eager to replace us on this contract."

Pinari still refused to deliver the ammunition. Podrizki didn't know it, but part of the problem was that Diveroli had yet to pay MEICO for the rounds in advance, as the agreement required.

Exasperated, Podrizki decided he needed help—not because the ammo was Chinese but because he couldn't get the Albanians to deliver. He was staying at the Hotel Broadway, just off the city's main square. The US Embassy was nearby, a building surrounded by barbed wire, barricades, and scores of armed Albanian and American soldiers. Podrizki presented his passport to a guard at the gate and asked to speak to an official. He was told he wasn't allowed to enter the embassy. But a political/military-affairs attaché named Victor Myev agreed to talk to him on the phone. Podrizki explained the situation to Myev, describing the contract and the inexplicable behavior of Pinari and the Ministry of Defense. Could the embassy put pressure on the Albanians?

"MEICO isn't delivering," Podrizki said. "I need help."

"I can't help unless there's an allegation of corruption," Myev said. Since AEY was a private company, even though it was doing business with both the American and Albanian governments, it would have to solve its troubles directly with the Albanians. But Myev sympathized. Doing business in Albania was frustrating, Myev allowed—especially inside the government. "That's just the way things are done here," Myev said, sighing.

Podrizki wrote to Diveroli to say he'd tried the US Embassy: "I spoke with the US Embassy to see if they could do something to help—like put pressure on Pinari, MEICO, or the Minister of Defense. Or all three. They said that unless something illegal is happening they can't do anything. They also said this type of treatment and attitude (laziness) is typical of the region and especially Albania."

Diveroli called Podrizki to discuss the situation.

"Listen, you might want to consider investing in some political capital," Podrizki said. It seemed to him that AEY's woes were essentially political. Diveroli needed a powerful American political voice—a senator, say, or a congressman—to make a few calls on his behalf. The Albanians would surely bend to American influence, especially with the much-desired ascension to NATO membership looming. The only way to resolve the kinds of obstacles AEY faced, Podrizki believed, was to purchase political power—and that meant giving money to powerful politicians.

"Don't give me a geography lesson. I know what I'm doing," Diveroli said condescendingly, as if Podrizki were talking down to him.

But Podrizki was right. If war was the continuation of politics by other means, as the military theorist Carl von Clausewitz maintained, then arms dealing was a business where the ends justify the means. AEY could—and should—have taken many political steps. The dudes should have told the purchasing officer in Rock Island about the "Chinese" ammunition. The Army could have been apprised of the choice it faced—enforce the Chinese ban and deny the Afghans sufficient ammo for the fighting season, or find a way around the ban and complete a critical mission in America's global war on terror. The dudes could—and should—donate money to a pro-military-minded senator, or pro-Albanian congressman—and there were many—to smooth the path.

As the pressure mounted, so did the absurdities. The Pentagon was an ungainly behemoth tied down by thousands of tiny rules and regulations. None alone were crippling, but the accumulation of these hastily drafted laws, written under the pressure of two losing wars, threatened to snarl the effort to supply arms to the Afghans.

But the drafters of the defense regulations had displayed the foresight to create a fallback position for such eventualities. The law governing AEY's contract specifically gave the secretary of defense the power to grant a waiver. The problem was getting word to Robert Gates.

Regardless, Diveroli didn't dare tell the Army about the Chinese ammo, let alone try to find a back channel to the Pentagon. Diveroli was sure that if he informed the procurement officers in Rock Island about what was happening they would say no to a waiver, no matter the circumstances.

It would later emerge that Diveroli was in fact correct. If he'd appealed to the Army, no variance would have been allowed, nor would the procurement officers have gone up the chain of command to find solutions to a legal and technical issue that threatened critical supplies. AEY had been notified that Chinese ammo was not permitted, and that was the end of the matter.

Large companies like Raytheon and Boeing spent fortunes paying lobbyists to guide them through circumstances like those AEY found itself in. Lockheed Martin alone dropped more than $15 million a year on Washington lobbyists. The revolving door between the military and the conglomerates profiting from the military-industrial complex was well oiled. For a connected DC operator, fixing AEY's dilemma would be easy. A well-placed phone call, a favor called in, an appeal to logic over lunch at a K Street steak house—the situation perfectly illustrated why lobbyists existed in the first place.

Comrades in arms: David Packouz and Efraim Diveroli at the American Gun Range, Miami, 2006.

Packouz at the Eurosatory arms show, Paris, playing war, 2006.

Diveroli at Eurosatory, Paris, 2006.

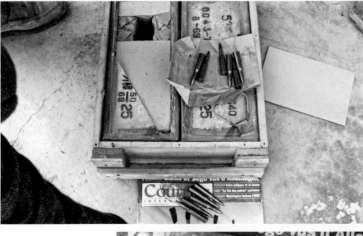

When Alex Podrizki arrived in Albania in April of 2007, he discovered much of the ammunition had been manufactured in China decades earlier.

Despite its age, the ammunition was in surprisingly good condition.

To disguise the Chinese origin of the ammo, the rounds were taken from their original packaging.

The ammo was put into lightweight cardboard boxes and palletized to be shipped from Albania to Afghanistan.

The Albanian arms company MEICO was run by an official named Ylli Pinari. *Credit: Gent Shkullaku*

The Albanian minister of defense Fatmir Mediu. *Credit: Gent Shkullaku*

A businessman named Mihail Delijorgji apparently outranked the defense minister on the pricing of the ammo. *Credit: Gent Shkullaku*

Also involved, the dudes discovered, was the prime minister's son, Shkelzen Berisha. *Credit: Gent Shkullaku*

The repacking was being done by an Albanian businessman named Kosta Trebicka.

Until Trebicka was kicked off the deal and went to the *New York Times* and federal prosecutors in America with claims of corruption involving powerful Albanians—and was soon found dead. *Credit: Gent Shkullaku*

Because of a lack of safety precautions in a deal run by the same politicians selling ammo to AEY, an ammunition dump in the Albanian village of Gërdec exploded, killing twenty-six civilians. *Credit: Gent Shkullaku*

On March 27, 2008, a front-page story in the *New York Times* appeared with a photograph of ammo AEY shipped to Afghanistan—though the rounds pictured weren't Chinese and they weren't from Albania.

The mug shots of Packouz and Diveroli that appeared in the *New York Times*. *Credit: Miami-Dade Police Department*

Diveroli was a kid in a hurry. He was convinced any sign of weakness or doubt—any trouble at all—would jeopardize the deal. He didn't dare seek real guidance. Nor did he spend the money to hire a top DC law firm to advise him. He had millions of dollars in the bank but none of the maturity or experience to know when it was important to spend some of that capital—as Alex Podrizki had suggested.

Unwilling to contact the Army directly, Diveroli instead wrote to the lawyers in the State Department who were assigned to answer questions from federal contractors. Was Chinese-manufactured ammunition in Albania outside the embargo against Chinese munitions if the rounds were manufactured before the ban? Diveroli asked. He didn't provide details or outline any of the compelling arguments a lawyer might have provided him. He asked the way a scared kid might—afraid he'd get in trouble if the grown-ups found out what he was up to.

The reply came swiftly, as if the matter required no consideration. No, the State Department's lawyer said, there was no such provision in the law. Under State's regime, the proposed transaction would not be authorized. "Exceptions to this policy require a presidential determination," the lawyer wrote.

The answer was incorrect: under the State Department's rules, the ammunition would in fact change nationality after five years. But that didn't matter. Diveroli was now convinced AEY was cornered.

To comply with the contract, the company had to ship the ammo to Kabul by Thursday. It was Tuesday.

"It looks like we have another reason to repack," Diveroli said to Packouz. "And this time it's not an option."

A meeting of AEY's team was convened in Miami: Diveroli, Packouz, and two other dudes from the yeshiva who were now working for AEY—Danny Doudnik and Levi Meyer.

"Well, this is it, boys," Diveroli said. "This is where we separate the boys from the men—the pussies from the big swinging dicks. We got no time to switch sources, and I'm not counting on President Bush to give a fuck about us. We can either go crying to the government that we fucked up or we can do what they want us to do anyway and deliver the motherfucking ammo."

The arms-dealing business had a term for the situation AEY confronted. The law could be followed. Or the law could be evaded—*circumvented*, in the argot of gunrunning. Men like Henri Thomet regularly faced these kinds of dilemmas. Embargoes and human-rights reports and the web of international laws often made it difficult for arms dealers to act strictly legally. In such circumstances, the result was circumvention.

Ironically, the same logic applied to the Pentagon in Iraq and Afghanistan. The established system for arming allies had been created over decades by the State Department. Designed during the Cold War, it provided for orderly and sustained policies of supplying weapons to NATO allies and countries like Israel and Egypt. Conflict in the age of terror presented a new set of challenges; standing up armies in Afghanistan and Iraq was far more difficult and urgent than anything State's laws anticipated. The Department of Defense procurement regimen had been constructed to speed the process—in effect to circumvent State's laws.

AEY was likewise caught in a desperate situation—and would likewise have to circumvent.

Diveroli demanded an update on the repacking job in Albania. The cardboard boxes hadn't been sourced yet, Packouz said. Nor had Alex Podrizki found someone able to physically repack the ammo, which appeared to be necessary, as the Albanian military refused to do the work. Packouz and the others reported on their search for companies in Eastern Europe that could do the job. But all the potential partners came with caveats and delays.

"We don't have time for that bullshit," Diveroli said. "We've got to get these fuckers to perform."

"Alex told me he's got a lead on a local guy in Albania," Packouz said. "He only talked to him on the phone, but Alex said the guy is pretty motivated. His name is Kosta Trebicka. He's some kind of paper manufacturer. This Trebicka guy claimed he could arrange delivery of the boxes quickly."

"Excellent," Diveroli said. "Now we're rolling. Get Alex to meet this Albanian dude immediately. We're dropping everything else until we get this resolved. If we don't get this done, we're all fucked."

Chapter Seven

GEGH

In early May of 2007, Alex Podrizki met the Albanian businessman Kosta Trebicka at the Illy Caffe in Tirana, a slick new place on Rruga Pandi Dardha. Trebicka was in his late forties, a former lawyer who'd turned himself into a prosperous entrepreneur. Years earlier, he'd lived in the United States, in Syracuse in upstate New York, with his first wife and their daughter. He spoke fluent English and considered himself knowledgeable about Americans. He'd also served in the Albanian military, rising to the rank of major and accumulating a significant fortune from the sale of state-owned assets after the collapse of Communism.

Trebicka listened intently as Podrizki told him he needed eighty thousand boxes to repack 100 million rounds of AK-47 ammo. Podrizki explained that the wooden pallets holding the ammo were too heavy to ship by plane. Fuel prices had made airfreight prohibitively expensive. Using reinforced cardboard and lighter pallets would save a significant amount of money on transportation. The US Army had approved the plan, Podrizki said.

Podrizki asked if Trebicka might be interested in doing the repacking job as well as supplying the boxes. Trebicka was indeed: he had access to a pool of workers and ambition to burn. Podrizki was excited and relieved: finding someone in Albania to do such an odd job had looked as if it would be extremely difficult, but Trebicka promised to solve both of AEY's problems at once.

The next day, Podrizki and Trebicka went to the military section of Tirana's airport, where 2 million rounds of ammo were stored in an open-air hangar. To begin, Trebicka brought along forty workers, drawn from the people who worked at his cardboard factory. Half of the ammo was Albanian-made, half had Chinese markings on the boxes. Podrizki told Trebicka to have the workers divide the crates into two piles—one Albanian, the other Chinese. Podrizki said to start with the Albanian rounds. Following Podrizki's instructions, Trebicka showed his crew how to remove the metal cans from the crates. Each can contained 640 rounds of ammo, with batches of twenty cartridges wrapped in stencil paper that indicated the place of manufacture, age, and caliber. For the Albanian rounds, the ammo could be put in the cardboard boxes still wrapped in paper, making the task relatively easy. The workers were instructed to inspect the ammunition to make sure it wasn't rusted, discolored, or obviously faulty; any rounds that were flawed were to be put aside.

Trebicka had his workers repack one pallet of ammo in order to assess the difficulty so he could come up with a quote. Trebicka then had an extended phone conversation about the cost with Diveroli in Miami. After the inevitable dickering they agreed on $240,000.

As Trebicka's team worked away, the supply of Albanian ammo quickly ran dry. A million rounds of Albanian ammo had been palletized and was ready to be shipped—as soon as AEY could get the logistics of the flight to Kabul organized.

But Ylli Pinari announced that MEICO would supply only Chinese ammunition from now on. The Chinese ammunition was in good condition, Podrizki could see—it was actually better quality than the Albanian rounds. But the repacking would have to be done differently, Podrizki explained to Trebicka. Instead of putting the Chinese ammunition in the cardboard boxes still wrapped in the stencil paper, the paper would have to be removed, too. Every round would still be inspected for quality, but instead of being in neatly wrapped stacks the ammo would be put loose into plastic bags.

"Be careful to make sure there are no Chinese markings on any of the material inside the cardboard boxes," Podrizki told Trebicka.

Trebicka agreed to follow Podrizki's new system—but with a quizzical look on his face. The stencil paper didn't add any weight, so why take it out? It made the job messier and more time-consuming, to no purpose that Trebicka could see.

Inspecting and repacking millions of rounds was proving to be maddeningly slow and difficult. After a few days of his workers' toiling away, Trebicka feared he'd seriously underbid his price. During breaks he complained that he was going to lose money if things didn't speed up. Podrizki said he could do nothing to change the price. Exasperated, Trebicka called Diveroli in Miami to try to renegotiate. Removing the ammo from the cans was a waste of time, Trebicka said; the cans didn't add significant weight. Why bother? Trebicka asked. AEY was going to have to pay him more, Trebicka said, or he would stack the cans inside the cardboard boxes, instead of removing all the rounds. The same was true for the stencil paper.

"Are there Chinese markings on the lids of the cans?" Diveroli asked.

"Yes," Trebicka replied.

"Are there Chinese markings on the paper wrappers?"

"Yes."

Diveroli said that the operation had to continue as instructed, even if it was going to cost more. A new price was agreed, granting the Albanian an extra $40,000 for his trouble. Trebicka was surprised by Diveroli's response—and suspicious. That evening, Trebicka and Podrizki went to a local restaurant for dinner. Both ordered fish soup, a traditional Albanian delicacy.

"This is a very strange thing to do," Trebicka said to Podrizki. "Why do you want to spend all this money for repacking the same ammunition?"

"Weight," Alex replied. "Everything is done to avoid wasting money on airfreight."

"But what is such a strong reason to hide the Chinese writings on the top of the cans?" Trebicka asked. "And the Chinese letters on the paper, too—why do this?"

"Don't worry, Kosta. The simple reason is that the ammo passes over different countries during transportation. If the authorities in another country stop the flight and see that part of the ammunition is from Albania and part is from China they will start an investigation. The difference will have to be explained. That will delay the shipments. We'll lose the contract if we don't deliver on time."

Trebicka didn't seem satisfied. Podrizki was a man of few words—the less said the better, he believed. But he realized he needed to be direct with Trebicka, or at least give him an explanation that was believable.

Leaning forward, Podrizki confided that the truth was that Chinese ammo wasn't allowed under the contract. He explained the situation as it had been explained to him—the ban and the fact that the ammo had been manufactured in China was a contractual issue between the Army and AEY. He said AEY was searching for alternative sources for the ammo, but it'd default on the whole contract if they didn't ship on time. AEY had no choice—it had to repack. Nothing about the repacking changed the quality of the rounds, or the urgency of the need in Kabul.

"I had my own personal reservations, but I kept moving forward, hoping things would work themselves out somehow," Podrizki recalled. "I wasn't ready to quit and go home. It was a problem to do with the terms of the contract—not the quality of the ammunition."

Trebicka listened silently, a serious expression on his face. He was quiet for maybe ten seconds.

"I imagined in those moments he drew the same conclusion that I had," Podrizki said. "He was going to keep going. He could understand the reasoning. It wasn't such a big deal. The ammo was good quality, even if it was old, so what was the difference if the Chinese markings were removed? It wasn't like we were hiding flaws in the ammunition to trick the American military. Every round was inspected for quality."

But privately Trebicka wasn't pleased by Podrizki's reassurance. Concerned that AEY might be breaking the law, Trebicka decided to reach out to a contact he had in the US Embassy, a diplomat he'd known for years. Robert Newsome was a State Department official who worked as an economic representative in Albania. Trebicka met Newsome at the Chocolate Café next to the US Embassy. Trebicka described AEY's arms contract and how the company had hired him to repack the AK-47 rounds. The ammunition was Chinese, Trebicka said. He explained how his workers were breaking down every wooden crate, putting the rounds into plastic bags, then putting the bags into the cardboard boxes.

"Why are they doing that?" Newsome asked.

Trebicka repeated what Podrizki had told him about weight and freight and the possibility that the flight would be grounded in a third country en route to Afghanistan—leaving out the possibility that Chinese ammo was forbidden under AEY's contract. Newsome asked for Alex's mobile phone number.

"Everything is okay," Newsome assured Trebicka. "The contract is a great help for the United States. We've been looking for funding to demolish most of the ammunition in Albania."

The next day Trebicka told Podrizki about his encounter with the State Department official.

"What did Newsome say when you told him the ammo was Chinese?" Podrizki asked.

"He said it was okay," Trebicka said. "He said it was a great idea to send the ammunition from Albania to Afghanistan so it doesn't have to be destroyed here."

This was great news: a senior American official apparently didn't care that "Chinese" ammunition was being transported to Kabul. Surely the diplomat knew about the ban and didn't think it mattered, or applied. Newsome called Podrizki later that day. The State Department attaché told Podrizki that he had firsthand knowledge of the situation in America's two war zones—how dire and desperate the need for ammunition really was. In wartime, bureaucratic niceties had to give way to the realities on the ground—and the reality was that standing up armies in Iraq and Afghanistan was a top strategic priority for the US government.

"I understand you're repacking and delivering Russian, Albanian, and Chinese ammunition to send to Afghanistan," Newsome said.

"No," Podrizki said. "We're only delivering Albanian and Chinese."

"I'm familiar with the ongoing war effort. I know what's going on."

Podrizki took this to be unspoken approval, the proverbial nudge and a wink. Finally talking to a friendly person, Podrizki described the troubles he faced. There were still delays in getting more of the ammo to the airport. Onerous fees had to be paid at the airport because the authorities were treating the flights as commercial instead of governmental. Could Newsome help get the fees waived?

"I can help," Newsome said. "I'll stay in touch with Trebicka and let you know how things progress."

///////

On May 16, 2007, AEY's first shipment of ammunition under the Afghanistan contract touched down in Kabul. But it wasn't the ammo from Albania—the repacking for the first planeload still wasn't complete, and the dudes hadn't been able to obtain the proper overflight permissions. Nor had they been able to find a reasonable price for the airfreight from Tirana to Kabul.

AEY's first shipment consisted of hand grenades—110,000 grenades from Bulgaria. An Azerbaijan airline called Silkway made the delivery, charging $130,000 for the flight. AEY could afford to pay the high price to Silkway for the shipment of grenades because the load was worth $3 million. With the AK-47 ammo, each load was worth only $300,000, so the exorbitant airfreight cost meant AEY would make no money on the deal.

"The first delivery was a huge relief for us," David Packouz recalled. "We were finally performing, even if the cost of airfreight was insane.

But there were still lots of problems getting overflight permissions. It was the hardest thing I'd ever tried to do."

To coordinate the flights from Albania, AEY hired a string of logistics companies that specialized in that business. The companies assured Packouz they could arrange the required permissions, but they'd call back a few days later saying they couldn't complete the contract. It was a mystery—as if invisible forces were interfering with AEY.

Taking up the job himself, Packouz called the American embassies in the countries where AEY was having a hard time—Macedonia, Bulgaria, Turkey, Georgia, Azerbaijan, and Turkmenistan. After weeks of cajoling, the military attachés were finally able to help Packouz get overflight permission for every country except Turkmenistan. For some reason, they couldn't get that one, so Packouz had the idea of using Turkmenistan's airline, and it worked—no lubricant was better than money for a gunrunner greasing the wheels of commerce.

In late May, an ancient Ilyushin 76 from Turkmenistan landed in Tirana and taxied to the military section of the airport, where the repacking was taking place. The giant cargo plane was in terrible condition, and US military officials stationed at the airport joked about its being unable to take off.

The pallets were finally ready to be loaded. But as preparations were made, Kosta Trebicka's ambitions appeared to be changing. He now had fifty workers busily taking AK-47 ammo from cans and putting it into plastic bags, placing the bags in cardboard boxes, then arranging the boxes on pallets. It was hard work and he was making a pittance, at least compared with Ylli Pinari of MEICO. Or so Trebicka surmised. Pinari was doing nothing but arranging for delivery of the ammo from stockpiles around the country. While Trebicka and his workers slaved away in the open-air hangar, all Pinari did was make a few phone calls and military trucks loaded with AK-47 ammo turned up at the airport. How much was Pinari personally making from the deal? Trebicka wondered—because in Albania he was certain that an unctuous official, like the head of MEICO, would be taking a cut.

As Trebicka drove Podrizki to the sea one day, on a sightseeing trip, he bad-mouthed the Albanian officials in MEICO, most especially Pinari—"little people," he called them. Trebicka claimed that he could "protect" AEY from Pinari.

Walking along the beach, Trebicka said that he'd done clandestine work for the CIA during the eighties and early nineties. He claimed he'd been instrumental in overthrowing the old Communist regime. He said he remained deeply connected to the American intelligence apparatus in Albania, an invisible network that had great influence in the country.

Podrizki didn't know what to make of Trebicka's new attitude, or his tales of intrigue. It sounded like empty boasting. Podrizki duly reported the offer to "protect" AEY to Diveroli, more as a joke than a serious matter.

Diveroli was intrigued by Trebicka's claims. If the Albanian businessman was so well connected, Diveroli said, perhaps he could find out what the Swiss arms dealer Henri Thomet was really paying MEICO for the ammo. Diveroli had long wondered what Thomet's true profit margin was.

Trying to squeeze every last dollar from the deal, Diveroli called Trebicka directly. The Albanian businessman was eager to ingratiate himself with the young gunrunner. Trebicka readily agreed to use his connections to find out the price Thomet was paying; Trebicka had a contact inside the Ministry of Defense who could do some sleuthing for him. A few days later, Trebicka called and told Diveroli that he'd discovered that MEICO was selling the ammo for $22 for every thousand rounds. That translated to 2.2 cents a round. Diveroli was stunned speechless, at least for a moment, as he did a quick calculation. AEY was paying $40 per thousand, or four cents a round. That meant Diveroli was paying nearly double what Thomet was paying. Thomet was making millions of dollars for doing literally nothing, while AEY was repacking the ammo and arranging for all the logistics of delivery—and taking all the risk on the China matter. Diveroli's profit margin was tiny, Thomet's huge.

"Fuck Thomet," Diveroli screamed. "He's a fucking thief."

"This is your business," Trebicka said. "Only you know what to do about it."

"You have lots of contacts in Albania," Diveroli said. "Can you have somebody go talk to the minister of defense to kick Thomet out and let us buy directly from MEICO?"

"I can do this. But I have to be paid properly for my unpacking and repacking the ammunition."

"How much?"

A deal was quickly struck, nearly doubling Trebicka's pay. A lengthy phone call with Ralph Merrill, in Utah, led the older businessman to write to Thomet (the Swiss broker had ceased replying to Diveroli's messages). Merrill's e-mail had to tread through a field littered with land mines of lies, half-truths, and subtle deceptions. "Circumvention concerns" was the title, alerting Thomet to the possibility that Diveroli might decide to cut him out of the deal entirely—this form of "circumvention" in the arms trade referring to going around a broker like Thomet to buy directly from the seller.

"Efraim is upset that you are making a lot of money and we are losing money," Merrill wrote. "He has received offers from the Ukraine, the Czech Republic, and Hungary, where there is enough ammo to fill the order. There is also the risk element regarding the reason for repacking. It seems to be a double negative to lose money and assume considerable risk."

Merrill turned to the question of the Chinese ammo, though without directly mentioning it in the e-mail. The matter was now simply referred to as "the problem." Merrill wrote, "Efraim is upset because he's checked all his e-mails from you and not found any mention of the problem. He thinks he's been set up."

Merrill proposed $27 per thousand as a fair price. "This would help with shipping, repacking, and the risks involved," he wrote, without overtly explaining the "risks" he was referring to. "Obviously we are not interested in donating to the war cause in Afghanistan, and are looking for a way out of this pit as soon as possible. Efraim awaits your response to this offer to save the Albanian connection."

But Thomet wouldn't budge on price—not under any circumstances. Diveroli decided he had to travel to Albania. He was going to negotiate the deal directly with the Ministry of Defense. He was going to get rid of the duplicitous Thomet, and he was going to force MEICO to lower the price.

Diveroli called Packouz into the hallway to talk confidentially, away from the staff: "Listen to me very carefully. I got to get to Albania to meet with that fat fuck Pinari. This is a make-it-or-break-it situation. So this is what I want you to do. Call the Ukrainians, the Hungarians, the Kazakhs, and get quotes from them. Then change the prices to make it look like we've got better options so I can beat that greedy fucker down. The documents have got to look good. But I know you're an artist, baby. When I land in Tirana, I need you to have sent me something beautiful."

Late that night, as Diveroli flew over the Atlantic, Packouz sat down to create another set of fake documents—and perhaps commit another fraud, he feared. By now Packouz knew that this kind of duplicity was all too common in arms dealing.

"I was very nervous," Packouz recalled. "I knew I was in really shady territory—possibly illegal, with a real paper trail. But I also felt excited that it might work—that we'd save the deal. And was it really so bad? We were lying to a sleazy Albanian tough guy to get a better price so we could deliver what the government needed. This was why the government needed us—they didn't want to have to do these kinds of things. In reality, they couldn't do these kinds of things because of the risks and complications, but they needed them done. So they sent us. It was how things worked—it was the nature of the business. In a way, the Pentagon was paying us for this exact service."

The next day, Alex Podrizki waited in the arrivals section of the airport in Tirana to greet Diveroli. Striding through the terminal, Diveroli was loud and brash, smirking at the bustle of the backward country. Driving into the city, Diveroli ridiculed the condition of the roads, the peasants walking donkeys next to the highway, the run-down houses and tiny, white pillboxes scattered all over the landscape.

"This place is like a jungle," Diveroli said. "Give me twenty men with guns and I could take this country."

The pair went to the Sheraton. They downed shots of raki, the colorless, high-alcohol Albanian eau-de-vie, sending shivers down their spines. Diveroli checked his e-mails and found the documents Packouz had doctored, showing false prices for AK-47 ammo. Packouz had done an excellent job changing the numbers, doctoring quotes from other suppliers to show the Hungarians and the Bulgarians could beat MEICO's price by a significant amount. Diveroli and Podrizki were ready.

The first stop was Ylli Pinari's office in the Ministry of Defense. More raki was poured and cigarettes were passed around. Diveroli placed a stack of documents on the table. He said they were quotes from other Eastern European countries for the same ammunition he was buying from MEICO.

"These are the standard prices," Diveroli said. "Any more than this, I will walk away."

Pinari inspected the sheet. He'd been in the business for decades. He knew the real prices of surplus nonstandard munitions. He looked up and shook his head with contempt. "These are fake."

Diveroli had been busted. Stumbling for what to say next, he forged on, "Your ammo is old. Some of it is nearly fifty years old. It doesn't warrant the price."

Pinari was unmoved.

"It's steel-cased, not brass," Diveroli said. "It's not as good."

Pinari said nothing.

"The only place you can sell your ammo is in Africa. The Africans can't afford to pay as much as the government of the United States."

The conversation was going nowhere, it seemed: Diveroli demanded a reduction, and Pinari insisted on the agreed terms. All the extra costs AEY had incurred, for the repacking, the higher airfreight prices, the unexpected licenses and fees at Tirana's airport—those were issues for Diveroli to take up with Henri Thomet, not MEICO, Pinari said.

Diveroli asked to see the Albanian minister of defense.

"If you want to change the price, you have to meet someone else," Pinari said finally.

Apparently, someone was more powerful than the minister—a strange assertion. Ylli Pinari escorted Diveroli and Podrizki to his Mercedes sedan. The pair were driven around the streets of Tirana in a seemingly deliberately confusing route, so the Americans wouldn't be able to re-create where they'd gone. Finally, they turned into an abandoned construction site for a partially completed office building. Pinari led the pair up a set of stairs and along a corridor until they reached a door. Stepping inside, they found a sleek, stylish office, like the suite of a corporate law firm in a skyscraper in Miami. The incongruity was disorienting. So was the sight of the man rising from his seat behind the desk. Instead of the kind of global businessman who might be expected to occupy such an office, there was a hard-looking man—a real thug, Podrizki thought, fear rising. *Gegh* was the Albanian word for such a man: muscular, dark-skinned, with what appeared to be prison tattoos on his forearms, a native of the tribal mountains.

This was Mihail Delijorgji. Diveroli and Podrizki then turned to see a young man around their age sitting in the corner. Dressed in a baseball cap and a sweater, he had dark hair, a soft chin, and sharklike eyes. He wasn't introduced. This was Shkëlzen Berisha, the son of the prime minister of Albania, they would later be told by Pinari. Shkëlzen was part of what was known in Albania as "the family," the tight-knit and extremely dangerous group that surrounded and lived at the beneficence of the prime minister, Sali Berisha.

Delijorgji didn't speak English, so Pinari translated Diveroli's reasons for wanting a price reduction. Diveroli's brash manner disappeared, as did his idea of cutting Thomet out of the deal. Diveroli and Podrizki were obviously in the presence of seriously connected men. Diveroli's complexion turned pale. Now his main complaint was that the vast majority of the rounds AEY was buying had steel casings. Brass casings were much more valuable, Diveroli claimed. Steel casings damaged the barrels of weapons, shortening their life span. Diveroli wanted to pay 3.7 cents a round.

Delijorgji said that if Diveroli wanted a discount he would have to change the arrangements for the repacking operation at the airport. If AEY was going to pay less for the ammo, the money would have to be made up another way—by giving the contract to repack to Delijorgji's company. The son of the prime minister remained silent. Henri Thomet's name was never mentioned. Nor was the fact that Diveroli knew MEICO was selling the rounds to Thomet for just over two cents a round.

Diveroli and Podrizki departed.

"That guy looked stupid enough to be dangerous," Diveroli said of Delijorgji.

"Did we just get out of a meeting with the Albanian mafia?" Podrizki joked.

"Absolutely. Absofuckinglutely."

Diveroli's swagger began to fade. He didn't say it out loud, but he was clearly scared. The dudes went to a local casino to gamble, and Diveroli pounded down his usual massive portion of alcohol. As ever, Diveroli acted the big shot, boasting about the contracts he was winning in Iraq and how gunrunning was a great business.

As the pair left the casino, Diveroli was anxious. The booze and bravado hadn't calmed him. He didn't want to be alone. He insisted that Podrizki sleep on the foldout couch in his hotel room. Who knew what the Albanian gangsters were capable of?

The next morning, Kosta Trebicka was pacing in the lobby of the

Sheraton, desperate to hear about Diveroli's meetings the day before. As ever eager to please, Trebicka provided a BMW and a driver for the rest of Diveroli's stay in Albania. Trebicka would also supply an attractive young woman for Diveroli's pleasure, an offer the young arms dealer gladly accepted.

Diveroli could have told Trebicka the truth about his encounter with Delijorgji: AEY would get a discount on the AK-47 rounds only if Delijorgji's company took over the repacking job—cutting Trebicka out of the deal. But Diveroli did what he'd become accustomed to doing: he dissembled. Diveroli said he'd been taken to a "hidden" place and threatened. The Albanians had said he'd be killed if he didn't go along with Thomet and Evdin as the middlemen. Diveroli told Trebicka that Ylli Pinari of MEICO had warned him to keep his mouth shut because the prime minister's son had been in the meeting.

Trebicka was outraged—something had to be done. He readily agreed to try to help Diveroli escape the clutches of men he considered gangsters. Trebicka arranged a meeting with an official in the Albanian Ministry of Defense who could supposedly help. But it turned out that the official was far too young and junior to do anything. Trebicka obviously wasn't as connected as he believed.

As they were driven through the busy streets of Tirana, Diveroli started to look even more nervous, it seemed to Podrizki. Diveroli was obviously out of his element. He hadn't been physically threatened, despite the tale he'd told Kosta Trebicka, but the risks of being in Albania were self-evident. If the wrong person was crossed, it would be easy to have someone killed and have it made to look like an accident. Sitting in the backseat of the car, Diveroli announced he wanted to leave Albania the next day. He dispatched Podrizki to the local travel agent to change his flight.

Trebicka had planned for Diveroli to meet with US Embassy officials, so they went for a sit-down in the lobby of the Sheraton. The diplomat Robert Newsome was in his late forties or early fifties and gave off the aura of being involved in the intelligence world. Newsome

was with military attaché Victor Myev, a former soldier turned diplomat nearing retirement age—the man Podrizki had talked to on the
phone weeks earlier.

Diveroli laid out the scam—or the slightly fictionalized version he
was willing to share with the government officials. Diveroli said the
Albanians were using a Cypriot company run by a Swiss arms dealer to
charge AEY nearly double the real price for 100 million rounds of AK-
47. Diveroli said his company was caught up in Albanian corruption.
He described the meeting the day before, with the prime minister's son
and Mihail Delijorgji, who were controlling the contract to sell the
ammo. Diveroli said that he'd been told that if he didn't pay bribes he
wouldn't be able to get delivery of the ammo, which would imperil
America's ability to arm the Afghans.

The story wasn't entirely true. He shaded certain inconvenient
facts, like the possibility that selling Albanian-Chinese ammo was
against the law. Or the reality that AEY had yet to pay MEICO for any
of the rounds, which would explain the delays in delivery. Or that
he'd cut Kosta Trebicka out of the deal. In essence, Diveroli didn't
want to disclose that he was actually trying to get a better price from
the Albanians, instead casting himself as the innocent victim of corruption.

Victor Myev and Robert Newsome listened with great interest. If
what Diveroli described was true, the United States faced a potential
diplomatic crisis involving the Albanian prime minister. Albania was
on the cusp of membership in NATO. What Diveroli was alleging
meant that corruption traveled to the highest reaches of the government. The American diplomats promised to make inquiries and do
what they could to assist Diveroli with the delivery of the ammo.

After the meeting, Myev wrote an e-mail to Andrew Winternitz in
the Policy section of Defense Secretary Gates's office in Washington,
DC. "Ammo for Afghanistan" was the subject line. "I want to report a
meeting we just had to see if you have any insight you might share with
us," Myev began. He explained the dubious structure of AEY's Alba-

nian deal and described how Diveroli had approached the embassy for support.

"Although we would normally not get involved in a contract negotiation like this, the element of supporting our efforts in Afghanistan, coupled with Albania's increasing support of NATO efforts there, makes us wonder if we might not want to at least show our presence.

"Any thoughts?"

"Sounds like the prologue for a good spy novel," Winternitz replied within hours. "CONFIDENTIAL" was written in large letters at the top of the e-mail, a document that would later be placed under seal by a federal judge. As a senior official, Winternitz wondered at the cloak-and-dagger nature of the situation. He made it clear he understood crucial geopolitical issues were at stake.

"As for insight, if Albania could provide the ammunition, it would be one more good data point that Albania is becoming a provider of international security rather than a consumer," Winternitz wrote.

The message was clear: the contract was a win-win-win, for America, Albania, and Afghanistan.

Robert Newsome likewise reached out to two senior officials in the State Department. The level of importance given to the e-mail on the government's closed-circuit system was "High."

"We have a Florida company here called AEY that has a Department of Defense contract to provide Soviet and Chinese arms to the Afghan government," Newsome wrote. "The validity of the contract has been verified. AEY contacted us because they are having problems ('informality' issues) with MEICO."

"Informality" was a reference to corruption allegations. Newsome said the embassy wouldn't intervene on AEY's behalf unless a request came from higher authorities in State or Defense.

"We're bringing this to your attention as AEY has a legitimate contract to provide arms to the Afghan government and the implications this might have for Coalition efforts in Afghanistan."

Newsome concluded, "Please respond on the classified side as you deem appropriate."

No further replies or guidance came from Washington—or if they did, the documents remain classified.

/////

On the far side of the Atlantic Ocean, in AEY's modest headquarters in Miami Beach, David Packouz had finally obtained all the permissions necessary to ship 5 million rounds of AK-47 ammo from Hungary to Afghanistan. On the evening of May 24, 2007, while his friends were gambling and drinking in a casino in Albania, Packouz received an e-mail from AEY's freight forwarder confirming that a cargo plane carrying eighty pallets of AK-47 ammunition had taken off and was banking east over the Black Sea toward Kyrgyzstan.

Relieved, Packouz drove home to his condo in the Flamingo, smoked a bowl of weed with his new electronic Volcano, and headed to a place called Sushi Samba for dinner. In the middle of the meal, AEY's freight forwarder called from New York to tell Packouz that the Hungarian AK-47 ammo had been seized in Kyrgyzstan. The rounds were being held hostage, the freight forwarder explained in a panicked voice, and the Kyrgyz KGB was demanding payment of $300,000 for every day the goods remained at the airport in Bishkek. Stoned, baffled, once again in over his head like his buddies in Albania, Packouz stepped outside to get away from the restaurant's pounding music.

"Tell the Kyrgyz KGB that ammo needs to get to Afghanistan right now," he shouted at the freight forwarder. "This contract is part of a vital mission in the global war on terrorism. Tell them that if they fuck with us they're fucking with the government of the United States!"

/////

Packouz reached Diveroli in the middle of the night, Albanian time. The prostitute supplied by Kosta Trebicka was slumbering next to him in bed. As Packouz told him what had happened, Diveroli told Packouz to contact the embassy in Bishkek to enlist the support of the military attaché.

"Now, if you'll excuse me, I'm going to get back to fucking this hooker," Diveroli concluded with fake aplomb.

In the morning, Diveroli circulated an e-mail to the company's minuscule team: "URGENT/STRATEGIES REGARDING THE KYRGYZSTAN SITUATION, Please work on this immediately!!!!!!" Diveroli outlined the questions that needed to be answered. "WE MUST SEND AN OFFICIAL SIGNED REQUEST ON LETTERHEAD TO THE AMERICAN EMBASSY AND THE AMBASSADOR REQUESTING THEIR IMMEDIATE INTERVENTION!!!!!!!!"

Arriving at Diveroli's hotel, Podrizki shook his head as he watched the now frantic arms dealer yell and scream instructions back to Miami. Diveroli wanted AEY to write an e-mail to the Kyrgyz military that was forged to look as if it came from the US military—the dudes could threaten all kinds of dire consequences that way. Podrizki was sure that Diveroli's juvenile shenanigans, and his reflexive way of trying to lie his way out of trouble, wouldn't work. The Kyrgyz weren't going to be fooled by a kid in panic mode. The same was true of the Albanians they were dealing with. Arms dealing wasn't a game, as Diveroli apparently believed it was. Again, Podrizki told Diveroli that the problem was political and that he ought to invest some of the money he'd made acquiring "friends" who could help. Podrizki explained that AEY needed a senator or a congressman to make calls on their behalf. Diveroli needed to "share the spoils" from his gunrunning business, through political contributions, if he was going to get what he wanted. It was how the system worked. Diveroli looked at Podrizki like he was an idiot and went back to ranting at Packouz to get the American embassy to intervene.

At noon, Diveroli headed for Tirana's airport. Podrizki accompanied him. When they reached customs, Diveroli embraced Podrizki, a strong hug that seemed meant to convey both respect for his bravery and concern for his safety.

"I'll send you a ballistics vest and a pistol when I get back to Miami," Diveroli promised.

The bulletproof vest never arrived. Nor did the handgun. Podrizki was on his own once again.

/////

In Miami Beach, the days that followed were a blur. Packouz contacted the military officer in the US Embassy in Bishkek—a Colonel Plumb. Packouz put on his best military voice as he explained that the plane had been seized because AEY supposedly didn't have the correct paperwork.

"It's a very serious problem," Packouz told Colonel Plumb. "We have a 747 loaded with five million rounds of 7.62x39 ammo bound for the Afghan army. The Kyrgyz are telling us they're going to charge us three hundred thousand dollars per day for every day the aircraft stays on the runway—at the same time as they're not allowing the plane to leave. It's extortion. It's going to destroy our business. But more importantly, it's stopping munitions from getting to our allies and hurting a crucial mission in the global war on terrorism."

"Three hundred thousand dollars a day." Colonel Plumb whistled. "Holy cow. We've never had a problem with the Kyrgyz before. We're constantly shipping stuff to Afghanistan through here. There are never any fees. We pay them enough damn rent to use the air base as it is. Let me make some calls and get back to you."

"You're a lifesaver, sir. Thank you!"

Soon after, Colonel Plumb reported to Packouz that the Russians had been involved in the "precoordination" of the flight—meaning they'd arranged to disrupt the American shipment. "We don't have clear visibility into what they are currently doing, and what they are planning on doing," Plumb wrote to the dozen or more Army officers now assisting in getting AEY's ammo released. "We are trying to determine exactly what the Kyrgyz concerns are."

Packouz was learning that intentions were rarely declared in the opaque world of gunrunning. Duplicity, double-dealing, hidden motives, were the everyday reality. The American embargo on Russian arms had denied Putin's proxies a lucrative payday on the Afghan deal. The Russians had considered the ban tantamount to a declaration of war. Now that the American contractor was trying to fulfill the deal, Putin was having his revenge—and doing it in an exquisitely deniable way.

AEY's woes weren't the only concern for the US government in Kyrgyzstan. The airport in Bishkek was a strategic staging point for the war in Afghanistan. Stopping to refuel before traveling on to Afghanistan was a necessity for many cargo planes; the airport also provided a safe haven to manage cargo away from the perils of Kabul's besieged tarmac. It was imperative the dispute be resolved promptly. Defense Secretary Robert Gates traveled to Bishkek to get AEY's ammo released, and the Americans quickly agreed to double the rent they were paying to use the airport.*

Both Packouz and Diveroli were used to telling Army officials they dealt with that they were working on a "contract vital to the global war on terror." Packouz had regarded this rhetorical trick as slightly comic in its feigned hyperpatriotism. But now Packouz could see it was true. AEY's munitions would be released and delivered to Kabul weeks later, though he could only guess at what had happened behind closed doors. He was still a kid, but Packouz could feel himself at the center of world events in a way he'd never imagined—and that he was ill prepared for.

The vast divide between the complexities of the task AEY was undertaking and the naïveté of AEY's staff was beginning to dawn on the Army's procurement officers in Rock Island. In the middle of the Kyrgyz crisis, a memorandum was drafted by the civilian in charge of AEY's contract to put the company on notice that the seizure had

---

* Gates described his dealings with the "amazingly corrupt" Kyrgyzstan government as one of the most despicable experiences of his career—but still the American government did business with Kurmanbek Bakiyev, because it had no choice: *Duty: Memoirs of a Secretary at War* (Knopf, 2014), 194–95.

caused a stir in the Pentagon—all the way up to the secretary of defense. "Because of this incident, we have received concerns that this type of incident may happen again in another country and the confidence level in your company's ability to deliver without incident is very low," the civilian contracting officer wrote. "You need to be sensitive to the volatile political relations in the region and the relations between the United States and foreign countries."

But the memorandum was never sent, as the civilian's superiors deemed it inappropriate to scold a contractor in such a manner—even one as transparently unqualified as AEY.

"I never did find out what really happened, or why the plane was seized in the first place," Packouz recalled. "It was how things were done in international arms dealing. The defense industry and politics were extremely entwined—you couldn't do business with one without dealing with the other. Your fate depended entirely on political machinations. You didn't even know whose side you're on—who you were helping and who you were hurting. There were these shadowy forces out there, and it was obvious there were a lot of perils we didn't understand."

Chapter Eight

GJAKMARRJA

President George W. Bush arrived in Albania on June 10, 2007. It was the only foreign trip the president dared to take to mark the end of his second term. Fear of mass protests and social unrest had kept Bush from going to even the friendliest nations. Not Albania. It was a quasi national holiday as Bush swept down Rruga Demokracia in Tirana, cheered on by tens of thousands of jubilant Albanians, many dressed in Uncle Sam costumes and waving the Stars and Stripes. Giddy at the genuine affection of his admirers, Bush leaped from his limousine and posed for snapshots—to the dismay of the Secret Service. But no place on earth was safer for an American president than in the ecstatic embrace of the Albanian people as the nation neared the historic milestone of joining NATO.*

Alex Podrizki watched the parade in wonder. He'd never witnessed such fevered pro-American sentiment—not even in the United States on Super Bowl Sunday. Through the crowd he caught a glimpse of Bush's waving hand. Standing in a sea of Albanians, Podrizki felt that he had truly embarked on a great adventure—one of many to come, he hoped.

In early June, Podrizki was enjoying a rare break from the frantic pace of acting as AEY's agent in Albania. The repacking effort had been

---

* Video footage can be seen at http://www.youtube.com/watch?v=PKDdF6vfjoo.

stopped days before Bush's arrival. The Secret Service and representatives of the US military had come to the airport and demanded that the ammo be moved to a hangar farther from the area where the president would be arriving. The Albanian military had complied, shifting the AK-47 ammo to a hardened shelter to the west of the airfield, where it was determined the rounds no longer represented a risk to the president.

That American officials had open access to the repacking operation provided Podrizki with yet more comfort that nothing was seriously amiss with shipping "Chinese" rounds to Afghanistan. The military section of the airport had been teeming with federal agents before Bush's visit. No one had said a word about the giant stack of old crates with Chinese markings on the tarmac or AEY's repacking operation.

After returning to Miami, Diveroli had come to an agreement with the Albanians. AEY would receive a discount of two-tenths of a penny on each round of ammo, reducing the price to 3.8 cents. In return, Diveroli had agreed to cut Trebicka out of the repacking job, which was now being done by a company called Alb-Demil,* an entity seemingly controlled by the prime minister's son and Mihail Delijorgji. The process was now moving much more quickly and efficiently. A short, stocky tough guy named Tony was in charge at the airport. As many as 7 million rounds were being unpacked, inspected, and repacked every week, enough for three or four planeloads to fly to Kabul.

During the day, Podrizki came by to observe the work and make sure that quality controls were being enforced—and they were. Any substandard rounds were put aside. The vast majority of the ammo was old but in pristine condition and easily met the contractual standard of *serviceable without qualification*. The best proof was the Army signatures on the growing number of deliveries accepted in Kabul without

---

* The name combined *Alb* for "Albania" with *demil* for "demilitarization."

complaint, apart from a small dispute about the thickness of the card-board boxes the ammo was placed in—a typical contractor-government issue in the world of FedBizOpps.

In Albania, Podrizki still had to deal with "informality" issues from time to time. To receive permission for AEY's planes to land, for example, Podrizki had to pay a bribe of 2,000 euros to civil aviation authorities. One night three officers in the Albanian army's transportation brigade that was trucking the ammo to the airport invited Podrizki out for a drink. They'd grown friendly, Podrizki thought. As they sat down, the Albanians said they couldn't truck any more ammo to the airport unless he was paid a tribute for their efforts. By now Podrizki was an old hand in the Balkans, in a way.

"We're not paying you anything," Podrizki said. "If you have a problem, take it up with the Albanians doing the repacking."

Sometimes Podrizki thought about the "Chinese" ammunition question, but less and less often. The transaction was so obviously beneficial to all concerned.

"Bending the law is sometimes necessary, especially in a time of war," Podrizki recalled thinking. "There was the law, and then there was what the law was intended to accomplish. Ammo was needed in Afghanistan. Through no fault of our own, it turned out that most of the ammo was 'Chinese.' But the contract wasn't benefiting anyone in China. It was benefiting the United States and Albania and the Afghans. There was a lot of pressure to deliver, because it was peak of the fighting season. We were getting the job done."

In Afghanistan the summer of 2007 was the most violent in years. An assassination attempt against President Karzai was averted. Thirty-five civilians were killed when a bus exploded in Kabul, an event followed by the death of nearly a hundred innocent people in an American bombardment in the village of Hyderabad, in the south of the country. Based in sanctuaries in Pakistan, the Taliban and Al Qaeda turned frontier provinces like Kunar into killing fields.

But at least the Afghanistan security forces finally had ample supplies of ammunition for their AK-47s. After months of excruciating pressure, the Afghanistan contract was running like clockwork. Three dudes from Miami Beach were supplying millions of dollars' worth of ammunition to the Afghanistan army and police. Security forces going into battle during Operation Lastay Kulang, the struggle for Chora and the strike to kill Mullah Dadullah, were carrying AK-47 rounds from AEY. The security of a nation teetering on the brink of chaos was, in some good measure, in their hands.

For David Packouz, the summer of 2007 was a time of deliverance. After months of round-the-clock work, he could now handle the logistics of the Afghanistan deal with a few phone calls and e-mails every day. He began to relax, breathe easy, arriving at work late in the morning and leaving in midafternoon. Still surviving on his life savings while awaiting payment from Diveroli, Packouz had stopped doing massages. He didn't have to worry about money in the same way as he had: on paper, he was rich. Packouz used his spare time to visit his daughter and compose music for the album he was going to call *Microcosm*. The songs came to him in a creative flurry—"Waiting for the Call," "Flickering Light," "Carpe Diem." For one of the numbers, "Change," the inspiration came in a dream, the sentiments perhaps unlikely for a gunrunner:

> We can change our future
> We can remake our world into something better
> No matter how difficult the way
> Never lose hope for a better day. . . .

Efraim Diveroli, meanwhile, didn't let up on his insane work schedule. As always, wake and bake was followed by eighteen-hour days scanning for opportunities on FedBizOpps. Rather than focus on the Afghan deal, Diveroli continued to expand AEY's horizons. He now had more than half a dozen people working FedBizOpps, searching for deals. He continued to win small contracts in Iraq, for helmets and ammo and military uniforms. No deal was too big or too small for Diveroli, with scores of contracts in various stages of performance—a high-wire act he was struggling to maintain.

The result was a constant state of siege in the offices of AEY. Like a contract to supply $5 million worth of small-caliber ammunition to Iraq. Packouz had advised his friend against bidding on that deal, as the ongoing distraction would jeopardize their performance on the Afghanistan deal. Diveroli didn't listen. Nothing was enough for Diveroli, Packouz was realizing, to his increasing dismay. Packouz was more than content with the $8 million or so he stood to make from the Afghan deal. Diveroli's ambition was bottomless.

So was Diveroli's greed—or so it seemed to Packouz. One day Diveroli announced that he wanted to renegotiate their agreement on the Afghan deal. They had initially agreed that Packouz would get 25 percent of the profits from the parts of the deal he sourced. Now Diveroli said he'd provided all the finance for the deal, along with the majority of the contacts. Why should Packouz benefit as if he were an owner when he'd never risked any of his own money? Diveroli asked. Another structure needed to be found, Diveroli said, one that recognized the reality of the situation—or how he saw it.

"I know what it's like to get fucked out of a lot of money, therefore I would never knowingly do that to somebody," Diveroli e-mailed to his friend. "However there is a huge difference between being dishonest and merely being greedy in the sense that I work hard and will collect ALL monies which I am rightfully entitled under the normal code of business practices."

"I have been working for zero salary for nearly two years," Packouz replied. "I now have a child to support. Is an extra 2% or 4% of net profit, or whatever it is you're trying to squeeze me for, really worth souring our relationship? Am I worth that little to you?"

"I will not be guilt-tripped if you end up making less than you had in mind," Diveroli replied. "I strongly believe the biggest issue here is that you got a little too big for your britches."

Packouz recalled that Diveroli started looking at him differently. Packouz could tell Diveroli was working things over in his head. Now that real money was in AEY's bank account—millions and millions— Diveroli was about to be forced to pay Packouz a big chunk of change. Before Diveroli departed for Ukraine, to try to bargain for cheaper airfreight prices, he stopped by Packouz's desk. Packouz recognized the look on Diveroli's face—the one he had whenever he renegotiated a contract.

"Listen, buddy, you and me, we got to talk," Diveroli said. "I've been hearing a lot of complaints around the office lately. People are asking why you're getting paid so much money."

"Who's saying that?" Packouz asked, certain that Diveroli wasn't telling the truth—why would the others at AEY care what Packouz was making?

"Doesn't matter. I can't have my staff demoralized. I expect you to pull your weight."

"I'm running the Afghanistan deal basically on my own. It's going great. I don't need to work twenty hours a day to get it done."

"You see the team working on the Iraq contracts and you don't jump in and help."

"I only get paid on the deals I work," Packouz said. "If you want to bid on more contracts, that's your business. But it doesn't involve me."

"If AEY goes down, everyone goes down."

"I told you not to bid on the Iraq contracts. You should focus on the three-hundred-million-dollar deal, not some five-million-dollar contract. It's a waste of time, so I'm not really interested."

"It might interest you to know that the employees think I should pay you a hundred grand and cut you loose."

"So you want to fuck me over?"

"I didn't say that's what I want to do. I'm sure we can find a reasonable compromise."

Packouz knew he was trapped. He hadn't been paid yet—that would come when the contract was completed. Diveroli now said he didn't want to "give" Packouz all of the money he was claiming. It was as if Diveroli didn't think Packouz had earned the money—and that it was up to his discretion to decide how much to pay him. It seemed to Packouz that Diveroli was doing what he'd said his uncle had done to him years before, by refusing to pay him his share. But how could Packouz stop him? How could Packouz have been so foolish not to see that Diveroli would turn on him someday?

"You're just looking for any excuse to squeeze down my share," Packouz said.

Diveroli shrugged. When he returned from the Ukraine in July, tensions escalated. Packouz stopped coming to the office, preferring to work from his pad in the Flamingo. Diveroli called and insisted that Packouz wasn't entitled to the millions they'd agreed on. Diveroli said he'd "give" Packouz $280,000, a sum he considered to be more than generous for less than a year's work on the Afghanistan deal.

Packouz exploded. "If you fuck me, I will destroy you," he screamed into the phone. He hung up.

Worried, Diveroli called Alex Podrizki in Albania to mediate. Diveroli wanted to know what Packouz meant by saying he was going to "destroy" him. Podrizki called his friend, and Packouz explained that he was going to tell suppliers in the Balkans what Diveroli was really being paid by the Army, so they'd see his profit margin.

"They'd know what a liar he was," Packouz recalled. "I would tell them about the forged documents. Second, I was going to tell the Internal Revenue Service about his accounting bullshit. I didn't know exactly what his problem with the IRS was, but I knew he was terrified of them. Lastly, I was going to tell the Army about the Chinese ammunition from Albania."

Podrizki was stunned. Not by Packouz's threats: this was Podrizki's first indication that repacking the Chinese ammo presented a potentially serious legal problem. Podrizki had understood from the beginning that Chinese rounds weren't permitted, at least technically, but Diveroli had assured him that it was purely a contractual and civil-law matter. After Podrizki's conversations with Robert Newsome of the US Embassy in Tirana, Podrizki had assumed that AEY had the tacit approval of the government. He'd explicitly talked about the Chinese ammo with Newsome, and he'd urged Podrizki to continue the good work. But things were not as they seemed, he was realizing.

The same day, Podrizki relayed Packouz's threats to Diveroli, sending the dispute to yet another level.

"You tell him that if he does those things I can't guarantee his safety. Tell him I will fucking kill him."

Podrizki reported back that Diveroli had made his own threats. Packouz decided to end the discussion.

"You have threatened me, and that is something I can never forgive," Packouz wrote by e-mail. "Our business and personal relationship is over."

"As a businessman I have learned to never be threatened as you have repeatedly done in the last few days," Diveroli replied, denying he'd threatened Packouz. "As your best friend, who's really hurt by this situation, I would like to sit down and work this out without getting any nastier with each other."

"Unfortunately, threats are the only thing that keep you from fucking me," Packouz replied. "If you fuck me, I have nothing to lose and you have everything to lose. The consequences will be MUCH MORE DIRE for you. I promise you that. The more you push me, the angrier I get. So do yourself a favor and end it now. Otherwise, prepare for war."

The pair needed an intervention. In July of 2007, Packouz and Diveroli agreed to sit down with each of their lawyers. Before the meeting they had a quick exchange in the hallway.

"Listen, dude, you fuck me, I'm going to fuck you," Packouz said.

"Whatever," said Diveroli.

"You don't want the IRS to come and look around."

"Calm down. Don't throw around three-letter words like *IRS*. We can find a settlement."

"We both know you're shipping Chinese."

A deal was struck. The settlement would be as Diveroli proposed, $280,000 in cash. Packouz believed the lack of a written agreement made it impossible to prove their real deal. Something was better than nothing, Packouz reasoned. Payment was to be spread over two years, to ensure that Packouz didn't sabotage the Afghanistan contract as he'd threatened.

The last point of contention was Diveroli's demand that Packouz sign a noncompete agreement. Packouz refused. Under no circumstances would he execute a document that forbade him from going into the arms business. In fact, his intention was to use the money he was getting from Diveroli to start bidding on federal contracts on his own, using the tricks he'd learned at AEY.

For the rest of the summer, Packouz worked on setting up his business, named Dynacore Industries—he thought it sounded sexy. He applied for the relevant licenses—DUNS number, CAGE code, ATF Class 8 import permit. He put up a website for his new company, grandly outlining all the work Dynacore's "staff" had done on Army contracts in Iraq and Afghanistan.

"Sometimes you have to fake it until you make it," Packouz recalled.

Then he got lucky. When he'd traveled to Abu Dhabi a few months earlier, he'd met a Nigerian colonel who'd been lingering around the small-arms exhibit in the booth of a Russian arms company, but he'd been ignored. Packouz had taken the opportunity to introduce himself and tell the colonel that he would be happy to source any nonstandard munitions he wanted. The gambit had paid off. Soon after Packouz fell out with Diveroli, the Nigerian e-mailed to say he was looking for a large supply of AK-47s and ammunition for the country's navy. Packouz approached Yugoimport, the Serbian company that both Diveroli and Thomet used, and they happily agreed to sell the guns. With a few e-mails and phone calls, Packouz had his first deal lined up—$1.5 million worth of Kalashnikovs and ammo, with a profit of $200,000 coming his way.

With the Nigerian deal pending, Packouz decided to take a few weeks off. He lazed by the pool at the Flamingo, even if it meant risking running into Diveroli. He took his infant daughter to the zoo and for strolls along South Beach. As weeks passed, Packouz was developing a new sense of himself. He was a serious gunrunner now, wearing his wraparound sunglasses, carrying his silver briefcase, slipping through the streets of Miami Beach in his Audi. Then Packouz went a step further. He reasoned that Diveroli might calculate that it was cheaper to hire someone to kill him than to pay the money he owed. To protect himself, Packouz bought a .357 Taurus revolver, the first gun he'd ever owned.

All the while, Diveroli continued accumulating enemies. One of his favorite sayings was "You can screw just about anybody once." His cavalier attitude illustrated his immaturity: he miscalculated the risks he took by enraging the people he discarded. Like Kosta Trebicka. After the Albanian businessman had been cut out of the repacking deal months earlier, he'd complained constantly to Diveroli, calling and e-mailing to try to be put back on the deal, or at least to be paid for the thousands of dollars' worth of useless cardboard boxes he'd been left stuck with.

Refusing to go away quietly, Trebicka had initially tried to cause trouble for the Albanians who'd taken over the repacking job. He'd told the workers he'd hired that they were being fired because of corruption inside the Ministry of Defense. Trebicka's incitement had led to protests and a few burned tires in the village where most of the workers came from. But it was impossible to sustain their anger; Trebicka had been wronged, not the workers.

After losing the contract, Trebicka continued to stalk Podrizki in Tirana, claiming that they were "friends," muttering about exacting revenge against Ylli Pinari, trying to find a way to get back in on the deal.

Podrizki finally lost his patience and told him, "You fucked up. You overstepped your boundaries. You got what you deserved."

"I'm going to kill Pinari," Trebicka said.

The threat was empty, perhaps. But when Podrizki next saw Ylli Pinari, he felt obligated to warn him: "I don't want to get in the middle of this, but Trebicka's been talking about killing you."

"Everybody says this in Albania," Pinari replied dismissively. "Trebicka is a nothing person."

But as the weeks passed and AEY's shipments from Albania continued apace, Trebicka's anger was hardening into something more dangerous. *Gjakmarrja* was the Albanian word for "blood feud." In the *Kanun*, the ancient text that codifies Albania's traditional laws, men have a moral and social obligation to avenge the loss of honor. But Trebicka wasn't a violent man—not really. He was a lawyer and a businessman. His payback would be calculated. If everyone else was going to play dirty, so would he.

One June afternoon, Trebicka called Diveroli in Miami Beach. Trebicka was secretly recording the call on his Nokia cell phone. His aim was to lure Diveroli into talking about corrupt Albanian officials—then leak the proof of their dishonesty to the press. Diveroli had no idea he was being set up.

"So what's happening with your pal Pinari?" Trebicka began.

"I don't know," Diveroli said. "You tell me. Did you make a deal with him for the boxes?"

"I don't want to make a deal with him. You know that he's a crook. You told me before that he's a Mafia guy, didn't you?"

"I think he is. Either he's Mafia or the Mafia is controlling him. Either way, he's a problem. The problem is, I don't have a choice. I have to deal with him. The US government is expecting the products. I have no decision to make."

Diveroli assured Trebicka that he would push hard to broker a deal. "I did not remove you from this job. I had nothing to do with this. Nothing. I have never supported this decision. I'm very, very upset about this. I'm very concerned."

Diveroli wasn't telling the truth: Diveroli had done nothing to protect Trebicka, preferring to take a price discount of two-tenths of a penny per round—a fact that would further anger the Albanian if he ever found out.

"Are you still working with Henri Thomet?" Trebicka asked.

"I have to work with Thomet. I'm different from Thomet. I can't play monkey business with the Mafia—Delijorgji and all those fucking Mafia guys in Albania. I'm a US company. Everyone is watching me. Pinari needs a guy like Thomet in the middle to take care of him and his buddies. It's none of my business. I don't want to know about it. I want to know about legitimate businesses."

"I understand."

"How is everything with you?" Diveroli asked.

"It's okay. I'm quiet. I have other businesses to take care of. We had a good reception for your president."

"I heard it was a good meeting."

"Probably I will be invited to Washington, DC, from the CIA guys. In one or two weeks, I will come to Florida to shake hands and discuss future deals."

This was an implicit threat. Trebicka wanted Diveroli to know that he wasn't going to quietly go away. He wanted Diveroli to know that he was going to talk to the US government—and could talk about the re-packing job in Albania.

Diveroli urged Trebicka to try to find an accommodation. "Why don't you kiss Pinari's ass one more time? Call him up, beg him, kiss him, send one of your girls to fuck him. Let's get him happy. Maybe he gives you a chance to do the job. Maybe you give him a little money. He's not going to get much from this deal. If he gets twenty thousand dollars from you, I'm okay with that."

"I understand," Trebicka said, luring Diveroli further into his plot.

"The more it went up higher, to the prime minister, to his son—this Mafia is too strong for me," Diveroli said. "I can't fight this Mafia. It got too big. The animals got too out of control."

Trebicka had what he wanted. In the days that followed, he approached one of the leading Albanian dailies, a newspaper called *Shekulli*. He told the editor his story of AEY's contract, the profit margin MEICO was siphoning off, and Defense Minister Fatmir Mediu's apparent role in the scheme. Then he played the recording of Diveroli. The editor was extremely interested. Trebicka gave him Alex Podrizki's e-mail address. In a note to Podrizki, the editor from *Shekulli* wrote:

> We have reasons to believe that this is a big corruption scandal and this money of commission are taken by the corrupted politicians that are in head of Ministry of Defense and other officials in a government that is claiming itself to be, "Government who is doing big fight against organized crime." We need to know your version of this story because we will publish this information in our newspaper very soon. Please contact us as soon as possible, because this is becoming a very sensitive problem in Albania.

Podrizki ignored the e-mail. He knew that it was foolish, perhaps even fatal, to anger those behind the arms deal—including the politicians. Without Podrizki's cooperation, the Albanian story never ran.

Trebicka realized he had to up the ante. He knew an Albanian-American man in New York City, Gary Kokalari, who would be interested in anything that pointed to corruption in the government of Albania. Kokalari was the child of Albanian parents, though he'd grown up in New Jersey. An investment banker, he was successful, smart, and obsessed with Prime Minister Sali Berisha and the shady men who carried out his orders—though *obsession* didn't describe the depth of Kokalari's hatred for a man he considered "evil."

Talking to Kokalari in New York through a broken line from Albania, Trebicka poured out his story: ammunition, kickbacks to Albanian politicians, a Swiss arms dealer named Henri Thomet, a company from Miami called AEY repacking AK-47 ammo in Tirana.

Trying to make sense of what Trebicka was saying, Kokalari became convinced he had evidence of an American company bribing Albanians—and that the US Embassy in Tirana was ignoring the corruption. Kokalari was going to ensure the story went public. But if it did, Trebicka would be making many powerful enemies.

"Are you sure you want to proceed?" Kokalari asked. "Once we let the genie out of the bottle, you can't get it back in."

"Yes," Trebicka said. "I am sure."

Kokalari started to develop a plan. "I know how to harm powerful people," Kokalari recalled. "I have done it in the past, and I will do it in the future."

Kokalari's first call was to Congress, to the House Oversight Committee. Investigators there had subpoena power and could force AEY to disclose what it was doing. Kokalari then tried the *Wall Street Journal*, where there was some initial interest. But the story was complicated and it was about Albania, a tiny, obscure country. Kokalari turned to the State Department and the Pentagon to alert them to the corruption in Albania and how the American government was being defrauded by radically overpaying for the ammunition it was purchasing from AEY.

As Kokalari continued to research journalists he could pitch, one name kept popping up. C. J. Chivers of the *New York Times* was one of his generation's leading war reporters. An ex-Marine, Chivers routinely covered conflict, but he also wrote long investigative articles with an emphasis on military affairs. He sounded perfect.

"I have been somewhat of a gadfly to the current and former Albanian governments with my efforts to help curtail the crime and corruption that are at epidemic proportions in that country," Kokalari wrote to Chivers. Kokalari laid out Trebicka's narrative, as he understood it. The main point for Kokalari was to expose corruption in Albania, and US complicity in doing nothing to stop the theft. Was Chivers interested in the story?

The reply from the *Times* reporter was brief but prompt and exciting: "Why wouldn't I be interested?"

Kokalari didn't know it, but he'd tracked down one of the world's foremost experts on the AK-47. At the time, Chivers was at work on the definitive book on the Russian weapons designer Mikhail Kalashnikov. If anyone would understand the technical aspects of AEY's contract, it would be Chivers. He also had on-the-ground knowledge about recent ammunition shortages in Afghanistan. He'd been in Kabul in 2006 when the Combined Security Transition Command had decided to supply the Afghan National Army and Afghan National Police with a massive amount of ammo. A list of munitions had been drawn up, Chivers knew, with the hope of creating deep stores that would enable an eventual handoff to the Afghans.

Kokalari followed up with a long e-mail to Chivers. Kokalari didn't have the facts straight in some instances. He thought Albania was supplying all the ammo for the $300 million contract, whereas the AK rounds were only a small part of the overall dollar amount. Kokalari knew that the repacking was being done because of the Chinese markings. But he didn't know the real reason AEY was going to such trouble—because it was breaking the Chinese ban.

In his note to Chivers, Kokalari described how a Cyprus company named Evdin was paying the Albanians $22 per carton and then selling the same ammo to AEY for $40—without so much as touching the rounds. Trebicka had told Kokalari about Diveroli's trip to Albania and how he'd met with Mihail Delijorgji and the prime minister's son. Kokalari told Chivers that Diveroli had also met with US Embassy officials in Tirana to describe how he was being forced to pay kickbacks.

"I can tell you from my own experience in my dealings with our embassy in Albania," Kokalari wrote, "that because of Albania's cooperation with bigger picture issues like the war on terror, the U.S. government has been all too willing to look the other way when it comes to the corrupt practices of Albanian officials."

Chivers replied that he needed to get clearance from his editor and he'd need the promise of exclusivity. But he was definitely intrigued. Chivers wanted to know why the United States was using an intermediary, AEY, instead of buying the ammunition directly? He also wondered if the American government was overpaying for the ammunition.

To check the veracity of Kokalari's account, Chivers contacted the Army in Rock Island, Illinois, to see if AEY's contract was legitimate. It was. Chivers called Kosta Trebicka in Tirana. The Albanian confirmed Kokalari's allegations about the "Chinese" ammunition, adding details about AEY's repacking and corruption inside MEICO. Trebicka was eager to talk; he even volunteered to fly to New York. Chivers assured Trebicka that he was going to continue to report the story.

Chivers reached out to an arms researcher named Hugh Griffiths. Since Griffiths had started studying small-arms proliferation as a result of the wars in Iraq and Afghanistan, he'd tried to interest the *Times* in covering the way the US government was doing business with arms dealers like Thomet—which amounted to a scandal, in his view. Griffiths's research had revealed that private contractors like AEY were selling large amounts of substandard weapons with no serial numbers to the US military—and no one was seriously examining what the proliferation of small weapons meant for innocent civilians as thousands upon thousands of AK-47s fell into the hands of warlords and insurgents in Iraq and Afghanistan and elsewhere.

Griffiths wasn't surprised by the Albanian story as outlined by Chivers. Griffiths knew about Henri Thomet, the mysterious Swiss broker, and how he used the same methods the CIA had used in Iran-contra in the 1980s: cutout companies like Evdin and offshore banks in financial havens like Cyprus. Griffiths told Chivers that Thomet was also exporting arms to Niger and Chad and Mali—areas with extremist Islamist elements allied to Al Qaeda. In effect, the US government was using AEY as a proxy to deal with Thomet—even as Thomet was arming US enemies. This kind of governmental circumvention was exactly what American and international arms-dealing regimens were designed to avoid, Griffiths said. The Army was enriching and legitimizing gunrunners through a desperate attempt to stand up armies in Iraq and Afghanistan, even as this practice became a major contributor to the proliferation of small arms in war zones around the world.

"I told Chivers that AEY wasn't an anomaly," Griffiths recalled. "It was an example of what was going on. AEY's deal was how the gray market worked. Virtually every arms shipment coming out of Albania was illegal in one way or another. But the Albanians didn't give a flying fuck about the law. The lack of safety, the way things weren't done by the book—it was classic. Thomet was using the AEY kids as part of his strategy to do business with the United States. It was all about the money. The AEY kids were fucking idiots."

Chapter Nine

22 BUNKERS

The screaming fights were followed by makeup sex, quickly leading to another fight: I love you, I hate you, come here, go away. Efraim Diveroli's tempestuous relationship with his girlfriend Suzie was doomed. The police had been called once, when Diveroli threw Suzie's clothes into the hallway at the Flamingo and told her to get out. The police had found the girl crying in the hallway, but she denied she'd been assaulted and no charges were filed. Still, the police recorded the incident, adding it to Diveroli's increasingly checkered history, including the restraining order a prior girlfriend had taken out. The relationship was obviously out of control—like Diveroli's consumption of alcohol and cocaine, his lust for money, and his never-ending pursuit of contracts on FedBizOpps.

The affair had to end, and so it did. Newly single, Diveroli did what twentysomethings all over America did at the time when they wanted to meet someone new: he created a profile on Myspace.

"Well of course I'm a super nice guy!!!" Diveroli began. He described himself as easygoing, with a good sense of humor, though he allowed he'd had problems in high school so he'd worked from a young age. "I probably grew up way too fast. I finally got a decent apartment and I'm content for the moment, however I definitely have the desire to be very successful in my business and this does take up a lot of my time." He concluded, "Who I'd like to meet: a sweet pretty girl with a good attitude and love for life, a woman that will stand by her man because she knows he'd do the same for her, no matter the circumstance."

Romance aside, Diveroli was prospering, in his manner. The boiler-room model he'd created at AEY was cutthroat, as everyone was paid solely on commission. As usual, Diveroli micromanaged all aspects of the operation, screaming and yelling and flying into rages—only to step outside to smoke a joint and regain his composure. The main quality Diveroli looked for in his staff was greed. The desire for money was a motive he understood and believed he could control. But it meant that there was no loyalty.

As AEY's "team" tried to beat each other to deals, Diveroli ventured deeper into a dictatorial mode, unwilling to listen to others, overly certain of his own good judgment, and contemptuous of those who weren't willing to take the kinds of risks he encountered every day as a real-life gunrunner.

After months of dickering, Diveroli had finally reached an arrangement with Henri Thomet and MEICO, and the Afghanistan contract was running smoothly, even in Packouz's absence. In Bountiful, Utah, the Mormon businessman Ralph Merrill was following Diveroli's progress with admiration. AEY really was delivering on the $300 million contract. With the profits split fifty-fifty, Merrill stood to make millions. It all depended on Diveroli's final profit margins, which would be determined by an audit at the end of the contract.

"I thought Diveroli was performing well, all things considered," Merrill recalled. "He'd gained experience with the Iraq contracts, and he seemed to be in complete control. All of the problems I was aware of appeared to be external, and he was handling them as best as one could, given the circumstances. So I was pleased."

But Diveroli had other plans for Merrill. From the start, Diveroli had always wanted his "financier" to know as little as possible about his business. When he spoke with Merrill, in an uncharacteristically quiet and reasoned tone, Diveroli would be alone, in his office. But as the

Afghanistan contract proceeded, Diveroli's attitude began to change. Deference was replaced with desperation—or at least that was how Diveroli represented himself to Merrill. The money AEY had been paid by the government was supposed to be reinvested to finance further arms purchases until the Afghan deal was completed. But now Diveroli pretended he was barely breaking even and that AEY was in danger of losing the entire contract because he didn't have adequate funds to finance the various deals. In fact, the opposite was true: Diveroli's profits and the factoring agreement with Wells Fargo meant that he was no longer dependent on Merrill's money.

"Diveroli had been lying to Merrill about AEY's profits for years," David Packouz recalled. "Diveroli would often complain that Merrill was sitting on his ass in Utah while we were slaving away. He said he refused to be 'Ralph's workhorse,' and that everyone should be rewarded in proportion to the work they put in—not the deal they'd struck with him. That's how Diveroli justified his sleazy behavior to himself. So he decided he was going to squeeze Merrill's share down—just like he'd done with mine."

Diveroli concocted a phantom investor named Danny, a ploy he aimed to use to deceive Merrill and radically reduce his share of the profits. Danny was based on a real dude, Danny Doudnik, who was now Diveroli's main confidant at AEY. Like many of the people Diveroli worked with, Doudnik had gone to the Hebrew Academy in Miami Beach. The pair hadn't seen each other again for years, until they were both twenty years old and Diveroli was established as an arms dealer. At the time, Doudnik was working as a paralegal for a real estate company in Aventura, Florida, a dreary job with a modest salary and no real prospect of advancement or fulfillment. But Doudnik had a skill that was useful for Diveroli: born in the former Soviet Union, he was fluent in Russian. When the Kyrgyz intelligence agency had seized AEY's ammo, Diveroli had asked his old buddy to translate some of the documents. Diveroli had paid him $150 for the job. After that, Doudnik had occasionally done small translation jobs. Diveroli tried to recruit him to work full-time for AEY, saying he was always looking for "good people." Doudnik had steered clear of Diveroli for a simple reason—he thought he was a psychopath.

Finally, like David Packouz and Alex Podrizki before him, Doudnik had succumbed, however reluctantly, to Diveroli's inducements—including a salary of $100,000 a year. The experience had proved extremely trying, far more so than Doudnik had anticipated. The temper tantrums and disorganization and substance abuse were hard enough to deal with. So were the hours Diveroli demanded of his staff, with the office doing business in a variety of time zones and the company woefully understaffed. But nothing topped Diveroli's outrageous behavior on the trip he took with Doudnik to Ukraine. The aim was to negotiate lower prices with the air-cargo company shipping AEY's munitions to Afghanistan. Doudnik went along to translate. But he'd been horrified when Diveroli approached pretty women on the streets of Kiev as if all of them were prostitutes. Diveroli would simply walk up to a beautiful woman and ask, "How much?"—an inquiry Doudnik had refused to translate.

Ralph Merrill recalled that Diveroli told him that Doudnik was a phantom investor willing to put money into AEY—but only on very onerous terms.

"Danny says he can put three million dollars in, but he wants seventy percent of the profit in return," Diveroli said. "He drives a hard bargain. But he's the only source I've been able to find."

"That's disproportionate to what I have in the contract," Merrill said. "Tell him it's too much."

Diveroli promised to try. But he soon called Merrill back with melancholy news. His fictional investor wouldn't budge.

"I think we're going to have to take the deal," Diveroli said. "We definitely need more money. That will leave thirty percent for us to split. We'll just have to be content with that."

"You can't find any other institution that will lend against a government contract?"

"I don't know of any. We have no collateral."

Merrill sighed in resignation. It seemed plausible that AEY needed more money to cover the $300 million contract. Thus, in one fell swoop, Diveroli reduced Merrill's take from 50 to 15 percent. Diveroli gambled that he would be able to doctor the audit when the time came; what mattered was that he'd managed to make millions more for himself, taking his own share from 50 to 85 percent.

/////

By the end of the summer of 2007, Alex Podrizki only went to the airport in Tirana to check on the repacking operation every few days, primarily just to show his face and protect AEY's interests and ensure quality control protocols for the ammo were being followed. But the operation was continuing to attract other attention. American Army master sergeant Kristoff Winemiller was assigned to the Defense Attaché Office in Tirana. As part of his duties, he regularly visited the airport in Tirana, including the military side of the facility. In early August, Winemiller went to the military hangar with his Albanian assistant, Tef. Wandering the hangar with Tef, Winemiller watched the repacking operation and wondered what was going on. Dozens of workers were busily taking AK-47 ammo from wooden crates, emptying the boxes, taking the rounds out of their paper wrappers, and then putting them in plastic bags and new cardboard boxes. Piled in the hangar were ammunition tins with Chinese lettering and shrink-wrapped cardboard boxes on pallets. In this manner, more than 30 million rounds of ammo had gone from Tirana to Kabul to be issued to Afghan troops.

Tef told Winemiller that ammo was being repacked by an American company named AEY. The rounds were to be shipped to Afghanistan, and Tef pointed to two ancient Ilyushin 76 airfreight carriers parked on the tarmac, ready to be loaded. Winemiller asked Tef why AEY was buying Chinese ammo. Tef said that the Chinese rounds were older and thus less expensive. Winemiller nodded in understanding—he had no idea about the embargo against Chinese munitions.

Winemiller's ignorance of the law against acquiring Chinese matériel was matched by that of others in the US Embassy in Albania. Many officials, military and diplomatic, were aware of AEY's contract and that the company was repacking old, surplus Chinese ammo. To embassy officials, AEY's contract looked like a great deal for all concerned. None of these officials apparently knew about the China ban— or cared. The same was true in Kabul. Diveroli had predicted that no one in Afghanistan would notice that the ammo was "Chinese." All that mattered was that the ammo actually got there.

Diveroli's assessment of the Pentagon's procurement process was startlingly accurate. Haphazard barely began to capture the disorder and desperation of the procurement system AEY was dealing with. The administration of the contracts was technically the responsibility of civilians in Rock Island, Illinois, a long way from the battlefield. But the ammunition was coming from a country outside America—OCONUS, Outside of Continental United States, in military jargon—so the Army's munitions team had nothing to do with actually running the contract. In reality, Rock Island was only responsible for processing payments.

Actual oversight was supposed to occur in Kabul. But after awarding the contract the civilians in the Army Sustainment Command in Illinois realized that they had no one on the ground in Kabul to monitor the quality of the ammunition AEY supplied. The contract required acceptance at *destination*, but it had been proposed that the deal be amended to provide for acceptance at *origin*. The Army would thus inspect AEY's shipments in the various countries of origin before it was loaded onto planes to be flown to Afghanistan. If that system had been adopted, American soldiers in Albania would have checked out the rounds at the airport in Tirana.

But no one was comfortable with signing off on AEY's rounds without proof that the ammo had actually reached Afghanistan. So Rock

Island had sent an e-mail to the Defense Contract Management Agency to see if anyone in Kabul could serve as their eyes on the ground for AEY's deliveries. The DCMA said nothing in the contract required it to get involved—and that the contract called for only "minimal surveillance." This was a way to avoid bureaucratic responsibility. But the DCMA then assigned Major Ronald Walck to monitor AEY's deliveries, despite the fact that he had no training in dealing with arms shipments, let alone old, surplus, nonstandard ammunition.

Thus, when AEY's ammo arrived in Kabul, Major Walck performed a "kind, count, and condition inspection," but the process on the tarmac was perfunctory because of the dangers of incoming enemy fire; counting the number of pallets, not the rounds, was all Walck could manage. Walck received Certificates of Conformance from AEY stating exactly what was in every delivery. The COC form had lines for quantity, number of pallets, and place and year of manufacture. The line for the provenance of the ammunition was headed "Manufacturer (point of origin)." In this space Diveroli wrote on dozens of COCs, "Ministry of Defense of Albania, MEICO—Military Export and Import Company." This was literally true, depending on how the word *origin* was interpreted, as Tirana was literally the place of "origin." But it meant eliding the fact that the manufacturer of the ammo was Chinese.

In Kabul, AEY's ammo was then trucked to a facility called 22 Bunkers. If soldiers there had inspected the headstamps of the ammo, they would have seen that the rounds were "Chinese." The Pentagon had a nonclassified publication called the "Small Caliber Ammunition Guide," which contained references to the meanings of the numbers on the headstamps of various rounds from around the world. The headstamps indicated the factories in the People's Republic of China where the rounds had been manufactured—specifically, plants numbered 31, 61, 71, and 661. But the Army officers at 22 Bunkers didn't look, as Diveroli had predicted. All they cared about was that the ammo worked—and it did.

The lax oversight wasn't limited to AEY's contract. In both Iraq and Afghanistan, billions upon billions of dollars were lost as a result of waste, fraud, and abuse. The ad hoc nature of the Army's efforts led to the kinds of logistical fiascoes that resulted in lost wars. In Iraq, for example, in 2007 the Pentagon's property books failed to account for 190,000 weapons shipped to Baghdad—110,000 AK-47s and 80,000 handguns. The Army had no consistent system to track weapons received, meaning it was likely even more weapons had been lost or stolen or sold to insurgents. The situation in Kabul was just as bad, if not worse. The American officers who were supposed to be developing systems to secure and track weapons had failed to issue instructions for their proper maintenance and control. No records existed for 87,000 of the 242,000 weapons shipped to Afghanistan—fully a third of the guns delivered. In this context there was zero chance that headstamps would be inspected: it was a war zone.

These statistics weren't aberrations. According to later investigations, as much as 30 percent of the $50 billion spent on defense contracts in Afghanistan between 2005 and 2011 involved corruption.* Trucking contracts to carry supplies from Karachi, Pakistan, to Kabul, to cite one instance, involved criminal networks, widespread pilferage, and little or no oversight.** The Host Nation Trucking program, funded at $2.2 billion, included a contract for $360 million awarded to Hamed Wardak, the son of the Afghan minister of defense. Wardak was in his twenties and attracted to South Beach's nightlife, much like Efraim Diveroli. He was reportedly paying massive bribes to Afghan warlords and the Taliban to ensure that his trucks wouldn't be attacked. The practice was commonplace, as American officials knew—in part because the Afghan intelligence services had provided a "very detailed"

---

* Moshe Schwartz, "Wartime Contracting in Afghanistan: Analysis and Issues for Congress" (CRS, 2011).

** John T. Tierney, "Warlord, Inc.: Extortion and Corruption Along the U.S. Supply Chain in Afghanistan" (Congressional Subcommittee on National Security and Foreign Affairs, 2010).

report on the epidemic of corruption. As much as 20 percent of the money the United States was spending on transport was thus going directly to fund the Taliban—and nothing was being done about it.

"The American soldier in me is repulsed by it," the commander of the Third Brigade of the Tenth Mountain Division later told investigators. "But I knew it was what it was. It was essentially paying the enemy, saying, 'Hey, don't hassle me.' I didn't like it, but it was what it was."*

As events in AEY's contract continued to play out in the fall of 2007, the Army issued the Gansler Report, an in-depth study of the government's weapons-procurement procedures. It said the Army's contracting staff was "understaffed, overworked, undertrained, undersupported, and, most important, undervalued." The report said that the Defense Federal Acquisition Regulation Supplement—DFARS, which governed AEY's contract and included the Chinese embargo—was impossible to adapt to fast-changing circumstances in a high-pressure environment. Rigid, legalistic interpretations and the lack of command and control over the process had led to contracting dysfunction on an epic scale.

There was a law-enforcement agency assigned to stop the rampant fraud and theft and incompetence destroying the Pentagon's procurement systems. The Defense Criminal Investigative Service—or DCIS—had been created in the early 1980s expressly to "protect the integrity of Department of Defense programs and operations by conducting relevant, objective, and timely investigations."

In this endeavor, the DCIS was failing spectacularly. In Afghanistan, private contractors from America had written to the Department of Defense, complaining about widespread extortion by warlords and how billions in American money was going to the Taliban. These complaints were met with "indifference," a congressional inquiry would later find. The American military units overseeing the Host Nation Trucking program claimed to have "zero visibility" of how the subcon-

---

* Aram Roston, "How the US Funds the Taliban," *Nation*, November 11, 2009.

tractors worked. Asked why no investigations were initiated, a lieutenant colonel said the decision was out of his control: "That was way, way, way, way above my level."*

But the DCIS would pursue one case with relentless determination. No expense would be spared. All available resources of the DCIS would be applied to ensure that this singular investigation was brought to a successful conclusion. The targets of this costly multiyear investigation were none other than a few stoners from Miami Beach.

In the fall of 2007, Efraim Diveroli was oblivious of this—as of so much else. To Diveroli, things had never been better. AEY appeared to be on its way to becoming the empire he'd fantasized about. The company would be awarded an astounding $201,707,453 in government contracts in 2007. The sheer scale of the business Diveroli was now operating might have daunted him, but it didn't.

Nor did his unscrupulous business practices give him pause. As his successes increased, Diveroli was accumulating enemies, foreign and domestic—at times bitter, unscrupulous, vicious enemies. In Albania, Kosta Trebicka had sworn revenge and set in motion the investigation of C. J. Chivers of the *New York Times*. In Baghdad, rival contractors continued a whispering campaign against AEY and Diveroli. They told procurement officers that Diveroli was a Miami drug dealer, using money from running cocaine to buy and sell arms. The cumulative impact of the gunrunner's youth, bravado, and cutthroat prices meant he was despised by many inside the small world of arms dealing.

Another unknown foe was the grandly titled Blane International Group. The company was in fact a one-man operation, run by Milton Blane, an older man who'd gone into the arms business late in life. After the invasion of Iraq, Blane had vied for contracts on FedBizOpps, frequently losing to AEY. Like the others in the various bidding wars Diveroli won, Blane was mystified by the young gunrunner's way of

---

* Aram Roston, "Congressional Investigation Confirms: US Military Funds Afghan Warlords," *Nation*, June 21, 2010.

winning deals. Diveroli was somehow able to source weapons and ammo for unbelievably low prices. Like others in the industry, Blane figured Diveroli had to be doing something illegitimate, unethical, or illegal—or all three.

In 2005, Blane had secretly approached the Department of State saying he believed that AEY was operating illegally. Blane alleged that Diveroli was labeling Chinese-made AK-47 guns as Eastern European to sell to the Iraq government. Blane claimed that the guns were being shipped from China to Bulgaria, where they were relabeled and re-packaged to appear as if they'd been manufactured in Sofia. The weapons were then flown to Baghdad, where unsuspecting officers unloaded the guns and issued them to Iraqis. Many of the weapons were junk, Blane said, and had been rejected by the Army.

If true, Blane's allegations would be explosive. If what he said was correct, it might explain how AEY had continually been able to underbid its competitors. If Diveroli really had been shipping cheap and shoddy Chinese guns to Baghdad, via Bulgaria, of course his prices would be lower. Chinese weapons were notoriously inexpensive, just as they were known to be inferior in quality to Russian-made guns.

In February 2006, DCIS investigators had traveled to the headquarters of Blane International—a private residence in a suburb of Atlanta—and dutifully recorded the older man's tale of Diveroli's plot to covertly sell Chinese guns.

"Blane stated that he was aware that AEY personnel traveled to China," the confidential DCIS report said. "Blane further stated that another reason he thought that AEY was acquiring the rifles from China was the price that they won the bid with was below any of the common sources for the rifles.

"Blane told the agents of the AEY/China/Bulgaria/Iraq statement as a possible scenario of what AEY might be up to. However, Blane stated that he had no firsthand knowledge of where AEY was obtaining the AK-47 rifles. The scenario is pure speculation on his part."

The consequences of this encounter were far-reaching: Blane's tip—his speculation—appeared to provide the basis for a wide-ranging, two-year federal investigation of Diveroli and AEY. As a result of Blane's assertions, Diveroli was secretly placed on the State Department's watch list as an arms dealer suspected of illegal activity. When Diveroli traveled internationally, his luggage was seized and searched at airports—like on his trips to Albania and Ukraine. His laptop computer was also seized. In this way, Diveroli's rights as a citizen had apparently been breached based on rumors spread by a rival.

But why?

Any investigator assigned to the AEY case should have paused as they listened to Blane's accusations. Why was Blane telling the DCIS about Diveroli, after all? Was Blane trying to use law enforcement to harm a competitor?

To begin with, Blane's story didn't add up. The price of transporting weapons constituted a huge part of the cost of arms dealing, as AEY had learned the hard way in Albania. It would be prohibitively expensive for AEY to fly the guns from China to Bulgaria, repack the arms, and then fly them back to Baghdad. Wouldn't an experienced investigator understand the practical realities of arms dealing, and see that it cast doubt on Blane's version of events?

But AEY's competitors got lucky—very, very lucky. The epic failure of the DCIS to stop fraud in Iraq and Afghanistan had made the agency highly susceptible to the kind of case AEY appeared to be. Diveroli was only twenty-one years old, an absurd fact on its face: How on earth was such a young man able to win a $300 million arms contract? For the DCIS, Diveroli must have looked like easy prey. Going after the serious fraud in Baghdad and Kabul was politically risky and physically dangerous. Pursuing cases there required travel to war zones. It required defying well-connected companies like General Dynamics and Boeing. It risked upsetting lobbyists, retired military officers who'd gone to work for Fortune 500 companies, and the congressmen who depended on the political donations of defense companies. Meddlesome investigations also could anger the Army itself, as an unnecessary distraction that might slow or stop desperately needed procurement contracts. In a time of war, all sorts of compromises needed to be made. Edicts had come down from the highest levels of government—perhaps even the White House—that law enforcement was not to interfere with the war effort.

By contrast, Efraim Diveroli had no political connections. He had no allies in the business. He had no lawyers or lobbyists. AEY was just down the road from the DCIS office in Tampa Bay—a safe and convenient car ride. The Global War on Terrorism was raging, and the DCIS needed to do its part—and a twenty-one-year-old with a bad reputation in the arms business looked like a perfect target: heedless, brazen, and defenseless.

Diveroli's rivals got even luckier when the case was assigned to a special agent named Michael Mentavlos. A former Air Force major who'd become a law-enforcement agent as a second career, Mentavlos was in his midthirties, with a pasty complexion, dark hair, a humorless, by-the-book affect, and the glint in his eye of a true believer. Mentavlos had spent the six previous years at Immigration and Customs Enforcement. Along the way, he boasted how he'd mastered the *reverse undercover sting*. The term referred to a law-enforcement tactic of inventing a criminal conspiracy and then using undercover operatives to entice suggestible people into participating in the plot and thus breaking the law. The strategy was commonly used in terrorism cases, where confidential informants were planted inside mosques with conspiracies concocted by law-enforcement agencies. This was the technique Mentavlos hoped to use in procurement-fraud cases—to lure unsuspecting marks into breaking the law.

Mentavlos had recently started working at the DCIS, and he was looking to make a big case. To begin his investigation of Diveroli, Mentavlos contacted the Army's Sustainment Command Center in Rock Island, Illinois, and requested copies of all AEY's contracts, task orders, and end-user certificates—a request that was ignored for months. But by February 2007, as Diveroli and Packouz were swapping snorts of cocaine to celebrate their great good fortune in winning the Afghanistan contract, the investigation begun by Blane's speculations was slithering through the DCIS with serpentine efficiency. Sitting in an office in Fort Lauderdale, Mentavlos had drafted an affidavit to justify federal agents' raiding AEY's headquarters. The DCIS was planning to seize all of AEY's files and computers. The agency seemed to be looking for a crime—any crime. A *fishing expedition* was the legal term for such a venture.

On August 23, 2007, the DCIS was ready to make its move. First thing that morning, Mentavlos and other agents stormed AEY's offices brandishing a search warrant and instructing the company's employees to freeze and touch nothing, lest they tamper with evidence. A SWAT team was on standby—though law enforcement found only a small gathering of kids working the Internet.

August 23 was also the day David Packouz was to receive the first installment of his settlement payment from Diveroli. At ten in the morning, he got a call from Diveroli's personal assistant, who said frantically, "The government just raided the office."

"What? The government? Which agency? Why?"

"I'm not sure. They just walked in and told everyone to step away from their computers and to leave the office. They boxed up all the paperwork and took it away."

"Holy shit. We are so fucked. Thanks for telling me. I really appreciate it."

Packouz hadn't been in the office for weeks, but he knew there were multiple reasons why AEY's headquarters might be raided. He also knew what the likely explanation was—even if the DCIS knew nothing about the Chinese ammunition being repacked in Albania before the raid.

"I figured it had to be the Chinese ammo," Packouz recalled. "I knew the e-mails about the Chinese repacking job were incredibly incriminating. I knew that once federal agents saw those, we'd be in trouble.

We were so stupid. If we didn't e-mail, we probably could've denied the whole thing. But there were names and dates. It was undeniable. I realized I was going to get caught no matter what I did, so I better turn myself in first."

Packouz called his friend Alex Podrizki in Albania and told him about the raid. Packouz told Podrizki how the agents were going to find the e-mails about the Chinese ammo and how it might be a federal crime.

Sitting in his room in Tirana, Podrizki reeled. First he needed to know what had really happened in Miami. Podrizki phoned Danny Doudnik, who'd become his main contact at AEY. Podrizki didn't mention that he knew about the raid; he was trying to see if Doudnik and Diveroli would tell him the truth. As they talked, Doudnik didn't mention the raid, so he plainly was not going to level with him. Podrizki told Doudnik he needed a bunch of documents quickly. Doudnik said he was out of the office and didn't have the papers with him and that it was going to take a while to get them.

"Why not go to the office?" Podrizki asked. "It's urgent."

"I can't."

The stress in Doudnik's voice was palpable.

"What's the matter?" Podrizki asked.

Podrizki could hear murmuring in the background. "Tell him there was a bomb threat," he heard Diveroli whisper.

Doudnik repeated the lie.

"Are you guys okay?" Podrizki asked, feigning concern.

"It's okay," Doudnik said.

Podrizki hung up. He had to make a plan. Now. The Albanian police could be outside his door, for all he knew. First, he needed to get out of Albania and away from what suddenly appeared to be a crime scene at the repacking operation at the airport. Catching a plane was too risky, Podrizki decided. He was too well known at the airport. Leaving his meager belongings behind, he caught a cab to the edge of Tirana and got out. After the cab had driven away, he hailed another and directed the driver to take him to the port city of Durrës. Podrizki was now off the grid: no one would know where he was.

At Durrës, Podrizki bought a ticket for the ferry to Italy. He paid cash. As the ship put out to sea, he sat in the bar downing raki after raki and considered running to a country that had no extradition treaty with the United States. He replayed events from the past few months. He recalled how strange it was that Diveroli hadn't gone to the airport to see the repacking when he was in Albania. He remembered how Diveroli had borrowed his laptop for half an hour one day. Now he realized that Diveroli could've planted incriminating evidence on the hard drive. Diveroli could have been scheming to lay the whole repacking plot on Podrizki. There was no way of knowing how ruthless Diveroli could be. It was every man for himself, Podrizki realized.

Podrizki stepped out of the bar onto the deck of the ferry. He looked around to be sure no one was watching. He quietly slipped his laptop overboard, the computer disappearing into the black Adriatic Sea.

In Miami, David Packouz hired a lawyer and tried to figure out if he had a defense. Was the repacking really illegal? Was the ammo really "Chinese"? Did the federal government know it was receiving Chinese ammo? He had many possible arguments he could try to make, Packouz's lawyer said. But it was extremely expensive to mount a legal defense against the limitless resources of the federal government.

"You got two options," the lawyer said. "You can fight, which is going to cost a minimum of two hundred thousand dollars. Or you can plead guilty. Your parents got a house they can put a second mortgage on?"

"I'm not doing that to my parents," Packouz said. "What about a public defender?"

"You mean 'public pretender.' You'll be one of two hundred cases he's working. You'll be lucky if he remembers your name."

"You're saying I can only effectively defend myself if I have lots of money?"

"That's the system—how much justice can you afford."

"What happens if I plead guilty?"

"You become the government's bitch. Pretty much, you're pulling down your pants and begging them not to fuck you too hard."

"But I'm already bent over."

"The way of the world."

The lawyer arranged for a sit-down with Michael Mentavlos of the DCIS. An agent from the Immigration and Customs Enforcement agency named Oscar Garcia was working the case with Mentavlos. Garcia was older, near retirement, a veteran. Garcia led the meeting. He explained to Packouz that he had to confess to every crime he'd committed. A guilty plea applied to all possible forms of guilt.

"Keep in my mind we have all of AEY's files, computers, and e-mail accounts," Garcia said. "We're going to find everything eventually. If you omit anything or lie about anything, we'll come down on you like a ton of bricks."

"What if I forget something?" Packouz asked.

"Then it'll be a judgment call for us. Don't put us in that position."

Packouz had prepared with his lawyer. He might be charged with fraud, he understood, but his lawyer believed that with a full confession he might be able to avoid indictment. Packouz spoke slowly as he tried to recall everything he'd seen and done that might possibly be illegal. He told them how Diveroli had ordered him to falsify documents to send to arms companies in Bulgaria and Albania. He described the bait-and-switch tactics Diveroli used with Army procurement officers, bidding with brand-name Belgian guns and then persuading them to accept cheap Korean knockoffs. He told them about Diveroli's Save the King Package and the attempt to sell arms to Nepal. The investigators took careful notes. Mentavlos had a habit of frowning at Packouz, as if trying to intimidate him.

"Now I'll tell you the thing that makes me most nervous," Packouz said.

"Saving the best for last, huh?" Garcia said.

Packouz laid out how AEY had repacked the ammunition in Albania—the Chinese markings, the weight of the pallets and crates, the way they'd changed the packaging of the AK-47 ammo, first to save money, then to save the contract.

Mentavlos and Garcia exchanged a glance and burst out laughing.

"If it makes you feel any better, we already know about the Chinese ammo," Garcia said. "We found a to-do list in Diveroli's papers, and one of the items was 'Repackage Chinese ammo.'"

"That sounds incriminating," Packouz said.

"No kidding." Garcia laughed. "Now this is very important. I want you to think hard. Did any government official know about what you were doing? Were they involved, getting paid or anything else?"

"Not that I know of."

Afterward, Packouz prayed he wouldn't get indicted. He prayed he wouldn't go to prison, though he'd been told he could face years behind bars. The prospect of doing time in a federal penitentiary because of repacked "Chinese" ammo seemed crazy to Packouz—and Garcia seemed to agree, though he was careful not to make any promises. Packouz's lawyer said he felt that he could deal with Garcia—he was mature and levelheaded. But Mentavlos was another matter—he seemed unpredictable.

Packouz was now at the mercy of the government. So was Alex Podrizki, who'd returned to Miami, hired a lawyer, and confessed all to the federal agents. Special Agent Mentavlos promised to "go to bat" for them both. Diveroli was his real target, Mentavlos said. But Packouz and Podrizki thought there was something sinister in Mentavlos's gung ho attitude.

Packouz wanted to know what he could do to make a living—could he still work on arms deals? Mentavlos said that he could, provided he didn't break the law. Relieved, Packouz said he was working on a lead to sell a large number of AK-47s to a Nigerian colonel. A Serbian company was going to supply the weapons.

"Very interesting," Mentavlos said, sniffing the chance of making another case. He suggested Packouz help him set up a sting operation against the Nigerian. Packouz figured Mentavlos had simply assumed that the Nigerian had to be a fraudster—with no evidence whatsoever.

"Can you tell the Nigerian you've got a better source in the States?" Mentavlos asked. "Invite him here. We can set up a warehouse filled with AKs and bust him. That would really help your case."

"What?" Packouz asked. "The guy's totally legit. He's planning on going to Serbia any day to inspect the guns with Nigeria's top brass."

Mentavlos laughed. "Trust me. The guy's not legit. Can you set up a deal like that?"

"Everyone knows the cheapest prices for Eastern Bloc ammo come from Warsaw Pact countries. They'd never believe I got a better price in America."

"Okay. But you can't do the deal. You're an important witness in our case and we can't have you getting in trouble."

Packouz was crushed. The deal was perfectly legal. He'd obtained the necessary licenses and was counting on the $200,000 in profit he would make from the transaction, not least to pay his legal fees. The Nigerian deal also promised to lead to other African deals. But Mentavlos had killed that opportunity for no apparent reason, other than an unfounded assumption of criminal activity.

"Mentavlos wanted me to do a fake sting deal," Packouz recalled. "I didn't think the Nigerian was a criminal or a fraud. It seemed to me that Mentavlos would do anything to make a case. He wasn't trying to solve crimes—he was making them up. I thought it was pretty disgusting coming from someone with so much power."

As part of Packouz's cooperation deal, the DCIS put Packouz to work going through more than one hundred thousand e-mails, looking for evidence that further incriminated Diveroli. Day after day, Packouz read AEY's e-mail archives with amazement. Packouz read how Diveroli had attempted to squeeze Ralph Merrill out of the deal and then hide his profit margins from the older man. Merrill obviously had no idea of Diveroli's true margins or business practices.

The DCIS was delighted with Packouz's diligence. "You've saved us a lot of time and legwork," Mentavlos said. "All the agents here are fully supportive of keeping you and Podrizki out of the indictment."

"So Alex and I won't be indicted?" Packouz asked.

"We'll sure do everything we can for you guys. It's not up to us, of course. But they usually listen to what we have to say, so I'd say it's looking good for you guys."

"Wow. That's a huge relief."

"But that's contingent on us continuing to receive the same level of support and honesty from you."

"I'm one hundred percent on board. There's no going halfway on this."

"Exactly."

Packouz reenrolled in college and now aimed to complete a degree in science. But he was stone-cold broke and running up large legal bills; dealing with the DCIS required his lawyer to read through evidence and prosecution documents, even if he was never indicted, which was proving to be extremely expensive. To make a few bucks, Packouz was working as a masseur again, but he still had to figure out a way to support himself and his daughter.

Meanwhile, Diveroli was still rolling in money, Packouz knew, because of the millions he'd made with AEY, much of it legitimate earnings. Packouz reasoned that he'd missed out on his payment from Diveroli by a matter of hours—why not try to get at least some cash? He'd done perfectly legal deals with Diveroli—gun parts, scrap metal, propane for the Army. Leaving aside the Afghanistan deal, Packouz figured he was owed $17,000—money he needed badly.

Packouz called one of Diveroli's cousins and a meeting was arranged. The two estranged friends hadn't talked in months. After the raid, Diveroli had wondered if Packouz had betrayed him and snitched to the DCIS. Diveroli had finally decided Packouz wouldn't act against his best economic interests and jeopardize the money he had coming.

As they greeted each other, Diveroli behaved as if they were still best friends, giving Packouz a bear hug. A bong was produced and Packouz was offered a hit. He played along. Diveroli seemed just as cocky as ever, eager to pump him for information.

"Crazy shit going down, eh?" Diveroli said.

"Crazy," Packouz said, looking up from the bong.

"The government try to contact you?"

"I told them to talk to my lawyer," Packouz lied.

"Excellent! That's the way to handle these bastards. You can't let them run you over. If they smell blood in the water, they go into a feeding frenzy."

"You think you can freeze them out?" Packouz asked.

"I've got the best damn lawyers money can buy working on it. I'm going to crush those motherfuckers."

"You still delivering on the contract from Albania?"

"You think a federal investigation is going to slow us down? You know how we roll."

"Just be careful, dude. Sounds like serious trouble."

"Listen, buddy, you keep your head down and this shitstorm is going to pass. They'll forget about us. Then you and I can settle our business and you'll get the money you rightly deserve."

"I hope so."

Leaving the apartment, Packouz decided he should tell Mentavlos that he'd met with Diveroli. The investigator was furious. He ordered Packouz to tell him of any future meetings with Diveroli.

"Mentavlos wanted me to wear a wire on Diveroli," Packouz recalled. "In my mind, telling the government everything that had happened was one thing. But entrapping someone, even Diveroli—that was a whole new low. I wasn't willing to play along with Mentavlos's schemes, even though I could see that it would be in my interests. Mentavlos seemed like he'd do anything to get Diveroli."

The prospect of going to prison gave Packouz a new direction in life. All the fights with his girlfriend now seemed trivial. They'd reunited and were focused on their daughter, with Packouz taking the lead in child care.

"There's nothing like hardship to bring people together," Packouz said. "I savored spending as much time with my daughter as possible."

But darker voices still beckoned Packouz. He had his company, Dynacore, and the knowledge he'd obtained working with Diveroli. He'd lost the Nigerian deal, but mankind's thirst for weapons was never slaked, and Packouz figured he should try to cash in. The business was perfectly legal, after all, and it offered the chance to make a lot of money quickly. Packouz found a financier who was willing to back him on FedBizOpps deals, anything up to $5 million, which put Packouz back in the game. He was aiming to become an arms dealer in his own right. Like Henri Thomet. Like Diveroli.

"I told myself I'd make a few million—five was my goal—then I'd kick back and do what I loved to do," Packouz recalled. "I'd make music, play with my daughter, travel. But now I doubted that I'd stop if I reached the five-million-dollar mark. Diveroli already had that much money and it hadn't stopped him. He still worked like a dog. Once you're making millions, a large part of you is only concerned with making money. You want more and more. You make money for the sake of making money. I was afraid that was what I would become."

Chapter Ten

KORRUPSIONI

By October 2007, AEY had delivered more than 40 million rounds of AK-47 ammo from Albania to Afghanistan. Along the way, it appeared likely that the political operators and thugs controlling Albania's munitions had profited handsomely. *Korrupsioni* was the Albanian term for the phenomenon that pervaded every level of government, from street cops to politicians. As the anti-corruption fighter in New York Gary Kokalari expected, the US embassy in Tirana seemingly turned a blind eye to these crimes, despite the audacity of Albanian politicians.

In Miami Beach, Diveroli continued to oversee AEY's ongoing shipments, including the "Chinese" ammunition—despite the DCIS investigation. The Albanian deal was only a fraction of AEY's contract. RPGs and grenades and missiles were also arriving in Afghanistan in vast quantities. The raid had done nothing to dampen Diveroli's ambitions, or to hinder his performance.

The day after Alex Podrizki left Tirana, Diveroli had dispatched another young AEY employee, David Black, to Albania to oversee the repacking. Black had been told that the ammo was Chinese, but Diveroli said he shouldn't worry because it was coming from Albania. Diveroli had instructed Black to tell the Albanians that Podrizki had left so hastily because his mother fell ill. Black's pay went from $12 an hour to $1,000 a week, with the promise of a $20,000 bonus.

As the Albanian shipments continued apace, Diveroli's defiant attitude only appeared to further anger the DCIS. The illegal "Chinese" shipments had to cease, the agency fervently believed. To that end, Special Agent Mentavlos called the Army's procurement office in Rock Island, Illinois, and demanded that it stop accepting AK-47 ammunition from Albania from AEY. The procurement officers were unmoved. The Albanian ammunition was part of a crucial contract to supply the Afghans; the Army wouldn't stop shipments based on a dubious interpretation of the embargo against Chinese munitions.

Mentavlos was insistent. "Please put all 7.62x39 and 7.62x54 from Albania on hold," Mentavlos wrote to the procurement officers. "Please do not release this ammunition to the Afghan National Army, as it is part of our investigation and may become evidence in the future.

"Having recently returned from a military deployment in Afghanistan," Mentavlos continued, "I understand the requirement to get this ammunition into the hands of the ANA as soon as possible. We will discuss the situation with the State Department to determine if we can seize a small amount of ammunition and allow the rest to be distributed to the Afghan National Army."

The civilians charged with administering AEY's contract were flummoxed by the DCIS. The official in charge of AEY's contract, Melanie Johnson, wrote to Army lawyers to seek advice. She wanted to know what to do about ammunition that was apparently "Chinese" even though it was in Albania. "We really don't have inspectors and don't really know what authority, if any, we have over those at the receiving point," she wrote. "I don't know what course of action can or should be taken. I don't know if a contractor under criminal investigation is prevented from receiving other orders that don't relate to the AK-47 ammunition."

The procurement officials in Illinois then wrote to Lieutenant Colonel Loye Gau, in Kabul, to obtain his assessment of the situation on the ground. LTC Gau was asked what would happen if the Army suddenly prevented AEY from shipping the Chinese-Albanian ammo. Was it feasible to isolate the ammo AEY had shipped?

Gau replied that AEY's ammo was stored in a facility in Kabul called 22 Bunkers. He didn't comment on the "Chinese" question. Gau said he would do his best to figure out the logistics of complying with the DCIS's request, but stopping AEY's shipments, even in part, would have a terrible impact on the war effort.

"We will work up an estimate of how much pain will be involved in segregating the AEY-delivered ammo," Gau replied. "Some types of ammo are in high demand and operational necessity will trump any investigative procedure—some of this ammo is actually being used to kill bad guys. In particular, the 7.62x54 and RPG rounds will almost certainly not be held at 22 Bunkers as units in the field are experiencing critical shortages of both."

Operational necessity was a loaded term in the US military: it meant that AEY's mission was so important that lives would be endangered if the shipments were stopped. The 7.62x54 rounds coming from Albania were among the most urgently needed.

Then Gau got sarcastic. He said it would take fifty to sixty soldiers to isolate and inspect the ammunition and he didn't have the personnel to spare. If the DCIS was so determined to seize AEY's ammunition, Gau wrote, it was welcome to fly dozens of its agents to Kabul.

The DCIS wasn't chastened by Gau's tart reply. Once again, Mentavlos called the procurement officers in Rock Island and insisted on closing down AEY's Albanian shipments. This time the civilians agreed, however reluctantly. But they said first they needed a signed letter from Mentavlos explaining why the DCIS insisted on ceasing the delivery of the AK-47 ammo. There would thus be a record of what had transpired should a senior military officer ask why the Afghans were being sent to fight without ammunition—when perfectly good rounds were available. Or should a congressman or a journalist start asking questions about ammo shortages in Afghanistan. The DCIS refused to sign any such document.

The battle between the DCIS and Rock Island, which really amounted to a war, was as bitter as it was bureaucratic. The law was being broken by AEY, the DCIS maintained, and the ongoing knowing acceptance of "Chinese" ammunition had to cease. LTC Mentavlos sent word directly to Gau in Kabul, demanding that AEY's ammo be segregated and that samples be transported to his office. Gau refused. The American soldier on the front lines in Afghanistan flatly would not comply with a directive from the agency.

"Operational necessity will trump any investigative procedure," Gau wrote to Mentavlos.

Despite the resistance—perhaps because of the resistance—the DCIS persisted. In mid-October Mentavlos traveled to Illinois to meet with the procurement officials supervising AEY's contract. Once again, the Army said it would cease receiving AEY's ammo only if the DCIS provided a sworn statement detailing why it wanted the shipments to stop.

Seeking a way to circumvent Gau and the procurement officers in Rock Island—seeking a way to circumvent operational necessity and common sense—the DCIS decided to send Mentavlos to Albania. The DCIS needed irrefutable evidence that the AK-47 ammo was indeed "Chinese." Once Mentavlos had the actual rounds in hand, with the headstamps proving that they'd been manufactured in China and were thus subject to the embargo, no one could deny the DCIS had legal grounds for stopping Diveroli.

Before leaving, Mentavlos wrote to the US Embassy in Tirana explaining that the DCIS had been investigating AEY for more than two years and that he was going to seize "a handful" of the "Chinese"-made AK-47 ammo. "Since Chinese manufactured ammunition is strictly prohibited, AEY has hired a repacking company in Tirana to remove all Chinese markings," Mentavlos wrote.

In the e-mail, Mentavlos seemed to assure the embassy people that they didn't have to fear an investigation that might expose Albanian crimes or corruption. He didn't say it directly. The use of an ellipsis in a sentence appeared like a wink from Mentavlos: "The focus of our investigation is on AEY and its employees . . . we are not looking at any Albanian citizens."

As Mentavlos prepared to go to Albania, the DCIS investigation seemed to take on an inverse sense of proportion: the more dubious it appeared, legally and strategically, the harder the agency pushed. Fraud was rampant in Afghanistan, but the DCIS was pouring all its resources into a case based on a legal technicality. The more it appeared that the resources allocated to the case were completely unrelated to the substance of the alleged crimes, the more money and time and energy the DCIS poured into getting Efraim Diveroli.

In mid-October, Alex Podrizki was surprised to receive a call from his attorney saying that the DCIS wanted him to travel to Albania to assist Mentavlos. Podrizki met with Mentavlos and his partner Oscar Garcia at a law-enforcement office in Doral, Florida, where he was fingerprinted and told he was now considered a CI—confidential informant. Mentavlos made no promises, but helping him could evidently benefit Podrizki—and not helping could hurt him.

"I said I would talk about AEY and Diveroli because he'd left me twisting in the wind," Podrizki recalled. "And I would go to Albania to help because it might mean I wouldn't be indicted. But I wasn't going to turn in any Albanians. I was concerned for my safety."

At the end of October, Podrizki arrived in Albania by ship, at the port of Durrës, to avoid the airport in Tirana, where he was likely to be recognized. In Tirana he went to the Sheraton and asked for Mentavlos at the front desk, as he'd been instructed. An American man dressed entirely in black and faking a bad Australian accent approached and told Podrizki to follow him—but not to look at or talk to him.

"As we walked to my hotel, the guy in black told me that once I'd checked in he'd slip a note under the door to tell me what room he was staying in," Podrizki said. "He looked like a clown, he was so obviously an American in disguise. I guess he was supposed to be watching me. As we walked along, he suddenly turned away from me and vanished, like he was playing a game of secret agent. When I met with Mentavlos, he acted like he was the main character in a Tom Clancy novel—with all the intrigue and excitement. I tried to play it cool, but I was nervous the whole time and hated myself for doing it—but I felt like I had no choice."

Finally in Albania, Mentavlos seized samples of the "Chinese" ammunition. Before leaving the country, he went to meet with Kosta Trebicka at his sprawling house in the suburbs of Tirana. Trebicka was wary but willing to talk. In the interests of full disclosure, Trebicka said he'd been talking to the *New York Times*. Mentavlos reacted angrily, telling him not to talk to any journalists, in Albania or the United States. Above all else, Mentavlos said, Trebicka must cease communication with the *Times*.

"I have hired an Albanian lawyer to give information about AEY," Trebicka told Mentavlos.

"You are not to speak to the lawyer," Mentavlos said.

Trebicka was shocked. "Why?"

"You will harm a very serious investigation."

Trebicka wondered about Mentavlos's behavior. He had no jurisdiction in Albania, after all, so who was he to order Trebicka around? But Trebicka had lived in the United States and knew enough about the octopus-like powers of the federal government to realize he better be careful around an investigator who seemed to him to be unhinged in his desire to "get" Efraim Diveroli.

The American investigator said he wanted to take Kosta Trebicka's fingerprints. Now Trebicka was truly alarmed. Trebicka was an Albanian national and he had done nothing wrong. Evidently Mentavlos wanted to run Trebicka's prints through Interpol's global records to see if he had a criminal record. Trebicka submitted, but reluctantly.

As soon as Mentavlos departed, Trebicka called Gary Kokalari in New York.

Trebicka explained the fingerprinting and how the investigator had treated him like a common criminal. He was upset. All he'd done was report alleged illegal activity—both in Albania and in the United States.

"You don't have to do that," Kokalari said.

But it was too late.

Flying home in triumph, Special Agent Mentavlos had achieved his goal: he had a handful of "Chinese"-made AK-47 rounds. He literally had all the ammunition he needed to finally stop Efraim Diveroli.

/////

In the fall of 2007, the DCIS wasn't the only organization investigating AEY. The sheer improbability of what the three stoners from Miami Beach had attempted seemed to taunt the Fates, summoning forth the speculation of its rival Blane, the full force and might of the DCIS, and, finally, the world's leading source of investigative journalism. While the DCIS doggedly set out to keep AEY's ammunition from the Afghans, C. J. Chivers of the *New York Times* relentlessly pursued the AEY story. After weeks of reporting, Chivers had determined that his primary interest involved pricing. The doubling of the price at each level of the transaction from Thomet to AEY to the Army was suspicious. Why was the US military using intermediaries, instead of buying directly from the Albanians? Chivers wondered.

Relying on confidential sources, Chivers learned that AEY had sourced 9 million AK-47 cartridges for Iraq from the Czech Republic, through an arms dealer named Petr Bernatik. Chivers's unnamed source told him that Bernatik had been accused of shipping rocket-propelled grenades to the Congo, in violation of an international embargo. The informant told Chivers that Bernatik was on the State Department's watch list. So was AEY's Swiss broker, Henri Thomet, the owner of the mysterious company named Evdin.

This discovery pointed to AEY's being part of a much larger story about the American procurement process and the black market in arms. From his Moscow office, Chivers contacted Bernatik, who refused to comment in detail on his dealings with AEY. Alarmed by Chivers's call, Bernatik sent an e-mail to Efraim Diveroli in Miami

Beach: "Mr. Chivers asked if we are collaborating with AEY. Can you estimate why is *New York Times* collecting these informations?"

Then Chivers contacted Henri Thomet by e-mail. The canny Swiss arms dealer flatly denied any official role in Evdin. Thomet said allegations that he was on the State Department's watch list because of his involvement in illegal arms deals were based on "false statements by former competitors."

A *Times* stringer was dispatched to check Evdin's business address in Cyprus, only to discover that the headquarters was in an accounting office above a nightclub, a mailing address used for many shell companies. Evdin had been incorporated just one week after AEY bid on the Afghanistan contract.

Another *New York Times* Pulitzer Prize–winning journalist was assigned to travel to Miami and investigate AEY. Eric Schmitt obtained Efraim Diveroli's cell phone number and cold-called him. Caught by surprise, Diveroli had a brief exchange with the reporter.

"I know my company does everything on the up-and-up, and that's all I'm concerned about," Diveroli told Schmitt. "AEY is working on a moderately classified Department of Defense project. I really don't want to talk about the details."

Schmitt told Diveroli about the information Kosta Trebicka had provided to the *Times*, including the existence of the covertly recorded telephone conversation discussing corruption in Albania.

"What goes on in the Albanian Ministry of Defense?" Diveroli asked. "Who's clean? Who's dirty? Don't want to know about that."

For the *Times*, the last piece of the puzzle was Albania. Instead of sending Chivers to Tirana, the newspaper assigned a journalist based in the Balkans named Nick Wood. An Englishman with a refined accent that disguised a steely disposition, Wood had covered the war in Kosovo and nearly a decade's worth of instability since; he'd also specialized in reporting on small-arms proliferation from the region.

Only a month earlier, Wood had written a piece for the *Times* reporting what United Nations investigators had concluded about the business of a Serbian arms dealer named Tomislav Damnjanovic. Like Henri Thomet, the Serb had sold millions of dollars' worth of ammo and grenades and mortars to the US Army in Baghdad. The investigators reported that Damnjanovic had also falsified documents and sold arms to war criminals in Liberia and the Congo at the same time; forty-five tons of his weapons had gone to Islamic Courts Union forces in Somalia—direct allies of Al Qaeda. Thus Wood's article had illustrated how the Pentagon was doing business with allegedly illegal gunrunners spreading misery and death to innocent civilians in Africa.

When Wood arrived in Tirana, he went to meet Kosta Trebicka. The Albanian had summoned the courage to talk to the *Times* despite Mentavlos's express instruction to the contrary. Wood found a man who was obviously prosperous and intelligent—but also nervous. As Wood interviewed Trebicka, his eleven-year-old son from his second marriage was quietly doing his homework in the corner of the room. Wood's first concern was to measure how reliable Trebicka was. The Albanian said he wasn't sure if he was willing to speak on the record. (He would vacillate about this question for months.) He told Wood that he'd received threatening phone calls. He'd also been told by the defense minister to leave the matter alone—an ominous warning from such a powerful man. Trebicka had heard the allegation that the prime minister's son was involved in the AEY contract, another even more worrying sign. Wood saw that Trebicka knew he was taking an enormous risk in coming forward.

"We talked for four hours the first day," Wood recalled. "The next day I went to Trebicka's office. I continually went over my questions for him. He was consistent in his answers. I thought he had a good motive to talk. He was pissed off. He'd been cut out of the deal. He wanted revenge against the defense mafia in Albania."

On November 19, Wood went to interview Defense Minister Fatmir Mediu, accompanied by a young Albanian videographer hired to record the encounter. The minister's office was huge, with portraits of

Mediu standing with powerful Bush administration figures—Donald Rumsfeld, Colin Powell, Condoleezza Rice. The minister was stout, smiling, friendly, and cheerful. He evidently expected a glowing story about Albania's pending NATO membership.

"At first Mediu talked about all the American officials he'd met," Wood recalled. "He said Albania was a key ally in the war on terror. He talked openly about how he was helping with the contract to supply ammunition to Afghanistan."

"That's what I'd like to talk to you more about," Wood said to Mediu.

Wood took a breath and dived in, describing how Albanian officials were allegedly being paid kickbacks on AEY's contract, including Diveroli's recorded description of the Albanian "Mafia" and the prime minister's son.

Mediu exploded. "This is all lies!" he shouted.

"I would like to know the details of the AEY contract," Wood said. "Especially the pricing. The allegation is that MEICO is selling the ammunition for twenty-two dollars a crate to a Cyprus company, and that the price is marked up to forty dollars for each crate when it's sold to AEY. The money is being used to pay kickbacks."

"Lies!" Mediu screamed, beside himself with fury, as the videographer filmed the outburst.

"Turn off the camera," Mediu hissed.

The camera kept rolling.

"I know who you are," Mediu hissed at the cameraman. "I know who your father is."

In Albania, this constituted a serious threat. The camera was stopped. Wood and the cameraman departed. Later that night, Mediu met with the American ambassador to Albania to discuss Wood's interview. He also plotted to hide the repacking operation from the *New York Times* reporter, who was scheduled to visit the airport the following morning. On the minister's instructions, all of the Chinese boxes and packaging were moved from the airport to a nearby military base in the middle of the night.

At eight the next morning, Nick Wood of the *Times* went to the airport as planned. He was told he wouldn't be permitted to take any pictures in the restricted area. Nor could he bring his cell phone. Wood was escorted to an open-air hangar, where 3.5 million rounds of AEY's ammunition were sitting on pallets waiting to be loaded. The ammo was packed in plastic bags and cardboard boxes. Wood noted that the site was open to the elements—heat, rain, cold. But no crates with Chinese markings were lying around, nor any tins with Chinese markings.

Minutes later, the freelance videographer called Wood in a panic to say that men from the Defense Ministry had forcibly taken the video-tape of the interview with the minister.

Wood texted Mediu, "Mr. Mediu we need to talk. It is in your interest to do so."

Mediu replied, "You misspresented yourself, and I do not have anything else to talk. It was more than enaf."

"You have threatened the cameraman," Wood texted. "Your associates are stealing our tape from the interview. I suggest u call me. It was not my interest to write about u but I may do so now."

"I do not know what you are talking about. You are still misspresenting. You can write whatever you like."

There was no further communication.

The specter of the *New York Times* story now haunted the Albanian government. Trying to stave off negative publicity, Prime Minister Sali Berisha wrote to the owners of the *Times*. Defense Minister Mediu also contacted the newspaper, sending an angry personal letter to the executive editor, Bill Keller, claiming that he'd been ambushed by Wood:

> *Mr. Wood's comments were of an offensive nature, implying dishonesty on my part. His allegations were based on rumor and innuendo, twisting the actual facts, and impugning my reputation as a Minister. I endeavored to explain the facts but Mr.*

Wood was uninterested. His behavior was characterized by arrogance and rudeness that is typically associated with the worst examples of yellow journalism and tabloid sensationalism.

"*NY Times* might be doing a story on AEY and it might get ugly," an American official at the US Embassy in Tirana wrote to his colleagues. "Just a head's up. Ambassador is very concerned."

Chapter Eleven

OPERATIONAL NECESSITY

While Diveroli continued to work around the clock at AEY during the winter of 2007–8, David Packouz took a more laid-back approach to arms dealing. Scanning FedBizOpps for an hour or two each day, Packouz helped his girlfriend set up a spa, and they both did massages from the modest facility. When a solicitation for twenty-five thousand cleaning kits for M16s appeared on FedBizOpps, Packouz did a Google search and got quotes from companies in Italy, Missouri, and China (weapons were banned, but not accessories for arms). He bid $1.2 million, with a profit margin of 9 percent, but he lost. Another contract for ten thousand Pelican M6 2320 flashlights was posted, but Packouz wasn't able to find an approved source in time. A request for five hundred MP9 submachine guns led Packouz to approach a Swiss company called Brugger & Thomet—Thomet had formerly been a partner in the firm. It offered a price of $540,000. Packouz bid $595,000, but again he didn't win; Swiss arms were expensive because they were the best quality.

"I didn't have the single-minded obsession that Efraim had," Packouz recalled. "I didn't want to work eighteen-hour days bidding on every contract. I had other interests in life, like my daughter. I started to record my album, which was great. I wasn't in a state of constant panic and stress."

During this time, a young Pakistani arms broker named Usman

Masood contacted Packouz through his old AEY e-mail address and offered to supply a large amount of military equipment. Packouz and Masood began to exchange e-mails with quotes for various types of deals, like Russian-caliber machine guns, ballistic panels for armored vehicles, and twenty thousand AK-47 rifles for Sri Lanka—a country that was under a UN embargo because of the civil war then raging there.

"Dear Mr. David," Masood wrote in one e-mail, "please provide a quote for 8,000 Astra Cub pistol required by our esteemed client."

The Astra Cub was a small-caliber weapon, usually used by women for self-defense—a "purse gun," in the business. Packouz approached a Czech father-and-son team that he'd dealt with at AEY. The Czechs found a supplier in Spain and quoted $43 for each of the pistols—an amazingly low price. Packouz was going to sell the guns for $63, making a profit of $160,000 on the deal. But his broker's license required that he first contact the State Department to be approved to deal with parties in other countries. Before e-mailing State, Packouz asked Masood for the destination of the pistols. Somaliland, Masood said, a self-declared independent state on the Horn of Africa. Packouz did some research and discovered that Somaliland had broken away from Somalia after a series of massacres led to a civil war; a democratically elected government made it one of the most stable nations in the region, but it had yet to be internationally recognized. The State Department told Packouz that Somaliland was under a UN arms embargo, so he couldn't participate in the deal. As ever in the complicated and often capricious world of arms dealing, he'd flirted with breaking the law—but caught himself in time.

"The Somaliland deal was like the Chinese ammo in Albania," Packouz said. "The guns were for defenseless women to protect themselves. But there was an embargo. Doing the deal would break the letter of the law but not the spirit. I wasn't going to stick my neck out."

The letter of the law was very much on the mind of the DCIS as Special Agent Mentavlos returned from Albania, aiming to finally thwart AEY. Mentavlos sent an e-mail to the Army Sustainment Command in Rock Island, Illinois, stating that shipments had to cease forthwith.

On November 5, Melanie Johnson, the civilian administering AEY's contract, wrote to her superiors to explain the situation. Johnson began by pointing out that the sole accusation Mentavlos had against AEY was the supposed violation of the law by shipping "Chinese"-made ammunition. No allegations were made about the quality of the ammunition. As far as the Army was concerned, AEY was delivering ammunition in accordance with the contract. There had been some small questions related to the thickness of the cardboard AEY was using for the repacking, and some boxes had been jostled during the flights from Tirana to Kabul. The shortcomings were well within the normal course of business, especially given the situation in Afghanistan.

"Mentavlos asked if the contract had been terminated yet—these guys just don't get it," Johnson wrote to her colleagues. "He was told no. We want a sworn statement from the agent outlining what was seen, seized, etc. We are not taking any action until we receive something in writing."

So Mentavlos e-mailed his evidence—photographs of the Chinese markings on the ammo AEY was shipping to Kabul.

The Procurement Fraud division was forced into action.

On November 6, 2007, acceptance of AEY's shipments of AK-47 ammo from Albania to Afghanistan was suspended.

Inevitably, ammo shortages quickly followed in Kabul. Other companies were shipping limited amounts of ammo to Kabul, but AEY was supplying the vast majority. Ending AEY's shipments of AK-47 ammo from Albania would obviously lead to disaster.

Lieutenant Colonel Moises Gutierrez was assigned to NATO's logistics branch in Afghanistan. The specific goal of the logistics branch was to ensure that information was shared and that the military remained focused on *operational necessity*—the same metric the DCIS had encountered in its interactions with other American soldiers in

Afghanistan. For LTC Gutierrez, operational necessity meant getting AEY's AK-47 shipments started again—immediately. Winter was closing in, the only chance to lay in supplies for the coming fighting season, and he was anticipating a huge spike in demand. Weeks were passing and no small-caliber ammo was arriving in Afghanistan. From Kabul, it seemed as if investigators at the DCIS in Tampa Bay had lost their minds.

Then they ran out of ammo in 22 Bunkers. American officers embedded with Afghan forces contacted Gutierrez and furiously demanded that ammo be sent into the field—*downrange*, in the argot of the military. The soldiers were told that there was no ammo because the DCIS had stopped shipments.

Frustrated and astonished that Afghan soldiers were going into battle without ammunition because of an ill-begotten investigation in Florida, Gutierrez took his complaint up the chain of command. In January of 2008, he told his superiors about the lack of AK-47 ammo and how AEY's rounds were needed; that they were "Chinese" made absolutely no difference in combat. Gutierrez was informed that the shipments had been stopped and that the decision was final. Gutierrez didn't desist. He told his superiors that he was willing to take the risk of countermanding the DCIS. The only way to solve the problem, Gutierrez was instructed, was to put his request in writing. So Gutierrez sat down to explain to the Army how badly it was hurting its own cause:

> The Afghanistan National Security Force is moving into the spring fighting season and the ammunition is critically needed. The Afghanistan National Police has zero 7.62 x 54mm on hand and is urgently awaiting deliveries of this ammo. As such, we are requesting that Defense Contract Management be engaged as soon as possible to ensure quality product/packaging, but that deliveries continue given the criticality of the need.

The 7.62x54 ammunition Gutierrez referred to was used in sniper rifles and the PKM machine gun—weapons that were fundamental to the way war was waged in the mountains of Afghanistan. The memo-randum made it clear that the DCIS's investigation was morphing into a strategic threat.

Inside the Army, the number of officers copied on Gutierrez's e-mail exploded. Soldiers in the field were demanding the ammo, but it seemed as if nothing could legally be done to get AEY shipping again.

The procurement officials in Rock Island continued searching for a solution. The possibility of AEY's applying for a Supply Deviation Request was discussed. A general named Dowd stepped in and suppos-edly made it clear that no more shipments from Albania for AEY should be approved, no matter what American soldiers in Afghanistan said.

"How does LTC Gutierrez trump General Dowd?" one of the civil-ian women in Rock Island asked.

Gutierrez was in the war zone, came the reply, not Illinois, so he would know the facts on the ground.

A "huddle" was called in Rock Island to determine a way forward. The deputy director of the Acquisitions Center circulated a memoran-dum before the meeting. "I don't think General Dowd said to stop ship-ments," Debra Collins wrote. Dowd, it was now contended, had merely "suggested" that the Army get someone on the ground in Albania to ensure the packing was properly done, solving the cardboard strength but ignoring the "Chinese" origin of the ammo. "I would feel a lot more comfortable if we had someone higher up in the food-chain that wants AEY to continue shipping."

After weeks of uncertainty, the civilians in Rock Island finally hatched a plan. The first step was to get a "head nod" from someone "SENIOR" on continuing AEY's shipments. An analysis of the reports on the deficiencies of AEY's shipments should quickly be completed to determine if any issues related to quality, not just to packing. The Army could then issue a "cure notice," requiring AEY to solve any identified problems. Finally: "Get AEY up here ASAP to review the issues and define their corrective action."

Within days, Diveroli traveled to Rock Island to meet with the contracting officer. Diveroli told her AEY would implement more stringent packing protocols and no longer use loose-pack ammunition.

Once all the details had been corrected, the Army planned to bring the snafu to the attention of Admiral William Fallon, the four-star officer who was in charge of Central Command. Fallon would surely see that the matter needed to be remedied—and that AEY's shipments should start again immediately. There was no other way to get the necessary ammunition to Kabul: AEY was the only supplier that was in a position to quickly solve the dire shortages. Fallon would surely overrule the DCIS.

But the plan would never be acted upon. For reasons that remain unknown, the documents needed to enable AEY to commence shipping again would never reach the desk of Admiral Fallon. AEY would never ship another round of ammunition from Albania to Afghanistan. Despite "operational necessity," the Afghans would be left with "zero" ammo, creating "critical shortages."

The DCIS still wasn't satisfied. Now Mentavlos wanted to seize whatever Chinese ammo from AEY remained in Afghanistan. At his direction, the DCIS's representatives in the war zone—Special Agent Albert Wiesner and his partner—were told to make the dangerous trip from the Bagram Airfield to 22 Bunkers. Because of the elevated threat level, particularly on the Muslim Sabbath, when insurgent attacks ran rampant, the investigators traveled through a blizzard in a convoy of up-armored, unmarked Land Rovers, both wearing body armor and carrying M4 carbines; Wiesner later admitted to being terrified. When they arrived at the outdoor ammunition-storage complex, they found the place was a mess, as might be expected in a rapidly deteriorating crisis: boxes of ammo were strewn on the ground, and the "structures" used for storage were nothing more than old, rusting shipping containers. In the driving snow, Wiesner was taken to the containers holding the remainder of AEY's ammo and seized nearly five hundred rounds. Careful to establish a good chain of custody, Wiesner took photographs for use as evidence against AEY. All of the rounds were in pristine condition. They represented the last remnants of the Army's effort to effectively arm the Afghans. But that didn't matter: the rounds were "Chinese."

Michael Mentavlos had won his war.

"DCIS has a large Global War on Terrorism case," a senior DCIS agent triumphantly wrote to a senior counterterrorism official, referring to AEY. "This case is extremely high profile with the DCIS, the Department of Defense, and the State Department."

For all the glee inside the DCIS, the AEY contract was emblematic of larger failures in Afghanistan and Iraq. America was losing both wars, for myriad reasons, not least of which was a lack of focus on winning—or any workable definition of what might amount to "winning." The Army was desperate for AK-47 ammo in Afghanistan—even as it had stopped millions of serviceable "Chinese" rounds of AK-47 ammo from reaching Kabul.

For months AEY had been trapped between two distinct and contradictory US government forces. In Florida, the DCIS and federal prosecutors were pursuing a highly legalistic case with all the might they could muster. At the same time, the Army was telling Diveroli to ship ammo—no matter what. There was no way to reconcile these divergent demands, certainly not under the pressures of a war spiraling out of control.

Even though the "Chinese" AK-47 rounds from Albania were disqualified, AEY was still expected to fulfill the rest of the contract, including the delivery of millions of rounds of AK-47 ammo—which would have to be sourced from other countries. The demands placed on Efraim Diveroli increased exponentially when Task Order 005 arrived, worth $22,560,384, and including grenade launchers, OG 40 mm fragmentation warheads, as well as nearly 5 million rounds of AK-47 ammo. The loss of the Albanian connection forced Diveroli into a frantic hunt for other suppliers of surplus AK-47 ammo in Hungary, Bulgaria, and the Czech Republic—wherever rounds could be bought cheaply and quickly. But the ammo he sourced from these countries was problematic: ironically, much of it was much worse in quality than the ancient "Chinese" rounds in Albania. Time limits meant that AEY couldn't inspect the rounds or search for better-quality ammo. Because of the DCIS investigation, AEY was now shipping AK-47 rounds that weren't serviceable—while serviceable ammo sat on the tarmac in Tirana.

Worried about AEY's ability to fulfill the contract, the Army sent a letter demanding a written plan. Diveroli replied that he was hunting for new sources. With "severely depleted" stores of ammunition for the PKM machine gun—a situation that would "impact the mission"—the contracting officer instructed AEY to make this kind of ammunition the "first priority." AEY was now delinquent on the entire contract, in large measure due to the DCIS investigation.

The situation devolved during the winter as AEY was reduced to shipping a cache of Bulgarian small-caliber ammo, which hadn't been physically inspected or tested. Diveroli had purchased the ammo sight unseen, in the belief that supplying something was better than supplying nothing. In desperation, the Army was allowing AEY to improvise. Getting the proper end-user certificates for the Bulgarian ammo could take weeks, or longer, so Diveroli was told he could use the approvals he'd received for the Albanian "Chinese" ammo—technically a breach of the law but an operational necessity.

"The government realizes AEY has experienced some difficulties in the performance of this contract," the contracting officer wrote to Diveroli. "However, this does not alleviate the dire need for all ammunition under the contract and the required schedules for ALL ammunition is not to be compromised."

The message to Diveroli was clear: do whatever is necessary to get the rounds to Kabul.

The swirl of contradictory messages from the US government had left the Albanians confused as well. The Army needed exactly the kind of ammunition the Albanians had in abundance. If the Albanians couldn't sell the ammo to their American friends, perhaps they could give it away. To this end, the Albanian prime minister, Sali Berisha, and Defense Minister Fatmir Mediu flew to Baghdad. Despite a worldwide shortage of AK-47 ammo, they had more than 5 million rounds sitting in a warehouse at Tirana International Airport neatly shrink-wrapped, packaged, palletized, and ready to be shipped. Millions of rounds were also stored in caves and caches scattered all over the country.

The Albanian politicians met with General David Petraeus, the commander of American forces in Iraq, as well as the American ambassador, Ryan Crocker. These were the two most powerful American officials in Iraq. The Albanians formally proposed the donation. But Petraeus and Crocker rejected the offer. The Albanian ammo was "Chinese," it was known, and thus couldn't be received under US law. The Albanians flew home dejected.

Into this chaos stepped C. J. Chivers of the *New York Times*. As the New Year dawned, Chivers was employing the many resources of the *Times* to try to get to the bottom of the AEY story. To obtain a firsthand look at the ammunition AEY was supplying, Chivers traveled to Afghanistan, to an outpost called Nawa along the Pakistan border. There he interviewed a colonel in the Afghan army as they inspected a cardboard box of ammunition split open on a dirt floor. The rounds had been supplied by AEY.

"This is what they give us for fighting," the Afghan colonel told Chivers. "It makes us worried, because too much of it is junk."

Chivers contacted the US military's public affairs officer in Kabul to ask about problems with the ammunition AEY was supplying. To reply to Chivers, the public affairs officer sought the input of the soldier in charge of CJ-4 Shop, the location at 22 Bunkers where AEY's ammo was stored and issued. The soldier contacted was none other than Lieutenant Colonel Gutierrez—the officer who was fighting tooth and nail to get AEY's shipments started again. LTC Gutierrez was asked about any reports of shipping deficiencies related to AEY. Gutierrez could have replied that the rounds were serviceable—but he'd run out of ammo. Instead, he didn't bother replying to the press query. Later, when asked why he failed to answer, Gutierrez claimed that the request "fell through the cracks."

After months of reporting, Chivers's take on the AEY story was coming into focus. Chivers was appalled that the kids who ran AEY were apparently selling the Army junk surplus ammunition, putting Afghan soldiers at risk. Chivers believed Packouz and Diveroli were young, irresponsible, and obviously unqualified to carry out the Afghanistan contract. AEY was also possibly defrauding the US government by selling ammunition that was subject to a ban—if, indeed, the ammo was deemed to be "Chinese."

"I'm told that after AEY won the award, many people in the industry were flabbergasted, and complained to the Army," Chivers wrote to the Army's Sustainment Command in Rock Island. "Can you verify these complaints and their substance?"

"The contracting officer debriefed all unsuccessful offerors" came the reply. "There were no protests received. Industry did not complain to the contracting officer."

Chivers then asked about the quality of the ammunition AEY was supplying. The Army replied that there were "no serviceability issues."

Why had AEY been selected? Chivers asked.

The reply was as succinct as it was seemingly ridiculous: "AEY's proposal represented the best value to the government."

Chapter Twelve

GËRDEC

On January 22, 2008, Solicitation W52P1J-08-R-0044 appeared on FedBizOpps. This contract to supply ammunition to Afghanistan called for 1,480,000 rounds of 12.7x108 mm ammo for the NSV heavy machine gun, along with 370,000 tracer cartridges of the same caliber, which produced a streak of light when shot and were usually used for training. The Russian-designed NSV operated from a variety of mounts and was ideal for battles in mountainous regions like Afghanistan. An amendment to the regulations now required that the ammunition be no more than twenty years old—a clause inserted in response to AEY's shipping ancient rounds from Albania.

David Packouz, the sole operator of Dynacore Industries, was sitting in his underwear on a couch in an apartment in Miami's Little Havana when he saw the solicitation. His daughter was on a blanket on the floor with her toys, while her mother was at work in a local spa doing hair extensions. Every morning, Packouz would wake, make coffee, and then fire up his Toshiba laptop and begin scanning FedBizOpps, looking for new deals to bid on. Working harder as his money began to run short, he'd scan as many as one hundred contracts in a day, solicitations for items like tanks, mattresses, and socks for soldiers. He picked the deals he thought he had a chance of winning with the first criterion to find products he'd sourced when he was working with Diveroli, which largely meant military equipment.

In the months since he'd left AEY, Packouz had failed to win any of the contracts, but he wasn't discouraged. In that time he'd married his girlfriend, Sara, and moved out of the Flamingo into his wife's place. He was also working as a masseur once again, but mostly he was in charge of child care while his wife was the main breadwinner.

The moment Packouz saw the solicitation for millions of rounds of 12.7x108, he knew exactly whom to contact to supply and transport the ammo. Packouz figured that Diveroli would bid on the contract, too. The former partners were now rivals, but Packouz had the advantage of knowing Diveroli's tricks. Packouz e-mailed Henri Thomet in Europe to get a price quote. Thomet was more than happy to do business with Packouz, as were the other suppliers he'd dealt with while at AEY; Packouz was considered the sane, decent arms dealer at AEY; many suppliers had long ago stopped talking to Diveroli. Packouz then wrote to Yugoimport, the Serbian arms company, an arms manufacturer in Hungary, and a broker from Ukraine whom he'd met in Abu Dhabi when he'd traveled there after AEY had won the Afghan contract. The quotes Packouz received were for new-production ammo, not surplus, apart from the Ukrainian, who had access to a cache of old rounds that fell within the twenty-year age limit. The Ukrainian was the cheapest by far, as surplus ammo was much less expensive than new munitions. But Packouz was struggling with the amount he should bid using the Ukrainian quote, given Diveroli's usual 9 percent profit margin; Packouz was thinking of using 8 percent, or perhaps a lower percentage.

Packouz's proposal had to be in by February 26. He'd remained in contact with some of the people he'd worked with at AEY, including the Haitian man who was the office manager. Packouz happened to talk to him the day before he had to submit his price, and the Haitian told him that Diveroli was up to his usual antics: screaming and yelling and driving everyone at AEY crazy. The Haitian said that a bid for an Afghan ammo deal was due the next day, and Diveroli was furious that all the prices were for new rounds, not surplus.

A lightbulb went off: Packouz instantly recognized the importance of this information. The deal the Haitian was referring to had to be the same one Packouz was about to bid on: there was only one Afghan ammo deal up the next day. Packouz also knew that Diveroli had excellent contacts all over Eastern Europe. If Diveroli hadn't been able to find surplus ammo—if he was forced to bid using prices for new rounds—Packouz figured no one else had either.

"Diveroli didn't know my Ukraine source because I'd met him by myself," Packouz recalled. "That meant there was a very good chance I was the only who'd been able to source surplus cartridges."

This was very exciting news. If he was right, Packouz realized he had a lot of leeway with his bid, because the Ukrainian surplus rounds were far less expensive than new ammunition. Then there was the cost of transportation. After the debacle with Thomet's airfreight prices on the Afghan deal, Packouz no longer trusted any quotes for chartering flights. The Ukrainian wanted $660,000 for the ammo, and Packouz estimated he'd need seven flights at a cost of $130,000 each, for a total cost of $1.57 million. Normally he would have tacked on a modest return. But now he calculated that everyone else was bidding using the cost of new-production ammunition, so he averaged the prices he'd been quoted for new rounds as the basis for his bid. To be extremely conservative Packouz left out the cost of transportation as well as any profit margin. The other bids would have to be in excess of $5 million, more if the cost of air transportation was included. A bid of $4 million was sure to win. To play it safe—to not get greedy—Packouz bid $3.5 million. If accepted, his profit margin was nearly $2 million—a thought that made him giddy.

"That was the kind of money you could make on FedBizOpps if you knew what you were doing," Packouz said.

The ploy worked. Packouz was at home, his infant daughter on his lap, when he received an e-mail from the Army telling him that they were doing a pre-award audit on Dynacore; they had a list of questions they wanted answered. Despite Packouz's fear, they didn't mention

AEY, the Albanian "Chinese" ammo, or the federal fraud investigation of the Afghanistan contract. To his amazement, the procurement officers in Rock Island, Illinois, didn't make the connection—or have any system to effectively vet contractors, even ones subject to a major fraud investigation.

"I felt great," Packouz recalled. "After months of failed bids I'd landed a big one. I was going to make a lot of money, which would enable me to bid on bigger arms deals. I was proving that I really didn't need Diveroli to win contracts. It was incredible to know that I could do it by myself—that I could beat Diveroli at his own game. I'd even set up a deal to finance the contract with Wells Fargo, using the same guy who'd done Diveroli's deals. He was excited to do business with me. It was a serious, complicated arms deal, and I'd put all the pieces together. I was ready to go to Kiev to inspect the stuff. I was thrilled."

While Packouz was riding high, Alex Podrizki wasn't so fortunate. After he returned to Miami, he'd enrolled in college to study Arabic, but his legal bills left him broke and he wasn't able to find part-time work. In the evenings, Podrizki often met with Packouz at his place to drink beer and discuss their legal situation.

The pair were paranoid about the government's having them under surveillance. They wished the government would see that the repacking wasn't all about the money—it was also about doing what was necessary to complete the contract. The Army had accepted the rounds without a single complaint about their quality.

"The whole case against us didn't make sense, but that didn't seem to matter," Podrizki recalled. "David and I agreed that if we were going to be sent to prison for more than two years, then escaping the country would be a real option. David apologized to me, but I told him I'd made my own decisions and only had myself to blame. It seemed to me that our biggest mistake was not being politically savvy. I'd tried to tell Diveroli to build political connections to protect us, but he didn't listen."

The dudes didn't know it, but the AEY affair contained yet another layer of absurdity and deception—only this variety of venality would prove lethal. As soon as Alex Podrizki had discovered MEICO was selling them "Chinese" rounds, in April of 2007, he'd asked them to supply Albanian ammunition instead. He'd been told that it was impossible to fulfill the contract using Albanian ammo because it was scattered all over the country and thus too hard to truck to Tirana. Podrizki had strongly suspected he was being lied to—and he was correct. Ylli Pinari of MEICO didn't want to supply Albanian-made ammunition to AEY for a simple reason: he was selling it to someone else.

For the past year, an American company called Southern Ammunition had been demilitarizing millions of Albanian-manufactured AK-47 rounds at a small military base on the edge of the village of Gërdec. The whole "Chinese" Albanian supply fiasco could have been avoided if Pinari had allowed AEY to ship these rounds to Afghanistan. But the Albanians didn't want to sell those rounds to AEY because they had brass casings, not the steel jackets like most of the "Chinese" cartridges. The brass was worth half a million dollars to the Albanians if they sold the rounds to Southern Ammunition for scrap metal—money they wouldn't make if the cartridges were sold to AEY.

Greed was the dark truth at the heart of the arms-dealing world. Efraim Diveroli's greed had led to Kosta Trebicka's blood vendetta, just as Henri Thomet's greed had helped lead AEY into buying "Chinese" ammo in the first place. Now the greed of the Albanians, killing AEY's deal for 100 million rounds to make an extra five hundred grand, was about to cause new and disturbing consequences.

By the end of 2007, Southern Ammunition's demilitarization operation was at an end, as the supplies of brass-cased AK-47 ammo had run out. But Defense Minister Mediu had plans for Albania's remaining stockpiles. Trying to squeeze every dollar from the nation's stockpile, the Albanians decided to take apart large-caliber ammunition to salvage the brass casings.

Safely demilitarizing large-caliber ammunition was highly skilled work—and very different from taking apart AK-47 ammo. Sophisticated equipment was required to disarm explosives. Strict protocols needed to be followed, overseen by experts. A complex web of treaties and international laws and practices had to be adhered to.

The original plan—the official plan—had been for the United States and other NATO countries to assist the Albanians in ridding the country of its stockpile of a hundred tons of large-caliber ammunition. But now the Albanians were going to do it on their own. There was a catch: the operation was in violation of Albanian law and had to be kept secret.

In January of 2008, Mediu issued secret orders commanding that all of Albania's large-caliber, brass-cased rounds be transported to a military base in the village of Gërdec. Trucks were soon rumbling toward the village carrying rocket warheads and artillery shells and sea mines. Like the small-caliber ammo AEY had bought, the ammunition represented a serious danger to civilians in Albania. In 1997, when it emerged that the financial system in Albania was a vast Ponzi scheme and civilians lost more than $1 billion in investments in a matter of days, a rebellion resulted in the looting of the country's stockpiles of weapons; 656,000 weapons of various types had been stolen, along with 1.5 billion rounds of ammunition and 3.5 million grenades. More than two thousand people died in the ensuing chaos.

Getting rid of Albania's ammunition was a strategic necessity—but not in the manner planned by politicians aiming to personally profit from the operation. Instead of following standard precautions, the demilitarization project was done with heedless abandon; workers had no training and there was none of the proper equipment for the volatile munitions. Then there was the pace of the work: the Albanians were racing against the clock to salvage as much brass as possible before the country joined NATO and new, strict rules would govern the military.

The village of Gërdec was the perfect place to secretly take apart ammunition for salvage. Only ten miles from Tirana, the obscure settlement was tucked away in the countryside, both centrally located and far from prying eyes. During the winter of 2008, every morning scores of locals gathered at the gate of the base and clamored to be chosen to work by the overseer. Pay was $20 per day, decent money in Albania. Women and teenage girls were mostly chosen, as their hands were small and thus better for the finicky work.

Saturday, March 15, 2008, was a beautiful spring day in Albania, the blue sky flecked with clouds and the air warmed by a gentle Adriatic breeze. But at noon there was a terrifying sight—a fire racing across the ground on the military base. The fire was small, maybe six inches high, but it was moving like lightning toward the large shed where thousands of tons of large-caliber ammo were stored. Dozens of sacks of gunpowder were also in the shed, making it literally a powder keg.

Hundreds of peasant workers began to flee as smoke rose and the *pop-pop* of smaller rounds going off drowned their screams. No one knew what started the fire—a spark, a cigarette, sabotage. Spontaneous combustion was a real possibility, given the degraded and unstable nature of the ammunition.

Then the main shed exploded, sending debris flying like a scene in a Hollywood action movie. The explosion injured many and buried others alive under the rubble. Those who were unhurt took refuge in the hills, while a few braver souls returned to the base and tried to help the wounded and trapped. Single rounds of ammo continued to fire randomly, *pow-pow*. The worst was over, it seemed.

Fifteen minutes passed.

The second explosion was an almighty blast with murderous, apocalyptic force. Missile warheads, large-caliber artillery shells, tons and tons of gunpowder—the mother lode went off all at once. The concussive cataclysm sent dozens of people flying hundreds of feet into the air. A bloodred fireball shot skyward, followed by a Hiroshima-like black mushroom cloud. It was one of the largest non-nuclear explosions since World War Two. The sound could be heard a hundred miles away, and windows shattered in the capital city.

Twenty-six people died in Gërdec. Many were women and children. Like eight-year-old Erison Durdaj, who'd been sent to take his mother lunch and who was standing at the gate when the second explosion hurtled him through the air. Three hundred more were injured. More than four thousand homes and businesses were damaged or destroyed.

The catastrophe in Gërdec caused an outrage in Albania. Defense Minister Fatmir Mediu was forced to resign. Ylli Pinari and Mihail Delijorgji of Alb-Demil were cast as the villains. An independent prosecutor drafted a five-hundred-page indictment. It seemed as if the truth would emerge. But the investigation soon faltered. The world media hardly bothered to cover the story—the 2008 primary battle between Barack Obama and Hillary Clinton was crowding the headlines, along with the insurgencies in Afghanistan and Iraq. The explosion soon vanished from world news.

But the explosion in Gërdec and AEY were directly linked. The same Albanian politicians and officials were involved. It seemed likely that the *New York Times* would make the connection between AEY and Gërdec—as well as possibly reveal the knowledge of officials in the US Embassy in Tirana and the Pentagon.

Bracing for the coming *Times* article, in March of 2008 the US military claimed it had conducted a full-scale investigation of AEY's shipments to Afghanistan. The Army's own investigation—as opposed to the DCIS investigation of Michael Mentavlos—discovered no complaints about the quality of AEY's rounds, either officially or informally. But the Army wanted to be able to prove it had done its due diligence and issued forty-four shipping-deficiency reports on AEY. All of the reports were written at the same time, in March, months after the ammunition had been accepted and issued by the Army. None of the supposed deficiencies related to the quality of the rounds AEY had supplied. The reports were entirely revisionist: "Cardboard boxes are falling apart and cannot survive transportation," the newly minted documents all said. "Reports from the field state that amounts do not reflect what was supposed to be in each box. Therefore it is impossible to know the actual amounts received without counting millions of rounds in each shipment."

The Army then announced that it was reforming its wartime-purchasing process to combat fraud. In mid-March, an Associated Press article appeared, potentially stealing some of the thunder from C. J. Chivers's pending scoop. "The Army is ordering a major overhaul of the way it buys supplies for troops in combat zones," the AP piece said.

As a final piece of reporting, Chivers asked the Army to fully explain the vetting process used in awarding the contract to AEY. The reply said that contracting officers had checked the Army's "excluded parties list" and found that AEY's name didn't appear there. Days before his article was to appear, Chivers wrote to the Army to say he was particularly interested in Henri Thomet, as he'd been told that Thomet's name didn't appear on lists of brokers barred from doing business with the Pentagon.

"Are there any other processes to make sure that entities suspected of arms smuggling do not become brokers or subcontractors in American government business?" Chivers asked. "What assurances does the Department of Defense have that its contracts are not bringing business to international arms smugglers?"

Chivers had reached the heart of the matter. The answer was simple: the Pentagon did nothing to vet subcontractors. But that wasn't what the Army said.

"After looking at your query, we've determined that your questions need to be answered by the Department of Defense and the State Department" was the reply to Chivers's e-mail.

The internal response from the Army instructed the officials responsible for replying to Chivers's questions to end the paper trail: "Stop any work you were doing on them."

A high-level meeting was convened to discuss what would happen if AEY's entire contract was canceled before the *Times* story ran—not just the Albanian "Chinese" AK-47 rounds but all of the other kinds of ammunition that was being legitimately delivered. Was there enough evidence to terminate the whole contract for default? Had AEY been given the opportunity to correct problems? How long would it take to get another contractor up and running to meet the most urgent demands?

On March 18, AEY was notified that a portion of small-caliber ammo the company had shipped to Afghanistan had been found to be "unacceptable." "The ammunition is not in serviceable condition," the letter said. "Ammunition is corroded, rusted, and coated with oily material. This ammunition is not useable and poses a danger to those who have to work around it."

A photograph was attached. The rounds weren't the "Chinese" ammo shipped from Albania but the Bulgarian ammo Diveroli had recently purchased sight unseen in an attempt to get rounds to Kabul, and it was indeed in bad condition. The Army demanded AEY take immediate corrective action.

Diveroli panicked. The ammo was very evidently substandard—or "shit," according to AEY's internal communications. A plan was hatched to get the Bulgarians to send people to Kabul on the next flight to inspect every box, to determine what was good and what needed to be destroyed. AEY's memorandum ended, "This is an ABSOLUTE EMERGENCY."

But time was up. Three days later, AEY received another letter from the Army, declaring that the company had been suspended from any further contracting with the federal government. The seven-page letter had sixteen attachments, detailing how Diveroli had signed false Certificates of Conformance regarding the "Chinese" AK-47 ammo coming from Albania. The certificates required Diveroli to state "Manufacturer (point of origin)" for each shipment. Diveroli had entered MEICO's address in Albania on dozens of certificates. The disclosure was arguably true, in an artful way, but designed to deceive the Army.

On March 27, 2008, the day before the *Times* story was to appear, the Pentagon issued a press release saying it had suspended AEY: the company had lost its Afghan contract because it had supplied "Chinese" ammo and failed to follow "best commercial practices" in packaging the ammunition. No issues were related to the quality of the ammunition, the release said. Nor would the cancellation of the contract deny the Afghans sufficient ammo. "There's no shortage of ammunition already in Afghanistan," the Army's spokesperson said, despite the fact that this statement was patently untrue, according to the repeated pleas of Army officers in Afghanistan. "This will have no impact."

Chapter Thirteen

THE FRAME

"Supplier Under Scrutiny on Arms for Afghans," read the headline on the front page of the *New York Times* on March 28, 2008. A large photograph of a jumble of small-caliber ammunition showed rusty, discolored, substandard rounds. The caption said that AEY had supplied the ammunition, which was true, but the image was misleading. The substance of the story was about the millions of rounds of ancient "Chinese" Albanian ammo AEY had sold to the Army. But the photograph wasn't of the rounds from Albania—it was from the small amount of Bulgarian ammo AEY had shipped to Afghanistan, ammo the Army had rejected. The Bulgarian rounds amounted to thirty thousand of the tens of millions of rounds AEY transported to Kabul, less than .0001% of the total. But that didn't matter: the strong inference was that the faulty Bulgarian ammo was a representative example of the quality of rounds AEY had sold to the Army.

Looking at the *Times* article, David Packouz's heart sank. Accompanying the story were photographs of him and Efraim Diveroli. They weren't ordinary pictures, though: the newspaper had published mug shots of the duo, taken more than a year earlier on the night they got into a fight with the valet at the Flamingo. The *Times* rarely published mug shots, generally reserving such prejudicial images for stories about convicted criminals or fugitives. Packouz and Diveroli had been convicted of nothing; they hadn't even been indicted. But the pair stared balefully through bloodshot eyes in the pages of the *Times*.

"Diveroli and I looked like hardened criminals in the mug shots," Packouz recalled. "I knew that was a very bad sign."

In the first few sentences, Chivers described how dependent the Afghans were on the US military for logistics and munitions in the war against the Taliban and Al Qaeda. "But to arm the Afghan forces that it hopes will lead this fight, the American military has relied since early last year on a fledgling company led by a 22-year-old man whose vice president was a licensed masseur," the *Times* reported. "With the award of a federal contract worth as much as $300 million, the company, AEY Inc., which operates out of an unmarked office in Miami Beach, became the main supplier of munitions to Afghanistan's army and police forces."

Packouz felt a growing sense of dread. Chivers quoted military and government officials questioning how "Diveroli and a small group of men principally in their twenties and without extensive military or procurement experiences landed so much vital government work." According to Chivers, AEY was an "immature company" allowed to "enter the murky world of international arms dealing on the Pentagon's behalf—and do so with minimal vetting and through a vaguely written contract with few restrictions." The *Times* said that the problems could have been avoided "if the Army had written the contracts and examined bidders more carefully."

Chivers noted that much of the ammunition AEY had shipped from Albania to Afghanistan was forty years old and had been manufactured in China, making its procurement a possible violation of American law. To illustrate the poor quality of the ammunition AEY had supplied, Chivers quoted an Afghan colonel saying much of it was "junk." Chivers also quoted a munitions expert saying Albania's stockpile was "substandard for sure," along with an Army press spokesperson in Kabul who said that "while there were no reports of ammunition misfiring, some of it was in such poor condition the military decided not to issue it."

Chivers contrasted the Army's contract and AEY's performance with NATO and Russian standards for handling munitions, which required methodical ballistics testing and measures to protect ammunition against aging, humidity, and environmental conditions. "But when the Army wrote its Afghan contract, it did not enforce either NATO or Russian standards," Chivers wrote—as if the lax requirements had been a matter of negligence by the Army, not a deliberate policy.

Chivers noted the importance of the State Department's watch list, "used to prevent American dealers from engaging suspicious traders in their business, in part to prevent legal arms companies from enriching or legitimizing black-market networks." Chivers's reporting questioned whether the Pentagon was adequately vetting business done in its name.

"Put very simply, many of the people involved in smuggling arms to Africa are also exactly the same as those involved in Pentagon-supported deals, like AEY's shipments to Afghanistan and Iraq," Chivers quoted the arms researcher Hugh Griffiths as saying.

The explosion in Gërdec was mentioned, but only as an illustration of how shoddy and dangerous Albania's stockpile was. Instead, the story focused much of its attention on the "personal problems" of Efraim Diveroli. Chivers detailed Diveroli's record of misdeeds, from the fight with the valet at the Flamingo to the argument with his girlfriend that resulted in a call to the police; Diveroli had "stalked her and left threatening messages," the *Times* reported. Chivers recounted how Diveroli had once supposedly shoved another girlfriend to the ground and turned up at her house drunk and banging on windows and doors—"allegations that were never ruled on." The cumulative effect was a portrait of Diveroli as a violent, out-of-control fraudster and con man, with Packouz as his comically unqualified partner.

"There were so many factual errors in the article," Packouz maintained. "Like the picture of Bulgarian ammo on the front page. The *Times* took the absolute-worst rounds, using ammo that had been rejected, as if it was typical of what we shipped. It seemed to me like Chivers was trying to discredit us. How could the government award such a huge contract to a kid and his masseur vice president?"

In his book *The Gun*, Chivers wrote eloquently about the durability and reliability of the Kalashnikov, noting that ancient weapons from the 1950s and 1960s could still be found in use in the mountains of Afghanistan. "The wooden stocks of these aged AK-47s showed dents and dings," Chivers wrote of the ancient Afghan guns. "Otherwise most of these rifles appeared to be in excellent order, ready to fire for decades more."

But Chivers didn't apply the same standards to the "Chinese" AK-47 rounds. The ammo was old and it wasn't pristine, like the new rounds issued to NATO soldiers. But it worked—millions upon millions of rounds had been accepted by the Army and fired by Afghan soldiers in combat, with no documented reports of misfirings or issues related to quality.

"Chivers made no mention of the fact that the vast majority of the ammo we supplied was fully functional, including the 'Chinese' rounds from Albania," Packouz said. "The *Times* was right. The surplus ammo was old, and we hadn't done rigorous ballistics testing, but the contract didn't require those things. Chivers focused on making the government look incompetent, instead of realizing that the government had made a calculated decision to get the cheapest possible ammo to the Afghans as quickly as possible.

"In truth, we were being paid to do what the Army couldn't do for itself. It was impossible to send American soldiers to Tirana to buy the AK-47 ammo. They'd get caught up in the corruption for sure—just like we did. But Chivers never wrote about that or put the story in the larger context of what the Army was doing standing up armies in Afghanistan and Iraq—how they were using private companies like ours to be gunrunners on their behalf."

The reaction to the *Times* story was swift. The time difference between New York and Tirana was six hours. The AEY article was posted at midnight, 6:00 a.m. in Tirana. At precisely 6:06, the regional security officer in the US Embassy in Albania circulated an e-mail to the power players in the embassy. The officer had speed-read the *Times* piece and had great news to report:

"No mention of embassy involvement—thank God!"

The dudes were no longer the only dudes. In the days that followed, it would emerge that the true dudes were now prosecutors and investigators and diplomats and military officers taking deep, heady hits on the bong of power. The Justice Department was now hell-bent on bringing indictments against as many of those involved as possible. The Pentagon was determined to defend its honor and avoid looking foolish, even as it dissembled and hid the more damning truth that AEY wasn't an aberration but a good representation of how the procurement system operated. The Army also hid the fact that there were serious ammunition shortages because of the prosecution. Likewise, the State Department was terrified that its long-standing knowledge of what AEY was doing in Albania would emerge, along with evidence of possible American complicity in Gërdec. In effect, the *Times* story's most proximate consequence was a series of byzantine overlapping and self-contradicting attempts inside the government to shift blame, bury evidence, and feign innocence—like teenagers afraid their stash of weed would be found.

Against the limitless resources of the US government, Packouz, Diveroli, Podrizki, and Ralph Merrill didn't stand a chance. AEY's woes had always been as much political as legal. If Diveroli had invested in a high-end Washington lobbyist or attorney, the company would likely have found a solution to its Albanian problem long ago. Now the situation was overtly political, in myriad ways, including as a means for the Democratic majority in the House of Representatives to attack the Bush administration. Thus, on the day the *Times* article appeared the chairman of the House Oversight Committee, Henry

Waxman, announced that he would be conducting an extensive investigation into the AEY affair.

The Army likewise mounted a political campaign. The *Times* had claimed that the quality of the AK-47 rounds was poor. This key assertion was belied by the facts, the Army said in a press release:

"Safety and performance are the Army's top priorities when it comes to ammunition, for both our allies and our own armed forces. First, is the ammunition safe? Second, does the ammunition work? To date, we have not received any reports, from our units in the field or our customers, the Afghan army, concerning the safety or performance of the ammunition provided through this contract."

On the same day, federal investigators working on the AEY case received a letter from the National Ground Intelligence Center (NGIC) in Virginia regarding the quality of AEY's Albanian "Chinese" ammunition. Investigators had sent the agency one hundred rounds of the AK-47 ammo to assess for quality.

The NGIC report stated that age wasn't the crucial question when it came to quality. "The NGIC has encountered ammunition from combat theaters that proved effective (in that it fired from a weapon) despite manufacturing dates as far back as the 1950's." The report said that packing was essential to the longevity of ammunition. "The rounds sent to NGIC displayed every indication of suitable storage (casings were clean, showed no signs of corrosion)."

The NGIC noted that the Albanian ammo had been stored in the best possible manner—triple-layered, first in waxed-paper wrappings, then in hermetically sealed metal tins, and finally inside crates. The NGIC wasn't asked to test-fire the ammunition—normally a routine part of providing an opinion about the quality of munitions—but testing the ammo would risk its being found to be perfectly functional.

Federal law enforcement and the Army were directly contradicting each other. Caught in the middle, Diveroli tried to resist the onslaught. Over his head, now to the point of drowning, Diveroli set out to counter the central thesis of the *Times* article when he hired a company called

HP White Laboratory Inc. to test-fire the ammo AEY had purchased in Albania. The results were conclusive: the "Chinese" ammunition AEY had been selling to the Army was serviceable without qualification.

But what was the view of the US Army in Kabul and, through it, the Afghan army and police? Chivers had quoted one Afghan soldier, but nothing indicated that the reporter had questioned the people who might know best—senior officials in the Combined Security Transition Command.

After the *Times* story appeared, the Army asked Colonel Howard Davis, director of logistics in Afghanistan, to report on the "status" of the ammo AEY had delivered.

"The ammunition from AEY has been of good quality," Colonel Davis replied. "When queried, the senior mentors in each Afghanistan region reported that they have not received any complaints from the ANA or ANP concerning the quality of the ammunition received."

Sitting in his office in Bountiful, Utah, the Mormon businessman Ralph Merrill read the *Times* article in dismay. Like the three dudes in Miami Beach, Merrill feared that he would be indicted, particularly after reading the piece. The story was written in a highly prejudicial manner, Merrill believed.

"The fact of the matter was that the Army kept ordering, using, reordering, and paying for the ammo for months after the raid on AEY's offices and it found the e-mails about Chinese rounds," Merrill recalled. "The Department of Defense was happy and satisfied with the matériel, and they were very reluctant to terminate the contract—an act which cost the government millions of dollars and caused serious damage on the battlefield in Afghanistan."

But the *New York Times* had framed the story—and in the middle of that frame were David Packouz and Efraim Diveroli, staring grimly out from their mug shots.

In the days after their faces appeared in the *Times*, the arms-dealing dudes became celebrities, in a bad way. Poster boys for the serial incompetence of the wars in Iraq and Afghanistan, they seemed to personify the entire war effort in Afghanistan.

Despite the story, the Afghans still needed a vast stockpile of ammunition: hundreds of millions of AK-47 rounds, half a million sniper cartridges, 3 million heavy-machine-gun bullets, along with thousands of mortar, howitzer, and rocket-launcher rounds. AEY was the only feasible supplier, and canceling the contract had caused severe shortages in Afghanistan. But none of that mattered in the end.

On March 29, 2008, a new request for proposals was posted on FedBizOpps.

The bidding process began anew.

/////

On the day the *Times* story appeared, Kosta Trebicka nervously checked the newspaper's website every five minutes on his computer in Tirana. Trebicka knew that he had an enormous amount riding on what Chivers wrote—and not just legal jeopardy. Trebicka had taken on the Albanian prime minister and the defense minister—two of the most powerful figures in a country infamous for its lawlessness and violence. Trebicka hoped that the publicity from the *Times* would provide him some form of protection in Albania. Perhaps the revelation of corruption inside the Albanian government would have consequences, Trebicka hoped, and officials would be held accountable.

In the weeks that followed, it seemed to Trebicka that the *Times* story had no impact in Albania. The only person who seemed to care about the article was Michael Mentavlos of the DCIS, who was outraged that Trebicka had disobeyed his direct order and talked to the *Times*. Soon after the article ran, Mentavlos flew to Tirana and called Trebicka, screaming and demanding a meeting. Afraid, Trebicka lied and said he was out of the country. Three days later, he gave over to the seemingly inevitable and met with Mentavlos. The investigator told Trebicka he had to travel to Florida to testify in the AEY investigation. To Trebicka, it appeared as if Mentavlos would do anything to convict Diveroli.

"Mentavlos said that when I am in front of the lawyers I have to say that Efraim Diveroli and Alex Podrizki did know that they were illegally selling Chinese ammo to Afghanistan," Trebicka later recalled. "I answered that I cannot do it, since they never had expressed themselves literally in my presence something like this."

Days later, Trebicka received an e-mail from congressional investigators. He called Mentavlos and told him about the House Oversight Committee's interest in talking to him.

"Mentavlos told me that in three days I have to be in Florida and not to stop in Washington, DC, or give any documents to the committee," Trebicka recalled. "Again, I was surprised by him."

Trebicka flew to the United States—but at his own expense, to avoid any connection to the DCIS. He first went to Washington to meet with congressional investigators and tell them what he knew about AEY and Gërdec and Mentavlos. Trebicka then flew to Miami, where he was given an odd reception. As he spoke to the prosecutors in Florida, describing the corruption in Albania, it began to dawn on him that their aggressive attitude signaled that he might be a target for indictment. The notion was bizarre to Trebicka: he was a whistle-blower, not a criminal.

But Trebicka was saying things law enforcement plainly didn't want to hear. Like Trebicka's version of his meeting with the American diplomat Robert Newsome in Tirana, in May of 2007, and how Trebicka said he'd told Newsome AEY was shipping "Chinese" ammunition to Afghanistan before a single round had arrived in Kabul.

"Our special witness Kosta Trebicka is up to new tricks," an embassy official in Tirana wrote to his colleagues. "He told Special Agent Mentavlos that he is going to testify in front of Congress that he told Robert Newsome about the Chinese ammunition in 2007 and that Rob told him it was legal and to go ahead with the contract."

"For the record, this is untrue," another American official in Tirana wrote to officials inside the embassy. "Trebicka may say it, but it is untrue. Flatly."

Newsome wrote, "To be very clear—I never told Trebicka any such thing."

Trebicka represented a threat to the entire case against the dudes because the truth was unwieldy and contradictory, and contained elements that might point away from a jury's reaching a guilty verdict—or, as was the case in 98 percent of federal prosecutions, guilty pleas that make a trial unnecessary. Prosecutors in Florida then told Trebicka that he was required to provide sworn testimony in front of the grand jury in the AEY case. Trebicka began to fear that he was being lured into a perjury trap and that it would be his word against the word of American government officials. It seemed to the bewildered Albanian that the strange and ruthless prosecutors would do whatever they needed to do to win—even put him in prison.

Unable to stand the pressure, Trebicka finally decided to flee the United States. He didn't tell anyone he was leaving the country—he simply boarded a plane for France. He stayed in Paris for a few days, lying low. The authorities in Miami tried to force Trebicka's hand. Assistant US Attorney Eloisa Fernandez e-mailed Trebicka to demand that he confirm his travel plans to return to Miami so she could set a date for his testimony before the grand jury. Mentavlos was copied on the e-mail.

"From now on we have to communicate through my lawyer," Trebicka replied. He would no longer voluntarily testify, as he was concerned for his own safety, legally and physically.

Returning to Albania, Trebicka wrote an e-mail to congressional investigators. The House was supposedly looking into the entire AEY affair—how the Army acquired weapons for Afghanistan, how the dudes from Miami Beach had won the contract, how illegal "Chinese" ammo had been shipped from Albania. But Trebicka suggested a new line of inquiry—the abuse of power by American investigators: "Now I think is time to tell the truth to everybody of how the investigator for the Department of Defense, Mr. Michael Mentavlos, tried (according to my personal opinion) to obstruct the justice."

Trebicka described his encounters with Mentavlos, beginning in October, when the Albanian had finally learned from the investigator that selling "Chinese" ammunition was illegal. Trebicka told how Mentavlos had instructed him not to talk to any journalists, most especially the *Times*. Trebicka said that Mentavlos had also told him not to talk to any lawyers—including lawyers in Albania. "I was surprised," Trebicka wrote. "I asked him why? He answered that it would harm a very serious investigation he had worked on for three years. I tried to believe, but it was a vague situation."

Then there was the matter of Gërdec. The lethal explosion was tied to the same politicians who'd profited from AEY's contract, Trebicka said. In his letter to congressional investigators, Trebicka asked why Mentavlos had done nothing to investigate Gërdec, after he'd received documents from Trebicka linking the Albanians involved in the AEY case to the disaster? Trebicka was one of the few people who could tie Defense Minister Mediu, Ylli Pinari of MEICO, and Mihail Delijorgji to both the AEY deal and the explosion in Gërdec.

Which was more important to the American government, Trebicka wanted to know, "nailing Diveroli, or stopping a tragedy?"

But Trebicka's letter had no impact—not in Albania and not in Washington. The congressional oversight committee issued a report condemning AEY for supplying faulty munitions, without mentioning critical ammunition shortages in Afghanistan, the explosion in Gërdec, or potential American complicity in corruption in Albania. As far as Trebicka could see, all that mattered to the prosecutors and investigators was putting Efraim Diveroli behind bars.

By the summer of 2008, Kosta Trebicka just wanted the whole affair to go away. He still had his various successful businesses and his wife and his children. But there were threats—phone calls in the night, hard looks on the streets of Tirana, whispers of warning. Trebicka took precautions, like changing his cell phone number regularly and using aliases when he stayed in hotels in Albania. He confided to family and friends that he was scared.

Trebicka was right to worry—the truths he had revealed did indeed threaten many powerful interests. On September 12, 2008, Kosta Trebicka's body was found in a field along a rural road near the village of Korcë. There appeared to have been a car accident—but it had occurred in the middle of nowhere, on a flat stretch of road with no other vehicles involved. Somehow, for no apparent reason, Trebicka's Jeep had suddenly flipped over, and his body had been catapulted through the air, landing an improbable fifty yards from the vehicle.

Casting more doubt on the situation, one of the first people to arrive on the scene was a former bodyguard for the prime minister. The authorities claimed that Trebicka had been on a hunting trip. A rifle and a dead partridge lay on the ground next to his body. But friends said that Trebicka never went hunting alone, and that the area where his body was found wasn't a good place to hunt.

Days after Trebicka's death, an American state trooper from Virginia, Kevin Teeter, was dispatched to Tirana to inspect the location of the incident. Torrential rain had erased tire tracks, so the investigator had to rely on evidence collected by the Albanian police. Inspecting photographs, sketches, and the damaged vehicle, Teeter concluded that Trebicka had indeed been killed in an accident. "The driver made an abrupt turn left, which caused the vehicle's weight to sharply shift to the right," he wrote in his report. "The vehicle overturned onto its right side shattering the passenger side door glass and ejecting the driver onto the ground through the open roof area."

The investigation Teeter undertook was limited. The investigator apparently didn't inspect the autopsy report, if one was conducted; as far as Teeter knew, Trebicka could have had a bullet in the back of his head. Still, the report had the stamp of the Virginia State Police on its cover, providing the imprimatur of American authority, a powerful symbol in Albania that effectively closed Trebicka's case forever.

"If it was an accident," said an Albanian activist who'd worked with Trebicka on his anticorruption campaign, "then it was a very strange kind."

Alex Podrizki agreed. When he was asked by prosecutors what he thought had happened, he said he didn't know—and no one would likely ever know, because of Albanian corruption. But he said that he was virtually certain it wasn't an accident.

"The prosecutors weren't happy with my answer," Podrizki said. "But Kosta's death was too convenient for too many people—Albanian and American. He had made a lot of enemies."

/////

Despite assurances from Special Agent Mentavlos, after the *New York Times* story ran both David Packouz and Alex Podrizki were indicted, along with Efraim Diveroli and Ralph Merrill. There were three investigators working the case before the story ran, Packouz was told, but a dozen more were assigned afterward. Despite the *Times* story, federal prosecutors in Florida never presented any evidence that the ammunition supplied by AEY was faulty or failed to meet the standards described in the contract. The simple reason was that the ammo was of good quality.

But that didn't stop the authorities from issuing press releases that wrongly claimed the contrary.

"When these contractors intentionally cut corners to line their own pockets, they risk the safety and lives of our men and women in uniform," US Attorney for the Southern District of Florida Alexander Acosta said. "Such callousness and disregard for the lives of our soldiers and allies will not be tolerated and will be vigorously prosecuted."

"In this day, when our soldiers and our coalition partners are fighting to keep us safe, it is reprehensible that greed and disregard for human safety have resulted in such dangerous fraud," the director of the DCIS said.

In fact, the opposite was true. The greatest peril to Afghanistan security forces wasn't AEY, as the government claimed. It was the US government itself.

The Pentagon had set out to circumvent domestic and international law by creating its own protocols to acquire weapons, to speed getting arms to Afghanistan—and then the Pentagon's own law-enforcement agency had thwarted that effort. No one responsible for the fiasco would be held accountable—apart from the fall guys.

The AEY case vividly illustrated the kaleidoscope-like nature of the disaster of the war effort in Afghanistan. Major Ronald Walck, the Army's logistics person who'd received AEY's ammo at the airport in Kabul, seemed to recognize this. In the aftermath of the AEY fiasco, he left Afghanistan and returned to school to write a master's thesis. His subject was failure. The epigraph was taken from Dietrich Dörner's classic book *The Logic of Failure*: "Failure does not strike like a bolt from the blue; it develops gradually according to its own logic. When we watch individuals attempt to solve problems, we will see that complicated situations seem to elicit habits of thought that set failure in motion from the beginning."

So the saga of AEY ended.

So the war in Afghanistan was lost—not in any great battle but in the quiet desperation of three dudes and a doomed cause.

EPILOGUE

At the time of writing, the Army's weapons-procurement process remains unchanged. "Notwithstanding any other provision of law," the statute begins, effectively exempting the Pentagon from all laws, foreign and domestic. There is no requirement for the Army to check watch lists designed to prevent the US government from dealing with brokers suspected of being illegal gunrunners. The United States continues to exploit this legal black hole, supplying arms to allies—however temporary or dubious in nature—with virtually no oversight or legal constraint.

In August of 2014, news reports appeared saying that the Albanian government had transferred 22 million rounds of surplus AK-47 ammunition to assist Kurdish forces in Iraq. Inevitably, the shipments were mostly—if not entirely—decades-old Chinese-manufactured ammunition. The Albanians were also giving the Kurdish Peshmerga 10,000 Kalashnikov guns, 15,000 hand grenades, and 32,000 artillery shells of different calibers—likely all surplus Chinese munitions, too. Subsequent reports revealed that at least one C-17 US Air Force transport plane, used by American forces to transfer arms, was seen leaving Tirana's airport—suggesting that the United States was providing the necessary logistical support. With the Chinese embargo still in place, the shipments would technically be in contravention of American law, but that went unreported. The Secretary of Defense was quoted thanking the Albanians for coming to the aid of the Kurds with "urgently needed arms and equipment." No mention was made of their place of manufacture.

In the summer of 2014, the office of the Special Inspector General for Afghanistan Reconstruction issued a report on the nearly 750,000 weapons shipped to Afghanistan since 2004. This included 465,000 small arms, like AK-47s, pistols, and machine guns. The arms had been accompanied by a veritable mountain of ammunition—a significant portion provided by AEY. The report found that nearly half of the weapons couldn't be accounted for by the US military, and the situation was "far more severe" once the arms were transferred to the Afghan military. The possibilities for fraud and theft were mind-bending, as was the likelihood that the weapons wound up in the hands of the Taliban, or fighters in other conflicts throughout the region—proliferation that went uninvestigated and unprosecuted, the implications of which will be understood only in the decades to come.

According to independent arms researchers, at the time of this writing Henri Thomet was based in the mountains of Montenegro, where he enjoyed political protection at the highest levels and continued to deal in weapons.

Faced with the threat of long prison terms if they went to trial, Efraim Diveroli, Alex Podrizki, and David Packouz all pleaded guilty to seventy counts of fraud and one count of conspiracy. The Utah businessman Ralph Merrill refused to plead guilty to a crime he believed he hadn't committed. One of the first issues stipulated by the government prior to the trial was that it would not allege AEY's rounds were of poor quality. As Merrill and his legal team readied for trial, the US Attorney's Office in Miami deluged them with more than a million documents—everything from take-out food menus to irrelevant printouts. Ruthless prosecutors commonly used this tactic: bury a defendant in paper so that his or her lawyers spend endless time going through irrelevant material. Merrill's lawyers did the hard work of sorting through the evidence and found a useful document—or at least part of a document. A memorandum from an American officer sta-tioned in Albania described the machinations in Tirana involving AEY. The officer described how embassy officials deliberately misled con-gressional investigators. The memorandum detailed how the officer and others had known about the AEY contract and "Chinese" ammo for months before the contract was canceled. He also detailed how he'd suspected American officials were taking bribes from Albanians to look the other way while the country's stockpile of munitions was looted.

The document was potentially devastating to the prosecution. It pointed to direct knowledge inside the US government of what AEY had done long before the contract had been terminated. If admitted as evidence, it offered a variety of promising defenses to Merrill. But Merrill wouldn't receive this measure of justice. The case was as-signed to Judge Joan Lenard, a former prosecutor. Lenard ruled that the only issue that mattered in Merrill's case was his specific knowl-edge regarding the "Chinese" ammo. Did Merrill know the ammo was "Chinese," and that it was illegal to sell it to the Pentagon under American law? Everything else was irrelevant, she held. Merrill wouldn't be permitted to present any evidence regarding embassy knowledge that the ammo was "Chinese." Nor could he give the jury a sense of the many elements in the case that might raise reasonable doubt, based on the government's actions, like how American offi-cials in Albania knew, or should have known, that AEY was inevitably buying "Chinese" ammo from MEICO. Or how many American offi-cials had seen the repacking at the airport in Tirana and done nothing to stop it. Or how there was no such thing as a "Communist Chinese military company" when the rounds were manufactured in the 1960s, making nonsense of the law under which Merrill was prosecuted. Or how many millions of rounds were gratefully accepted in Kabul, long after the raid on AEY's offices and after it was widely and specifically known inside the Pentagon that it was allegedly illegal to acquire the ammo.

According to the government, Merrill was the mastermind of the fraudulent repacking program, not a financier who'd been kept in the dark about AEY's plans. His first trial resulted in a hung jury. At the second trial, he was convicted. At both of Merrill's trials, the prosecution showed the jurors scores of photographs of the "Chinese" ammunition to impress upon them that Merrill had defrauded the government.

"Generally, what would you say the condition is of these rounds of ammunition?" Merrill's lawyer asked the State Department's leading expert on small-caliber ammunition.

"They're in good condition," the expert said.

"Do you have any reason to believe these rounds wouldn't operate properly?"

"No, I do not."

"If you took one of these rounds and put it in an AK-47 and pulled the trigger, would you expect the bullet to be projected from the barrel?"

"I actually did that test," the expert replied.

"What did the test result show?"

"I took the oldest ammunition—which was from 1958—and one of the most recent rounds, from 1974, and I test-fired them. They fired as they were designed to fire."

But this evidence counted for nothing. Merrill spent more than a million dollars on his defense and lost his business and life savings. At the time of this writing, he was serving a four-year sentence in federal prison and working on a petition to overturn the convictions of all four AEY defendants.

As David Packouz awaited sentencing, he started advertising his massage services on Craigslist again. Fearful that he would be sent to prison, Packouz took a job as a volunteer at a local charity in Miami Beach, hoping to impress the judge with a sign of his remorse. He also spent his spare time refining the songs he was writing for his album, *Microcosm*.

Once a week or so, Packouz went out to sing karaoke. One evening at the bar called Studio, in South Beach, he ran into his old friend and business partner Efraim Diveroli. Packouz had heard that Diveroli was still living hard, consuming vast amounts of alcohol and cocaine. This evening, Diveroli was in high spirits, drinking at the bar with his new girlfriend. He greeted Packouz warmly and bought a round of shots.

"To everyone getting off easy," Diveroli said, offering a toast. "And to putting this behind us."

The pair clinked shot glasses.

"Can we ever be friends again?" Diveroli asked.

"Are you going to pay me?"

"What we agreed, okay?"

Diveroli got up to sing, employing his usual fake rock-star bravado on Everclear's "I Will Buy You a New Life."

/////

Alex Podrizki and David Packouz were spared prison sentences; both were placed under house arrest for a number of months. Standing before Judge Lenard, Packouz expressed regret for the "embarrassment, stress, and heartache that I have caused." But Packouz's real regret was political in nature: he believed that he and Diveroli and the others were scapegoats, prosecuted not for breaking the law but for making the government of the United States look bad on the front page of the *New York Times*.

"We were the Army's favorite contractors when we got the deal— poster boys for President Bush's small-business initiative," Packouz said. "We saved the government millions. The ammunition we shipped was truly vital to the mission in Afghanistan. We were living the American dream, until it turned into a nightmare."

/////

In January 2011, Efraim Diveroli appeared in federal court in Miami to be sentenced. He was dressed in a tan, prison-issued jumpsuit. The court was packed with his relatives, who sat in silence as a rabbi said Diveroli had offered to pay him $1 million if he could say something to convince the judge to keep him out of prison. "Efraim needs to go to jail," the rabbi said. Diveroli's mother concurred: "I know you hate me for saying this, but you need to go to jail." Diveroli's shoulders slumped as he stood and described his regrets to Judge Lenard. When prison guards saw his file, he said, they often asked in amazement how such a young person had managed to win such a huge contract. "I have no answer," Diveroli told the court. "I have had many experiences in my short life. I have done more than most people can dream of. But I would have done it differently. All the notoriety in my industry and all the good times—and there were some—cannot make up for the damage."

The judge gazed at Diveroli for a long time. "If it wasn't so amazing, you would laugh," she said. Four years was the sentence imposed.

The Miami hearing was not the end of Diveroli's criminal woes. As a convicted felon, he was barred from selling arms—or even so much as holding a gun. But he was sitting on millions of rounds of perfectly legitimate ammunition stored in warehouses in America. Diveroli couldn't transact with the government, but that didn't mean he couldn't put his money to work.

Characteristically, Diveroli had a solution. In March of 2008, before he was indicted, he'd incorporated a company called Ammoworks. Since then, he'd used the company as a legal entity to sell ammunition to the general public. Diveroli called himself a "consultant" and had business associates conduct the actual transactions, a classic gunrunner evasion. In the spring of 2010, while awaiting sentencing, the irrepressible Diveroli contacted a gun dealer to see if he was interested in buying Korean-made ammunition magazines. The gun dealer was suspicious when Diveroli told him that he was banned from doing business with the federal government because he'd sold Chinese ammo to the Army. Diveroli was behaving legally, in all likelihood, as the magazines only fed the ammunition into the gun and thus didn't qualify as a weapon. But the deal kept him neck-deep in the duplicitous world of arms dealers, where the perils were often invisible and consequences unpredictable.

Concerned that Diveroli was breaking the law, the gun dealer reported Diveroli to the Bureau of Alcohol, Tobacco, Firearms, and Explosives. When the ATF ran Diveroli's name and realized that it had chanced upon the notorious arms dealer behind one of the largest federal fraud causes in recent years, the agency scarcely believed its good fortune. Diveroli unwittingly became the target of a reverse sting operation—instead of capturing him breaking the law, investigators would try to lure him into acting illegally.

For weeks, an ATF undercover agent posing as an arms dealer tried to wheedle Diveroli into selling him guns. Diveroli refused, telling the undercover agent about his legal woes and describing himself as a "convicted felon" who couldn't trade in arms anymore.

The ATF persisted: Diveroli's avowed desire not to break the law wouldn't stop law enforcement from seducing him toward their ends. As federal agents secretly recorded his conversations, Diveroli couldn't resist bragging about his exploits; he talked about hunting alligators and hogs in the Everglades with a .50-caliber, muzzle-loaded rifle. He boasted about the millions of dollars he'd made as an arms dealer, and how he owned pallets of ammunition, and that he could broker deals— but he wouldn't actually take delivery of any arms for fear of breaking the law.

Finally, the ATF agent enticed Diveroli to a meeting in a parking lot, asking him to provide guns to test the magazines. Diveroli didn't bring any weapons, as it would be against the law—once again refusing to cross the line. But the undercover ATF agent had a solution. He popped open the trunk of his car, where he had a small arsenal of arms, and handed Diveroli a Glock 9 mm semiautomatic pistol. The temptation was too much. Adopting his best tough-guy swagger, Diveroli cleared the chamber, to make sure it was unloaded, and inspected the weapon.

As always, the twenty-four-year-old arms dealer was the star of his own Hollywood movie. He'd tried not to break the law. But every time he tried to stop acting like a big-time arms dealer, he was pulled back—this time earning an extra two years in prison—a sentence he completed in the fall of 2014.

"Once a gunrunner," Diveroli told the ATF agent, "always a gunrunner."

////// ACKNOWLEDGMENTS //////

I would like to thank David Packouz and Alex Podrizki for telling me their stories. Likewise, I'm grateful to Efraim Diveroli for sharing as much of his tale as his lawyers would allow. The fourth defendant, the financier Ralph Merrill, was swept up by events nearly entirely beyond his control; I hope he feels that he has received a measure of justice by finally having the whole tale told.

Miami criminal attorney Ken Kukec provided the initial entrée to this case and I am grateful for his belief in me. I was also helped to navigate treacherous legal waters by defense lawyers Nathan Crane, Peter Stirba, Hy Shapiro, and Cynthia Hawkins. To assist me in understanding the inner workings of the global arms trade, Colby Goodman of the Center for International Policy provided invaluable insights, as did Hugh Griffith of the Stockholm International Peace Research Institute. Nick Wood was generous describing the background to his reporting in Albania for the *New York Times*, and Sharon Weinberger of the Woodrow Wilson International Center for Scholars was kind enough to share sources and leads. On the intricacies of life and death in Albania, I was guided by Gary Kokalari, Erion Veliaj, Gjergj Thanasi, Theo Alexandridis, and Dorian Matlija. Genta Trebicka also provided assistance; she and I both hope the truth about her father's death will one day be revealed.

This adventure began in midtown Manhattan, at lunch with my editors at *Rolling Stone*, Eric Bates and Will Dana. I thank them for their support, intelligence, and wit. I am also grateful to Alison Weinflash and Sacha Lecca at the magazine, along with the irrepressible owner Jann Wenner for providing a venue for this kind of journalism.

Many people had a hand in crafting this book. Three editors at Simon & Schuster worked with me: Karen Thompson started the project, Karyn Marcus helped shape the narrative, and Emily Graff saw it through to completion. I am grateful to all three for their care and diligence and creativity. Jonathan Karp acquired the book and provided an insightful and patient voice during the difficult days every author encounters; his sense of humor and proportion were vital and very much appreciated. I couldn't ask for a better publicist than Larry Hughes, and the marketing efforts of Cary Goldstein and social media campaign of Elina Vaysbeyn were exemplary. The manuscript required a careful legal edit, and Elisa Rivlin more than rose to the occasion. Publishing truly is a team sport and I am grateful for the efforts of all involved.

Finally, I would like to thank my siblings—Ben, Liza, Hugh—the Kaimal clan, the Arons, the O'Learys, Merrily Weisbord, Scott Anderson, Barry Berman, Charles Foran, the awesome gang at MKFIF, and all the many great friends who provide encouragement and laughter. To the smart, strong, and beautiful women in my life—to Lucy, to Anna, and to Maya—my love and gratitude are forever yours.